IDEA S

INSTITUTE FOR JEWISH
IDEAS AND IDEALS

ANGEL FOR SHABBAT

VOLUME TWO

MARC D. ANGEL

Thoughts on the Weekly Torah Portions

A Publication of the Institute for Jewish Ideas and Ideals, jewishideas.org

THE INSTITUTE FOR JEWISH IDEAS AND IDEALS fosters an intellectually vibrant, compassionate, and inclusive Orthodox Judaism. It respects legitimate diversity of opinion within the Torah tradition, and appreciates the importance of independent thought and speech solidly grounded in classic Jewish law and worldview.

The Institute's important work is made possible through the support of its members and contributors. Please visit our website www.jewishideas.org, and join our expanding community through your membership commitment.

ISBN: 978-0-615-75093-4
Copyright © 2013 by Marc D. Angel

Cover design by Benjamin Motola
Produced by Olivestone, Inc.

PRINTED IN THE UNITED STATES OF AMERICA

Introduction

𝔎 It is amazing that the Torah—dating back thousands of years—continues to yield new ideas and relevant insights for our generation. As we study the Torah portion of each week, we find an inexhaustible fountain of wisdom and inspiration.

For the past five years, I have written the "Angel for Shabbat" column for the website of the Institute for Jewish Ideas and Ideals (jewishideas.org). These columns have been sent by email to thousands of subscribers throughout the world, and many have also been translated into Hebrew, Spanish, Portuguese, and Ladino.

In 2010, the Institute published volume one of *Angel for Shabbat*, collecting the first few years of columns into book form. That volume was translated into Hebrew (2012) as *Malakh leShabbat*, and is currently also being prepared for publication in Portuguese and Spanish editions.

We are now happy to present volume two of *Angel for Shabbat*, a collection of columns published since the appearance of volume one. I hope that readers will enjoy these *Divrei Torah* and discuss them with family and friends. More importantly, I hope readers will be inspired to look more carefully at the text of the Torah so as to generate their own insights. The Torah has a message for each person in each generation and has the capacity to generate new and life-transforming ideas.

This publication is made possible by the **Norman S. Benzaquen Publication Fund** of the Institute for Jewish Ideas and Ideals. I thank Norman S. Benzaquen for his friendship, support, and ongoing commitment to the work of our Institute. The Institute fosters an intellectually vibrant, compassionate, and inclusive Orthodox Judaism.

I express sincere gratitude to Ronda Angel Arking for her excellent editorial assistance; and Benjamin Motola for his extraordinary artwork on behalf of the Institute, including the design for the cover of this volume. I thank David Olivestone, who has handled the publications of the Institute with skill and efficiency.

I especially thank my family, with whom I have discussed Torah and from whom I have learned so much: my beloved wife, Gilda; our children, Rabbi Hayyim and Maxine Angel; Ronda Angel and Dr. Dan Arking; Elana Angel and Dr. James Nussbaum; and our grandchildren Jake Nussbaum, Andrew Arking, Jonathan Arking, Max Nussbaum, Charles Nussbaum, Jeremy Arking, Kara

Nussbaum, Aviva Angel, and Dahlia Angel. I pray that our children, and our children's children for all generations, will always find the Torah at the center of their lives.

I thank the Almighty for having brought me to this special moment.

RABBI MARC D. ANGEL
17 Heshvan 5773

Thoughts on בראשית

Created in the Image of God

🕮 In describing God's creation of human beings, the Torah teaches that we were created "in the image of God." Philosophers and commentators have pondered the meaning of this phrase, and have given various explanations. What does it mean for humans to be created in God's image since God is an eternal, incorporeal being? Some have defined "image" as referring to intellect or will. Others have interpreted "image" to refer to humanity's spiritual quest. Still others have applied this verse to the teaching that human beings have infinite value, and that human life must be respected to the highest possible degree.

It is not always easy to detect the "image of God" in humanity. With billions of people on earth, it is difficult to focus on the divine worth of each of them. Moreover, there are a substantial number of hateful, murderous people—how are we to respect the "image of God" in such people?

Perhaps the Torah is teaching us an ideal concept about human potential. God created the first human beings, Adam and Eve, in "His image," as a lesson to subsequent human beings that they, too, can find this "image" within themselves. If they fully develop their human capacities, they will discover the image of God within themselves. However, this "image" is not an automatic birthright; it has to be earned. It exists in potential, and it is our task to realize that potential. Human beings who do not nourish the image of God within themselves thereby dehumanize themselves, and deprive themselves of their spiritual potential. Murderers, terrorists, and hate-mongers are examples of people who have, in a profound sense, forfeited their image of God. When the Torah teaches that humans were created in God's image this should be seen as a challenge and opportunity, not as an automatic gift that requires no further action on our part.

We develop the image of God within ourselves as we improve ourselves intellectually, morally, and spiritually. We come closer to God's ideal for humanity as we become more sensitive to the potential within all human beings, as we strive to increase understanding among humankind.

A story is told of Fiorello La Guardia, when he was presiding at police court in New York City. One winter day, a trembling old man was brought in for stealing a loaf of bread. The defendant said that he and his family were starving, and he had to steal the bread to survive. La Guardia said: "The law makes no exception. You stole. The fine is $10." But then La Guardia took $10 out of his own pocket and paid the fine! Then he said: "Now I'm going to fine everybody in this courtroom 50 cents for living in a town where a man has to steal bread in order to eat." The bailiff went around the room, collected the money, and gave it to the poor, incredulous man.

Seeing the image of God in others means that we strive to identify with their needs and feelings; that we seek to increase compassion and thoughtfulness in society; that we feel personal responsibility for others. By developing our own inner image of God, we make space for others to develop their own inner image of God—and this leads to a better, more spiritual humanity.

Torah and Evolution

❦ I recently received an email communication from an Orthodox Jewish organization stating in unequivocal terms that "Orthodox Judaism rejects the theory of evolution." In certain Orthodox circles, it is posited as a matter of faith that "true" Judaism does not and cannot accept evolution. God created the universe; God created Adam and Eve. This is clear from the first chapter of *Bereishith*, and there is nothing more to say on the subject. Any other position is heresy.

Actually, there is much more to say on the subject. I believe that it is religiously incorrect to state that "Orthodox Judaism rejects the theory of evolution." This is not only an invalid statement from an intellectual point of view, it is also invalid from an Orthodox religious point of view. The statement reflects obscurantism, not faith.

The first chapter of *Bereishith* presents a lofty, poetic account of creation. It does not present a scientific account of creation. It does not describe how God created things, only that He did indeed create the world.

It has been pointed out that the six "days" of creation are not 24-hour days as we know them today; the sun wasn't created until day four! Rather, the Torah poetically speaks of six periods of time—each of which could have been billions of years long—in which the universe came into being. Current scientific calculations place the "big bang" at a bit over 13 billion years ago. These calculations are not based on idle speculation but on carefully studied cosmic phenomena. Religious Jews, along with all thinking people, should feel comfortable embracing the findings of science. There is no contradiction at all between Torah and the "big bang" calculations.

The theory of evolution, which has a strong body of scientific support, posits that life emerged gradually, over the course of many millions of years. Simple life forms gradually evolved into more complex life forms. Human beings ultimately emerged from a long process of evolution. The Torah neither affirms nor denies the theory of evolution. It makes clear, though, that God created the world; things did not develop randomly. God could have created things in an instant; or He could have created things by a process of evolution spanning millions of years. When the Torah states that God created Adam from the dust of the earth, this could mean that God created Adam via a process of evolution spanning a vast period of time—beginning with the simplest cells found in the dust and ultimately developing into thinking human beings. The Torah simply does not provide us with scientific details about the formation of human beings.

Since the weight of scientific information indicates a gradual development of life, we can embrace this information without religious qualms or conflicts. The Torah tells us that God created the world; scientists have been trying to figure out the process of the creation. Thus, the theory of evolution poses no threat whatever to our religious tradition. Rather, it fills in scientific information that was not discussed in the Torah.

Our conflict is not with the theory of evolution per se. Our conflict is with those who claim that evolution happened entirely on its own, without any divine impetus. Religious Jews may properly accept the findings of science, but must always make clear that it was God who fashioned the universe, who set things in motion, and who indeed created the scientific phenomena upon which the scientists are drawing their conclusions.

During the Middle Ages, a conflict raged between science and religion on the question of the nature of matter. Science, as represented by Aristotle, argued for the eternity of matter. Religious tradition, based on the first chapter of *Bereishith*, argued for a created universe. Maimonides, in his *Guide of the Perplexed* 2:25, maintained the traditional religious view of God as creator. He argued that it is philosophically impossible to prove the eternity of matter. On the other hand, since it is philosophically plausible to posit God as creator of matter, we can safely rely on religious tradition to teach us that which science/philosophy cannot teach.

At the same time, Maimonides points out that if indeed it could be demonstrated that matter is eternal, then we would necessarily accept scientific truth. Since God is the Author of both Torah and Science, it is impossible for the two to be in conflict. If science could prove the eternity of matter, then the Torah would need to be re-interpreted accordingly:

> Know that our shunning the affirmation of the eternity of the world is not due to a text figuring in the Torah according to which the world has been produced in time. For the texts indicating that the world has been produced in time are not more numerous than those indicating that the deity is a body. Nor are the gates of figurative interpretation shut in our faces or impossible of access to us regarding the subject of the creation of the world in time. For we could interpret them as figurative, as we have done when denying His corporeality.

Maimonides' methodology is of profound significance. Religious texts do not and cannot conflict with demonstrated scientific truths. If the texts seem to conflict with scientific truth, then the texts need to be re-interpreted.

People are welcome to accept or reject the theory of evolution as they think best after they have actually studied the scientific data carefully. But regardless of their personal opinion, they are not entitled to say that "Orthodox Judaism rejects the theory of evolution." If the theory of evolution is scientifically valid, then religious Jews—along with all thinking people—should necessarily accept it—with the proviso that the process of evolution itself was God's means for creating life.

The Noahide Laws

🐚 Rabbinic tradition teaches that Noah and his descendants were given seven basic categories of law, and that "Noahides" fulfill their religious obligations through these Noahide laws. The Talmud (*Yebamot* 47a) states: "Our sages have said that seven commandments have been prescribed for the Sons of Noah: the first requires them to have judges; the other six forbid sacrilege, idolatry, incest, homicide, theft, and the consumption of a limb taken from a living animal."

The great nineteenth-century thinker, Rabbi Eliyahu Benamozegh, pointed out that the Noahide laws represent an important part of Jewish teaching. While Jews are obligated to observe all the commandments of the Torah due to their covenant with God, all non-Jewish human beings are bound by a divine covenant through the specific commandments given to them as Noahides. Thus, Judaism is a religion that maintains both a specific message to Jews and a universal message for all humankind.

Because non-Jews have access to God through the Noahide covenant, they are under no obligation to convert to Judaism in order to be "saved." "The authentic spirit of Judaism appears unambiguously when we find it affirming that there exist just men among the Gentiles, men loved by God, whose merits are responsible for the prosperity of the nations." (E. Benamozegh, *Israel and Humanity*, translated and edited by Maxwell Luria, Paulist Press, 1994, p. 349.) Those non-Jews who wish to convert to Judaism are welcome—but Jews have generally avoided active proselytizing, since non-Jews do not have to become Jewish in order to serve God properly. They need only adhere to the seven Noahide laws (and their derivatives), thereby living morally upright lives.

Judaism presents a religious message for humanity. It does not demand or expect that everyone convert to Judaism. It does not force Judaism on anyone. It respects non-Jews' spiritual integrity, and offers a religious worldview that is remarkably universal and humane. It only asks that all human beings—Jewish and non-Jewish—conduct their lives on a high moral level, based on recognition of One God who loves all humanity.

Maimonides (*Hilkhot Shemitah veYovel* 13:13) underscored the universal vision of Judaism: Not only the tribe of Levi but every single individual from among the world's inhabitants could rise to the highest spiritual levels and could become "totally consecrated, and God will be his portion and inheritance forever and ever."

Rabbi Benamozegh noted the irony: Christianity and Islam are considered "universal" religions; yet they have historically been intolerant of those not adhering to their particular religion. They engaged in forced conversion of "infidels," crusades, and religious wars in order to force others to accept their creeds. They have taught that only their religious adherents fulfill God's will and can share in the blessings of the world to come. Judaism, which is often (unfairly) portrayed as being parochial and particularistic, actually is the most universal religion—it teaches that God blesses all righteous people, that the world to come is available to all good people, Jewish or non-Jewish.

God's covenant with humanity—the Noahide laws—create the foundation for a world governed by justice and morality. Humanity still has a very long way to go to fulfill this covenant properly. In humankind's quest for a righteous world, the religious message of Judaism is a beacon of strength and hope.

Coming Out of the Cocoon

✣ Forecasters and marketers have come up with a word to describe a current trend: *cocooning*. This term refers to a growing phenomenon in which people increasingly strive for a sense of personal space by cutting themselves off from the outside world. They avoid social interactions by enclosing themselves in their own private world to the extent possible.

Here are some examples of cocooning:

• interacting socially only with people of the same socio-economic status

• playing computer games rather than interacting with friends

• communicating largely by email or texting, rather than in face-to-face conversations

• plugging into technological devices that render one oblivious of the people around him or her.

Cocooning is a way of enclosing ourselves in an environment where we don't have to interact as much with outside society. We can safely wrap ourselves in our own world, without having to deal with those whom we can keep comfortably away from us.

Cocooning is an appealing concept, in that it reflects the need to stay in control of our lives in a protected environment. We live in a noisy world, with many challenges and struggles, competition, ugliness, rudeness, exploitation. It's so nice to shut all those things out and build our own private ark of peace and quiet.

Yet, those who have studied the phenomenon of cocooning have also pointed out its negative features. People become more self-centered, more egotistic, more concerned with their own private comforts and pleasures. Their sense of responsibility for society diminishes. Their tolerance for others' opinions and viewpoints declines. People cocoon so that they don't have to worry about the needs or feelings of others. Only their comfort and safety matter, nothing else. Let others make their own cocoons. Let others worry about themselves.

Although forecasters and marketers describe cocooning as a relatively new trend, the Torah gives a prime example of this phenomenon going back thousands of years. The ultimate cocooner was Noah. When God informed Noah that He was going to bring a flood to destroy the world, Noah did not raise his voice in protest. Rather, he went to work building an ark to save himself and his family. He would safely ride out the storm in his "cocoon."

A Midrash imagines a conversation between Noah and God after the flood had wiped out the population. When leaving the ark, Noah was stunned by the devastation and the immense loss of life. He called out to God: "Lord, why did You do this? Why didn't you spare the people this calamity?" God replied: "Noah, why didn't you pray for the people when I first informed you of their impending destruction? If you would have spoken up then, I would not have brought the flood. You offered no protest or prayer: you only went off to build your ark."

Noah was a cocooner. He surely had a right and responsibility to look out for himself and for his family. Yet, by cocooning, he lost his sense of connection with society; he did not internalize a personal responsibility for others. Let others take care of themselves; it's their problem not mine.

The Midrash points out that Noah's cocooning ultimately played a role in the destruction of society. If he had been more involved with others, if he had taken their welfare seriously, he could have prayed to God to avert the flood—and God would have listened!

The Noah story goes on to tell that Noah became drunk after the flood. This may be understood to mean that Noah was overwhelmed by his situation. He wanted to escape his past and his future by becoming intoxicated. Cocooning had been a grievous error. It had given him and his family a short-lived feeling of safety and security; yet it contributed to the destruction of society.

There is nothing wrong with wanting to create safe space for oneself and one's family. There is nothing wrong with trying to shut out the unpleasant features of the "outside world." Yet, if we make cocoons that dull our sense of connection with others and that mar our commitment to society as a whole—then we fall into the pattern of Noah.

We all have a right to private space. But we all have a responsibility to the public at large. We need to be sure that we maintain a proper balance. We can begin by recognizing our own cocooning tendencies, and making sure that we don't let these tendencies close us off from the pulse of life outside of ourselves.

Here are a few simple suggestions.

Volunteer for a committee at your synagogue, UJA-Federation, or social service agency.

Make an effort to interact with people of different backgrounds, educational levels, economic statuses.

Don't talk on your cell phone or send text messages when you are in the presence of another human being. Rather, take the time and interest to speak to that person, even if only to say hello.

Think of ways you can help improve society—and then do something constructive according to your talents and means.

When you see injustice, don't stand idly by.

Don't follow Noah's example.

דוד

Hessed *in Deed;*
Hessed *in Thought*

 The Midrash teaches that Abraham and Sarah won many converts to their religious views. How did they succeed?

The Midrash offers a suggestion. Abraham and Sarah were models of *hessed*— kindness and compassion. They invited guests into their home, fed them, created a warm and loving environment. People were drawn to Abraham and Sarah as models of humanity at its best; and then, they went on to learn about the theology of Abraham and Sarah. The "strategy" of the Founding Couple of our tradition was to set a proper example of religious behavior, and to convince—not coerce—others of the truths of ethical monotheism.

Many people have first been attracted to Orthodox Judaism because they have had positive experiences with Orthodox Jews. They have been helped in times of difficulty; they have been offered hospitality; they have been warmly received in the synagogue; they have been treated with impeccable honesty and decency. Acts of *hessed* have the power of drawing people closer to oneself—and also to one's values and ideals. Once people feel comfortable with Orthodox Jews, they might then be curious to study the teachings of Orthodox Judaism.

Hessed doesn't only manifest itself in friendly, honest, and kind behavior. It also is reflected in our attitudes toward others. If we are imbued with *hessed*, we demonstrate respect for the feelings and thoughts of others. We enter respectful discussion with them. Our goal is to be helpful to them in their exploration of Jewish teachings, and to provide meaningful guidance in a gentle, thoughtful way. Discussion—not coercion—is the hallmark of *hessed*.

We sometimes (too often!) hear comments from Orthodox leaders and laypeople that do not reflect *hessed*. These statements convey the notion that the speaker alone has the Truth, and that others must listen and obey. The strategy of such people is closer to coercion than to open discussion. They say: do it our way or you are a sinner; obey our policies, or you will be disciplined.

They claim to be the sole spokespeople of God's Truth, and to have the right—and responsibility—to control the thoughts and actions of others. They prefer coercion to discussion. They aren't interested in other opinions, since they believe they alone have the Truth.

In his book, *Bein Yisrael laAmim* (published in 1954), Rabbi Haim David Halevy discussed the role of religion in the State of Israel. He obviously wanted the Jewish State to operate according to the teachings of Torah and halakha. Although he recognized the importance of involvement in the political process, he did not think that the religious nature of Israel could be guaranteed by political maneuvering or legislative coercion:

> We will not achieve our goal by these means [of political power]. All of our efforts to increase the presence of religious Jewry in the Knesset elected by the nation, can only be—in the best of circumstances—only a means to achieve the goal. . . . We will never be able to force our ideas and beliefs on the entire nation by means of legislation. (p. 85)

Rabbi Halevy stressed the need for the religious community to impact the larger society by setting proper moral examples, by teaching and convincing, by working with others in a spirit of *hessed*. Even if people can be forced to comply with religious legislation, this will ultimately backfire. People will resent the misuse of political power, and will ultimately cast off religion along with the coercive religious leadership. The truth of Rabbi Halevy's observations is easily substantiated by the many polls in Israel, which show a growing antagonism toward the "religious establishment" within Israeli society. Coercive power is abusive power: people will not put up with it indefinitely.

Abraham and Sarah set important models for us on how to reach out to others who do not share our views or beliefs. First, be a good person. Behave in such a way that people are naturally drawn to your goodness, kindness, and honesty. Then, be a respectful person who believes in discussion and exploration of ideas. Recognize that coercion not only reflects a bad attitude, but is actually a bad strategic choice. It drives people away, rather than bringing them closer. To create a religious community and society, we need to win hearts and minds. We need to think and discuss together, not to coerce or threaten each other. We need to demonstrate *hessed* in deed, and *hessed* in thought.

The Pursuit of Truth

❧ Some years ago, I had a conversation with a Hassidic Jew who assured me that his rebbe never committed any sins. He stated with certainty that his rebbe was endowed with a grand and holy soul, far superior to the soul of any other person.

When I pointed out to him that even Moses committed sins, he flatly denied that this was so. I reminded him that the Torah itself reports Moses's shortcomings. He said: You do not understand the Torah! It is impossible that Moses could have done anything wrong. He was perfect in every way.

The conversation came to an end, with both of us unhappy with the result. He felt I did not demonstrate enough faith in the perfection of saintly personalities, and I felt he was guilty of distorting the Torah's words and distorting the reality of the human condition.

This conversation came to mind recently when I received an email from a colleague, in which he included some important passages by Rabbi Samson Raphael Hirsch. The comments related specifically to stories reported in *Parashat Lekh Lekha*—but Rabbi Hirsch's point is of general relevance to our study of Torah...and to our evaluation of saintly individuals.

The Torah relates various problematic narratives about Abraham. For example, when going to Egypt, Abraham feared that the Egyptians would murder him and take his wife Sarah. Abraham told Sarah to say she was his sister, rather than his wife. In spite of (or because of!) this deception, Sarah was taken to Pharaoh. Abraham was given rewards, and he thrived in Egypt. When God punished Pharaoh and when Pharaoh realized that Sarah was really Abraham's wife, Pharaoh expressed outrage to Abraham over the deception. Pharaoh expelled Abraham and Sarah, who left Pharaoh's domain with much wealth.

This story surely does not cast Abraham in a good light. He asked his wife to participate in a deception. He let his wife be taken by the Egyptians. He reaped financial rewards while his wife was in captivity in Pharaoh's house.

Rabbi Hirsch makes a profoundly important point:

> The Torah does not attempt to hide from us the faults, errors and weaknesses of our great men, and precisely thereby it places the stamp of credibility upon the happenings it relates. The fact that we are told about their faults and weaknesses does not detract from our great men. Indeed, it adds to their stature and makes their life stories even more instructive. Had they all been portrayed to us as models of perfection we would have

believed that they had been endowed with a higher nature not give to us to attain. Had they been presented to us free of human passions and inner conflicts, their nature would seem to us merely the result of a loftier predisposition, not a product of their personal merit, and certainly no model we could ever hope to emulate.

Rabbi Hirsch goes on to say that "we must never attempt to whitewash the spiritual and moral heroes of our past. They are not in need of our apologetics, nor would they tolerate such attempts on our part. Truth is the seal of our Word of God, and truthfulness is the distinctive characteristic also of all its genuinely great teachers and commentators."

Our great biblical heroes, as well as our great spiritual heroes of all generations, were real human beings, not plaster saints. They had real feelings, real conflicts. Many times they performed admirably; on some occasions they fell short. To suggest that anyone is "perfect"—totally devoid of sin and error—is to misrepresent that person and to misrepresent truth.

There is a popular genre of "religious literature" that presents biographies of biblical and later religious luminaries as paragons of virtue, totally devoid of sin and inner conflict. In fact, such books are not authentic biographies, because they describe their heroes in an untruthful way. These personalities are drawn in such superlative terms, that readers will find it exceedingly difficult to identify with them or to emulate them.

There is an opposite tendency in some circles to point to every flaw and sin of our spiritual heroes, and to undermine their credibility as religious models. Our prophets and teachers are presented as though devoid of higher spiritual and moral qualities.

Just as it is false to overstate the perfection of our heroes, so it is false to undervalue their spiritual achievements. Rather, we must study their lives honestly, recognizing that these are remarkable individuals who reached great heights—and who had to struggle mightily to attain their levels of religious insight and righteousness. Their failings can be as instructive to us as their successes.

Just as Truth is the seal of the Word of God, so is the pursuit of Truth the proper objective of all students of Torah and Jewish tradition.

Humility and Strength of Character

🐚 When God informed Abraham that He was intending to destroy the wicked city of Sodom, Abraham immediately challenged the divine decision. Perhaps, argued Abraham, there were righteous people in the city: Should they perish along with the wicked people? "Will the Judge of all the world not act justly?"

Abraham demonstrated amazing *chutzpah* in confronting the Almighty. After all, what right did he have to challenge God? Why didn't he simply accept the decree, recognizing God's infinite wisdom and power? Doesn't true piety demand passive acquiescence to the will of God?

Abraham set a different model of faith that recognized the right of humans to voice their demands to God. Abraham acknowledged that he was only "dust and ashes"—that he was unworthy of arguing with the Almighty; yet he proceeded to challenge God.

Faith does not mandate passive subservience. Humility does not preclude standing up for one's views. Although we are only "dust and ashes," we are human beings created in God's image. Although we must always be aware of our ultimate smallness and insignificance, we must also always be aware of the divine spark within us. Vanity and arrogance are signs of foolishness. Silence in the face of injustice is a sign of defective moral development. Abraham showed that humility and strength of character go together.

Abraham presented himself before God as being "dust and ashes." Dust (i.e., the earth) is actually the source of life. Our food grows from the earth. Dust symbolizes the power of fruitfulness. It points to the future, to crops that will grow and sustain us in coming seasons and in coming years. On the other hand, ashes are the residue of things that have burnt out. Ashes symbolize the past, that which no longer exists. Abraham's words to God, then, might be paraphrased as follows: I know that my life only occupies an infinitesimal amount of time and space, and that You are the Eternal and the Infinite. But don't dismiss me due to the smallness of my existence. I am "dust," I am the forerunner of future generations, I symbolize the future of humanity. I am "ashes," I live with the memory of all the generations that came before me, I symbolize the past of humanity. I stand before you, God, as a human link between all that is past and all that is future. My life constitutes a cosmic instant—but I speak not due to my own worthiness, but as a representative of humanity, past and future. If I am speaking to You with *chutzpah*, it is because I speak on behalf of humanity's need to maintain an honest and forthright relationship with You.

In working on our own faith, we can learn much from Abraham's confrontation with God. We each come before God as dust and ashes. This underscores our need for humility. But it also underscores how each one of us represents the past and the future of humanity, and how we must develop the moral courage to stand up for what is right and just. Humility and strength of character go together.

Orthodoxy and Diversity

✒ *(This column is based on my article that appeared in* Liber Amicorum, *a book of essays in honor of Rabbi Nathan Lopes Cardozo, published in Jerusalem, 2006.)*

The Talmud (*Berakhot* 58a) teaches that one is required to recite a special blessing when witnessing a vast throng of Jews, praising the Almighty who is *hakham haRazim*, the One who understands the root and inner thoughts of each individual. "Their thoughts are not alike and their appearance is not alike." The Creator made each person as a unique being. He expected and wanted diversity of thought, and we bless Him for having created this diversity among us.

The antithesis of this ideal is represented by Sodom. Rabbinic teaching has it that the Sodomites placed visitors in a bed. If the person was too short, he was stretched until he fit the bed. If he was too tall, his legs were cut off so that he fit the bed. This parable is not, I think, merely referring to the desire for physical uniformity; the people of Sodom wanted everyone to fit the same pattern, to think alike, to conform to the mores of the Sodomites. They fostered and enforced conformity in an extreme way.

Respect for individuality and diversity is a sine qua non of healthy human life. We each have unique talents and insights, and we need the spiritual climate that allows us to grow, to be creative, and to contribute to humanity's treasury of ideas and knowledge.

Societies struggle to find a balance between individual freedom and communal standards of conduct. The Torah, while granting much freedom, also provides boundaries beyond which the individual may not trespass. When freedom becomes license, it can unsettle society. On the other hand, when authoritarianism quashes individual freedom, the dignity and sanctity of the individual are violated. I wish to focus on this latter tendency as it relates to contemporary Orthodox Jewish life.

Some years ago, I visited a great Torah luminary in Israel. Because of his independent and original views, he was increasingly isolated from the rabbinic establishment. He commented sadly: "Have you heard of the mafia? Well, we have a rabbinic mafia here." The issue is whether a rabbinic scholar has the right and responsibility to explore and discuss ideas, even when these ideas are not currently in fashion. To apply crude pressure to silence open discussion is inimical to the best interests of the Torah community. This is the way of Sodom.

Similar cases abound where pressure has been brought to bear on rabbis and scholars who espouse views not in conformity with the prevailing opinions of an inner circle of Orthodox rabbinic leaders. Over the years, I have been involved in the planning of a number of rabbinic conferences and conventions. Invariably questions are raised concerning who will be invited to speak. Someone says: If Rabbi so-and-so is put on the program, then certain other rabbis and speakers will refuse to participate. Someone says: if such-and-such a group is among the sponsors of the conference, other groups will boycott the event. What is happening in such instances is a subtle—and not so subtle—process of coercion. Decisions are being made as to which Orthodox individuals and groups are "acceptable" and which are not.

This process is insidious and is unhealthy for Orthodoxy. It deprives us of meaningful discussion and debate. It intimidates people from taking independent or original positions, for fear of being ostracized or isolated.

Many times I have heard intelligent people say: I believe thus-and-so but I can't say so openly for fear of being attacked by the "right." I support such-and-such proposal, but can't put my name in public support for fear of being reviled or discredited by this group or that group.

We must face this problem squarely and candidly: The narrowing of horizons is a reality within contemporary Orthodoxy. The fear to dissent from the "acceptable" positions is palpable. But if individuals are not allowed to think independently, if they may not ask questions and raise alternatives—then we as a community suffer a loss of vitality and dynamism. Fear and timidity become our hallmark.

This situation contrasts with the way a vibrant Torah community should function. Rabbi Yehiel Mikhel Epstein, in the introduction to *Hoshen Misphat* of his *Arukh haShulhan*, notes that difference of opinion among our sages constitutes the glory of Torah. "The entire Torah is called a song (*shira*), and the glory of a song is when the voices differ one from the other. This is the essence of its pleasantness."

Debates and disagreements have long been an accepted and valued part of the Jewish tradition. The Rama (see *Shulhan Arukh*, Y.D. 242:2,3) notes that it is even permissible for a student to dissent from his rabbi's ruling if he has proofs and arguments to uphold his opinion. Rabbi Hayyim Palachi, the great halakhic authority of nineteenth-century Izmir, wrote that

> the Torah gave permission to each person to express his opinion according to his understanding. . . . It is not good for a sage to withhold his words out of deference to the sages who preceded him if he finds in their

words a clear contradiction. . . . A sage who wishes to write his proofs against the kings and giants of Torah should not withhold his words nor suppress his prophecy, but should give his analysis as he has been guided by Heaven. (see *Hikekei Lev*, O.H. 6; and Y.D. 42)

The great twentieth-century sage, Rabbi Haim David Halevy, ruled:

Not only does a judge have the right to rule against his rabbis; he also has an obligation to do so [if he believes their decision to be incorrect and he has strong proofs to support his own position]. If the decision of those greater than he does not seem right to him, and he is not comfortable following it, and yet he follows that decision [in deference to their authority], then it is almost certain that he has rendered a false judgment." (*Aseh Lekha Rav*, 2:61)

Rabbi Moshe Feinstein, in rejecting an opinion of Rabbi Shelomo Kluger, wrote that "one must love truth more than anything" (*Iggrot Moshe*, Y. D., 3:88).

Orthodoxy needs to foster the love of truth. It must be alive to different intellectual currents, and receptive to open discussion. How do we, as a Modern Orthodox community, combat the tendency toward blind authoritarianism and obscurantism?

First, we must stand up and be counted on the side of freedom of expression. We, as a community, must give encouragement to all who have legitimate opinions to share. We must not tolerate intolerance. We must not yield to the tactics of coercion and intimidation.

Our schools and institutions must foster legitimate diversity within Orthodoxy. We must insist on intellectual openness, and resist efforts to impose conformity: we will not be fitted into the bed of Sodom. We must give communal support to diversity within the halakhic framework, so that people will not feel intimidated to say things publicly or sign their names to public documents.

Orthodoxy is large enough and great enough to include Rambam and the Ari; the Baal Shem Tov and the Gaon of Vilna; Rabbi Eliyahu Benamozegh and Rabbi Samson Raphael Hirsch; Rabbi Abraham Isaac Kook and Rabbi Benzion Uziel; Dona Gracia Nasi and Sarah Schnirer. We draw on the wisdom and inspiration of men and women spanning the generations, from communities throughout the world. The wide variety of Orthodox models deepens our own religiosity and understanding, thereby giving us a living, dynamic, intellectually alive way of life.

If the Modern Orthodox community does not have the will or courage to foster diversity, then who will? And if we do not do it now, we are missing a unique challenge of our generation.

Thoughts on חיי שרה

A Parable on Life's Meaning

🌿 (*The following is drawn from my book,* Losing the Rat Race, Winning at Life, *Urim Publications, 2005.*)

In this week's Torah portion, we read of the deaths of Sarah and Abraham—the founding couple of ethical monotheism and of the people of Israel. Their lives have left a profound imprint on human history; as we ponder their lives and deaths, it would be well to ponder the meaning of life for ourselves. A rabbinic parable offers a keen perspective:

A poor man was struggling to support his family. He learned of a faraway land that was filled with precious jewels. A ship would soon be leaving for this land and it had room for him as a passenger. But the ship would only return after an interval of unspecified length. His wife agreed that he should make the voyage, so as to be able to obtain valuable jewels to bring back to support his family in wealth and honor.

So the man boarded the ship and was off to make his fortune. Sure enough, the ship arrived at the faraway land, and it was indeed filled with treasures. The earth was covered with diamonds and all types of precious stones. He hurriedly filled his pockets with jewels; he stuffed his bags with gems. He was now an extraordinarily rich man. He rejoiced in the thought of how wealthy he and his family would be upon his return home.

But in the faraway land, the man soon realized that his precious stones were valueless. They were so abundant that no one paid any attention to them. None of the storekeepers would accept them as payment for merchandise. Rather, the currency of this land was wax candles. These were hard to come by, and were highly valued by the public. Everyone strove to accumulate as many wax candles as possible; their wealth and power were evaluated by the number of candles they possessed.

It did not take long for the man to recognize his need for wax candles. He worked hard to gain as many as he could. Soon, he had accumulated a large number of them. He emptied his pockets and bags of the diamonds, rubies and emeralds, and filled them instead with wax candles. In this new land, he became wealthy and prominent—very successful.

Time passed. It was now time for the man to return to his wife and family. The ship was ready to leave. Quickly, the man packed as many wax candles as he could. He proudly boarded the ship, laden with as many candles as he could possibly carry.

When he arrived home, his wife eagerly greeted him. She asked to see the treasures he had brought back. Proudly, the man opened his bags and emptied his pockets. He stacked up piles of wax candles. His wife was astonished. "You spent all that time in the faraway land, a land filled with precious jewels, and you brought back only piles of worthless wax candles?"

Suddenly, the man realized he had made a terrible mistake. When he had arrived in the faraway land, he knew he was supposed to gather precious gems—but he had soon forgotten his mission. Influenced by the people in that land, he had come to value candles and ignore jewels. He had thought that by accumulating candles, he had become successful. But now that he had returned home, he realized that he had missed his opportunity to bring back real treasures. Instead, he came back with a pile of nearly worthless candles.

We are placed on earth to attain transcendent treasures—wisdom, love, spiritual insight, moral courage, Torah and mitzvoth. If we can keep our lives focused on these goals, we can return to our heavenly home with genuine treasures. But in this world, people chase after "wax candles"—material wealth, fancy cars, glitz, hedonistic lifestyles. In this world, people are judged "successful" by the false standards of materialism. It is possible to lose sight of our real treasures and goals, to pursue the values that pervade our society. When we finally return home—to our heavenly home beyond—we may realize that we are bringing with us "wax candles" instead of precious jewels—that we had lived our lives chasing falsehoods and vanities, rather than pursuing goodness, truth, and piety.

Winning at life means keeping focused on what is truly important and not getting sidetracked by external glitz. Winning is not a one-time event, but an ongoing way of life.

The "JFK" Syndrome vs. the Real JFK

℣ I recently learned of a shorthand symbol used in online communications among Jewish singles. It is "JFK." For example: "Don't go out with him, he's 'JFK'." "He's not reliable, he's 'JFK'."

"JFK" stands for "Just for Kiddush." A person described as a "JFK" is one who skips synagogue services and shows up in time for Kiddush to enjoy free refreshments. Such a person lacks spiritual/religious values (skips prayer services); looks for free food (Kiddush); doesn't make commitments (shows up for food, but likely isn't a member of or contributor to the synagogue). A "JFK" mingles with the Kiddush crowd and tries to pass himself off as a respectable member of the community. In pre-computerese language, a "JFK" would be described as a sponge or a moocher, one looking for a free ride at someone else's expense.

A "JFK" can't be relied upon. Such a person lacks a basic sense of personal responsibility, commitment, self-respect. A "JFK" looks out for him or herself, not for others.

The Torah portion this week tells of Efron the Hittite, from whom Abraham bought a burial place for Sarah. While posing as a generous patron, Efron was in fact a self-centered man interested in gaining material advantage from others. Rashi comments about Efron: "He talked a lot, but didn't do even a little." He pretended to be a fine, upstanding person, but he was actually a person of deficient moral sense. He was an early version of a "JFK."

During the coming week, we will mark the anniversary of the assassination of President John F. Kennedy. It is fitting that we remember his famous words, words that reflect the real JFK and not the computerese shorthand "JFK": "Ask not what your country can do for you; ask what you can do for your country." President Kennedy tapped into the idealism of the American people as few presidents before or since have done. The real JFK spoke to the best in us, calling on us to give of ourselves for the betterment of our country, our society, the world at large.

In his book, *Profiles in Courage*, John F. Kennedy described individuals who displayed great integrity, who rose above selfish interests and political pressures in order to make proper moral judgments. They were willing to take risks and make sacrifices in order to promote what was right and just. The real JFK admired those who recognized personal responsibility toward the community and nation; who made commitments; who acted courageously and selflessly. He certainly did not think highly of the "Just for Kiddush" types.

We must all strive not to be a "JFK" who only shows up for Kiddush, who wants others to do all the work and pay all the bills, whose spiritual and moral life is so eminently deficient. Rather, we must all strive to reach for the ideals advanced by President John F. Kennedy, ideals that speak to the best in us, and that inspire us to grow in our integrity, sense of responsibility, and commitment to the welfare of our society.

Thoughts on תּוֹלְדוֹת

Hope and Despair

Rebecca was suffering with a very difficult pregnancy. She was so distraught that she questioned the value of her life. After reaching this point of deep despair, "she went to inquire of the Lord," i.e., she sought an explanation from God as to why she was enduring so much hardship. Once she was told that she was carrying twins who would be lifelong rivals, she ceased to complain. Even though the explanation of her suffering was not exactly wonderful, she seems to have been able to deal with it—as long as she felt she now had some control and understanding of the situation.

Researchers have found that when people feel helpless and hopeless, they are more prone to depression and physical illness. When they reach the point of questioning the very value of their lives, they not only suffer psychological stress but also a breakdown in their immune systems.

Stress and frustration are problematic features of life; but many people cope well and even thrive on stress. What separates those who are crushed by despair from those who overcome feelings of despair?

In his book, *Who Gets Sick*, Blair Justice discusses "transformational coping." This involves thinking about things optimistically, acting decisively, changing the situation into a less stressful one. It means taking control—to the extent possible—and not falling prey to feelings of helplessness and despair. Whatever the problem or challenge, one needs to foster a mindset that gives one hope and offers some positive resolution. Blair Justice quotes the results of a survey of 52,000 readers of *Psychology Today*, indicating that happiness "turns out to be more a matter of how you regard your circumstances than of what the circumstances are." It isn't the difficulties in themselves that can debilitate us, but our interpretation of the difficulties. If we feel overwhelmed and powerless, we are likely to surrender to depression and illness. If we feel that we can draw on our inner strengths to face our problems as optimistically and decisively as possible, then we can cope with the stresses and struggles that we face.

Researchers have found that people cope better when they have a network of loved ones who care for them, and who provide them with psychological support and encouragement. There is also much evidence that religious faith provides people with courage and optimism. When we pray, we come to a deeper spiritual inner peace that allows us to cope more effectively with the problems we face. By sharing our feelings with the Almighty, we link ourselves to the Eternal Source of all being.

We live in a stress-filled world, and face a constant stream of challenges. Optimism, decisive action, and spiritual calmness can help us with our "transformational coping"—our ability to respond well and effectively to the crises and problems that confront us.

I Want It NOW!!!

I have been reading a new book by Israeli Nobel Prize Winner Dr. Daniel Kahneman, *Thinking, Fast and Slow* (Farrar, Strauss and Giroux, New York, 2011). On p. 47, he cites a fascinating psychological experiment conducted some years ago by Walter Mischel and his students.

A group of four-year-old children were given a choice between a small reward (one Oreo cookie), which they could have at any time, or a larger reward (two cookies) for which they had to wait 15 minutes under difficult conditions. They were to remain alone in a room, facing a desk with two objects: a single cookie and a bell that the child could ring at any time to call in the experimenter and receive the one cookie. The room had no toys, books, or other potentially distracting items, so the children had to deal directly with the temptation to eat one cookie or to wait 15 minutes and thus be rewarded with two cookies. About half the children managed to wait the 15 minutes.

Dr. Kahneman reports on the follow up of this experiment:

> Ten or fifteen years later, a large gap had opened between those who had resisted temptation and those who had not. The resisters had higher measures of executive control in cognitive tasks, and especially the ability to reallocate their attention effectively. As young adults, they were less likely to take drugs. A significant difference in intellectual aptitude emerged: The children who had shown more self-control as four-year-olds had substantially higher scores on tests of intelligence.

This and other psychological experiments have demonstrated a strong correlation between self-control and personal development. Those who want instant gratification tend to under-perform in major aspects of life; those who are able to be patient often achieve greater rewards and self-fulfillment. One who can keep focused on larger goals, avoiding immediate diversionary temptations, has a far greater likelihood of living happily and successfully.

This discussion sheds light on this week's Torah portion. Our forefather Isaac preferred his son Esau over his son Jacob. He thought Esau had the strength to be a real leader of people, while Jacob was a quiet boy who stayed close to home. Yet the Torah describes Esau as an impetuous, tempestuous personality. When he came home from hunting, he was hungry. He wanted his food NOW. He excitedly said that if he didn't get his food right away, he would die! He sold his birthright for a bowl of lentil soup.

Esau was a classic example of one who wants instant gratification, and who cannot defer his immediate desires to achieve a larger or better goal. To him, satisfaction of his momentary hunger was more pressing than the long-term goal of inheriting the birthright and becoming the next link in the family's leadership.

Esau was stronger than Jacob. Esau was more energetic and more physically active than Jacob. But Esau is described as someone who says: I want it NOW! I can't wait. I'll take a bowl of soup now, rather than wait to inherit the birthright. He was like the child who chose one Oreo, instead of waiting fifteen minutes to get two cookies.

Esau's impetuosity was his undoing. It undermined his personal development and ultimately allowed the family leadership to devolve upon his younger brother, Jacob. Although Jacob was weaker and quieter than Esau, Jacob was able to keep focus, putting off immediate gratification in order to attain larger goals. Isaac came to realize that his wife, Rebecca, had made a sounder judgment about the future of their sons; she had understood that the quiet strengths of Jacob would eventually prevail over the impetuous strengths of Esau.

It often has been pointed out that the regimen of mitzvoth teaches us self-control and self-discipline. We may be tempted to eat this food or that food, but the mitzvoth instruct us to wait until we have kosher food and until we recite the appropriate blessings. We may be tempted to do this or that deed, but the mitzvoth instruct us to refrain from work on Shabbat and holidays, to refrain from immodest and unjust behaviors, to put off immediate "gains" for long-term commitment to our ideals and values. In short, the mitzvoth serve as a basic framework for helping us to fulfill our potentials, and to lead happy and meaningful lives. They teach us to avoid impetuosity and immediate gratification, and to stay focused on our long-range goals of living righteous and good lives.

Some people succumb to the "I want it NOW" syndrome; and most such people ultimately undermine their own potential success and happiness. The Torah and mitzvoth teach us to maintain our self-control and self-respect. If we keep in mind the vision of our ultimate goals and aspirations—and if we can be strong enough to overcome diversionary temptations—we can hope to achieve a life of personal fulfillment and happiness.

 Thoughts on

Making Room for Prayer in Our Synagogues

"How full of awe is this place! This is none other than the house of God, and this is the gate of heaven."
—BEREISHITH 28:17

🕊 A story is told of the great Hassidic master, Rabbi Levi Yitzhak of Berdichev. He had been visiting a town, and attended prayer services in the local synagogue. One day, he stopped at the synagogue door and did not enter the sanctuary. The many people who were accompanying him were perplexed. Why did the rabbi not enter the synagogue? Rabbi Levi Yitzhak told them: I am not entering the synagogue because it's too crowded. But the synagogue was empty! The rabbi explained: The synagogue is full of prayers, there's no room left for us. Usually, when we pray, our prayers ascend to the gate of heaven; however, in this synagogue, the prayers are recited without proper concentration and devotion, so the prayers don't reach heaven. In fact, they are trapped in the synagogue building—so there is no room left for us in the synagogue.

The people then understood. Our spiritual goal must be to raise our hearts and voices in prayer so that the prayers will ascend to the gate of heaven. This can only happen if we are sincerely engaged in our prayers. If we simply go through the motions, rattle off the words, and then rush off to our business—then the prayers remain in the synagogue, and the room becomes too crowded.

It is often suggested that people become more engaged in their prayers if they actively participate in the synagogue services. If they sing together, if they participate in the synagogue "honors"—then it is said that they reach a deeper spiritual level. The operational word is: "participation." The more we participate, the higher our prayers ascend.

While not discounting this approach, I think it is more fruitful to think differently about our prayers in synagogue. The key need not be participation in services, but rather finding spiritual space. We find spiritual space, oddly enough, when the synagogue service leaves us alone, when it doesn't call on us to participate, when it doesn't intrude on our quiet inner thoughts and meditations. The inconspicuous person sitting in the back row may be more spiritually alive and connected than those who are actively participating in the presentation of the synagogue ritual.

Surely, the prayer services require formal participation and involvement. Yet the ritual needs to be seen and experienced as a vehicle to help raise us spiritually. The words of our liturgy are bursting with meaning. The melodies of our prayers can lift us and inspire us. Participating externally in the services does not mean that we've felt the presence of God, or that we've really offered our prayers in such a way that they ascend to the gate of heaven. What we need more than participation is a sense of spiritual space, a sense that we have the freedom to express the feelings of our hearts, minds, and souls. Synagogue services that allow us this freedom to find our own spiritual space are those that help us raise our prayers to heaven.

Public worship offers us a framework for reaching out to God as a community. It is a vital component in a healthy religious life. But public worship is at its best when it inspires us to search deeper into our hearts and souls, when it allows us spiritual space for personal prayer and reflection. It's perfectly acceptable to pray quietly and inconspicuously. It's fine to request that our neighbors in synagogue refrain from chattering and disturbing our tranquility. It's okay to fall behind the service in order to focus more carefully on a passage that has captured our imagination. It doesn't matter where we are sitting in synagogue: We all have equal access to God, if we will only realize how powerfully true this is.

We don't want our synagogues to become "crowded with prayers" that are trapped within the sanctuary. We want to feel that we are in the house of God, and that our prayers can ascend to the gate of heaven. We need to make room for sincere prayer in our synagogues.

Mountains to Ascend

ℝ Two mountains are of special significance in our religious tradition.

Mount Sinai was the site of the Revelation of God to the people of Israel. This was the place where the Torah was given, where our religion was established. Yet, we do not actually know where Mount Sinai is! Some claim to identify this mountain, but we do not have a clear, unbroken tradition as to its actual location. We don't have major tours and excursions to this holiest of locations. We don't pray facing toward Mount Sinai.

Mount Moriah is identified in our tradition as the site of the binding of Isaac. In this week's Torah portion, Jacob is described as having had his wondrous dream—with a great ladder connecting heaven and earth, and with angels ascending and descending it—at "the place"—identified by rabbinic tradition as Mount Moriah. We know exactly where Mount Moriah is, and we visit it often. It is better known today as the Temple Mount, the place in Jerusalem where the ancient Temples stood, and where the Western Wall remains as a reminder of the sanctity of the place. When we pray, we face Mount Moriah.

Why is Mount Sinai—the place of the ultimate Revelation of God to the Israelites—so insignificant as an ongoing religious site, whereas Mount Moriah has continued to be a central feature of our religious life throughout the centuries?

In the case of Mount Sinai, the place of the Revelation is not the essential thing: the message is. The voice of God is everywhere and for all time, and is not limited to a particular mountain. Rabbinic teaching has it that each day a divine voice calls out from Sinai, reminding us to study Torah and be loyal to its words. We do not know where Mount Sinai is, because it is in fact a symbol of every place. We do not have tours to Mount Sinai because the voice of God is everywhere.

Mount Moriah—the location of the *Akedah* and of Jacob's dream—represents a different religious reality. If Mount Sinai symbolizes God speaking out to humans, Mount Moriah symbolizes frail human beings reaching out to God. Whereas the Revelation at Mount Sinai was witnessed by hundreds of thousands of Israelites, the *Akedah* and Jacob's dream were experienced privately, without public fanfare. If the Torah had not recorded these stories, we would never have known about them. Mount Moriah gained its sanctity and centrality not as the place where God dramatically spoke out to humans as at Sinai; but from the quiet, pious, sacrificial, and sturdy faith of lonely human beings crying out to God.

The site of the Temple Mount was sanctified by memories of the devotion, faith, and frailty of our forefathers. The Temple was where humans reached out to the Almighty, where they brought their first fruits in thanksgiving, where they brought sin offerings. The measure of the sacrificial service was determined by the sincerity of the people, by their joy and/or contrition—known only to themselves and to God. Mount Moriah is of eternal significance to us because it reflects our inner religious life and aspirations. It is symbolic of our reaching out to God in good times and bad.

Our tradition speaks of a third mountain: the Mountain of God. Psalm 24 asks: "Who shall ascend the Mountain of God, and who shall stand in His holy place?" It answers: "The clean of hands and pure of heart, who has not taken His name in vain nor sworn deceitfully."

Each one of us climbs his or her own mountain. Each of our lives is an attempt to ascend closer to the Lord, closer to personal fulfillment. Some people climb mountains that seem wonderful and strong—but are essentially hollow. Others climb mountains that seem quiet and un-extraordinary, but they are strong and lasting. The measure of our success is not our wealth, fame, or popularity; the measure is being clean of hands, pure of heart, sanctifying God's name, being honest and trustworthy.

Mount Sinai reminds us that God speaks to us. Mount Moriah reminds us that we long for God. The Mountain of God reminds us that we have lives to lead, mountains to climb, things to accomplish. These three mountains together help us structure our lives and our religious imaginations.

"I lift my eyes unto the mountains, whence comes my help? My help is from the Lord, Maker of heaven and earth" (*Tehillim* 121).

Thoughts on וישלח

Essential Humility

"I am not worthy of all the mercies and all the truth
which You have shown unto Your servant."
—BEREISHITH 32:11

🌱 Jacob had a remarkable curriculum vitae. He was the patriarch of a large family. He possessed an impressive amount of livestock and was quite wealthy. By external standards of success, Jacob had achieved a lot during his years with Lavan.

Many people, when feeling they have been successful, become egotistical. They take pride in their wealth, or power, or superiority in their field of endeavor. They may come to feel that they are somehow immune to the vagaries of life, that they aren't bound by the rules and regulations that govern the masses of people, that they have the right to impose their wills on others. Such people border on idolatry—the worship of their own selves!

Jacob, however, set a different example. Although exceptionally successful in his worldly endeavors, Jacob came before God with the admission of *"katonti"*—I am not worthy of all the blessings I have received. *"Katonti"* implies that Jacob thought of himself still as a child dependent upon God his Father. He did not become inflated with egotism and self-adulation. On the contrary, he continued to worry about the future challenges he would be facing; he recognized his limitations and his need to turn to the Almighty for help.

The 23rd Psalm ends with a puzzling verse: "Surely goodness and mercy shall follow me all the days of my life, and I shall dwell in the house of the Lord for length of days." Even if God had shown abundant kindness to David in the past, how could David be so certain that this goodness and mercy would surely follow him all the days of his life? I think the verse can properly be understood if we translate the word *akh* differently. Instead of meaning "surely," it should be translated "even if." The verse then should be understood as follows: Even if goodness and mercy shall follow me all the days of my life, I shall not abandon God; I shall not leave the presence of the Lord; I shall humbly receive these blessings and acknowledge God as their source. I will not become arrogant or egotistical, no matter how successful I may become in worldly matters.

In our morning prayers, we confess before God that we are cognizant of our ultimate smallness. "Are not the mightiest as naught before You, people of renown as if they were not, the wise as if without knowledge, the intelligent as if lacking in understanding?" This prayer reminds us to keep our lives in focus. No matter how much wisdom we have attained, no matter how powerful we are, no matter how much wealth we have accumulated—it is all as vanity in the face of eternity.

It is precisely when we understand our ultimate smallness that we can begin to relate more honestly to God and to our fellow human beings. We can do our best to serve God and humanity—not for the sake of glorifying ourselves, but for the greater glory of God.

The strife, violence, and warfare that plague humanity stem largely from human arrogance and egotism, from jealousy and greed, from the desire to exert power and demonstrate lordship. These qualities are evident in our every day interactions with fellow human beings, as well as in national and international relations. We cannot achieve redemption—not individually and not as nations—until we learn to say "*katonti*," until we learn basic humility, until we see our lives in context with the eternal God.

Confronting our Enemies

☙ In a recent lecture for the Institute for Jewish Ideas and Ideals, Professor Zvi Zohar quoted from the writings of Rabbi Ya'akov Moshe Toledano (1880–1960), who served as the Sephardic Chief Rabbi of Tel-Aviv from 1941 to 1960. Rabbi Toledano was critical of rabbis who called on Jews to accept their fate passively. These rabbis taught that Jews must bow to the harsh decree of Exile and servitude to the nations, until such time as the Almighty decides to grant us ultimate Redemption.

Rabbi Toledano wrote:

> Let me state outright, that—begging their pardon—they [these rabbis] caused the loss of individual lives and of entire communities of the Jewish people, who in many instances might have saved themselves from death and destruction, had the leaders and rabbis of the generation instructed them that they were obligated to defend themselves against aggressors. . . . (*Yam HaGadol*, H.M. 97)

He went on to praise the "flowers of this new generation who 'awoke and wakened' to revive oppressed hearts, to engirdle themselves with a courageous spirit, and to restore the crown of Israel's honor to its pristine glory."

During the many centuries when Jews passively accepted the injustices and cruelties committed against us, the oppressors took full advantage of our weakness. They confined us to ghettoes; they branded us as pariahs; they deprived us of basic freedoms; they committed acts of violence and murder against us; they planned and executed a Holocaust of European Jewry.

With the rise of modern Zionism, Jews decided that enough is enough. It was time—well past time—for the Jewish people to assert its own rights, to have its own sovereign homeland, to fight actively against those who oppress us.

The nations of the world were unaccustomed—and are still quite surprised—to see Jews who have shaken off the garb of passive victims, who have become politically active, who have created a strong and heroic State of Israel. If the historic levels of anti-Semitism have not declined in the modern period, at least everyone now knows that the Jews do not and will not accept anti-Semitism without fighting back.

As Rabbi Toledano noted, we may take pride in the heroism of the new generations of Jews who have demonstrated a courageous spirit and who have striven "to restore the crown of Israel's honor to its pristine glory."

Defending Jewish life and honor requires multiple strategies. We may gain insight from this week's Torah reading which describes Jacob's forthcoming confrontation with Esau. Jacob was returning home after many years in the domains of Lavan. Jacob had a large retinue with him—his family, his workers, his flocks. He learned that Esau was approaching with 400 men. Jacob well understood that Esau's forces were powerful and that Esau could wipe out Jacob and his entire retinue. How did Jacob prepare for his dangerous confrontation with Esau?

Drawing on the Torah's description of events, Rashi notes that Jacob adopted three strategies. First, he prayed to God. Second, he sent Esau gifts and engaged in diplomacy. Third, he prepared his company for possible battle. All three of these strategies, employed simultaneously, led to Jacob's success in his dealing with Esau.

Some think that praying alone is all that is necessary. We should accept whatever God wills. Such a philosophy, criticized so sharply by Rabbi Toledano, is still advanced by segments of the Orthodox community. It sounds as though it is pious—yet in fact it is self-destructive. It gives full sway to the enemy to wreak havoc on us. It surrenders human initiative, and leaves us at the mercy of those who would harm us.

Some think that we can achieve our goals solely by means of diplomacy. If we give enough of our property to the enemy, this will lead to peace. If we speak in diplomatic niceties, we will gain the goodwill and cooperation of others. However, such a policy is also self-destructive. The enemy is never satisfied with our concessions and always demands more. The enemy's goal isn't to gain a bit more property from us; their goal is to destroy us. Concessions and diplomacy alone cannot solve our problems.

Some think that we must rely on our military strength. If we have enough arms and missiles, we can force the enemy to submit to our will. We can overcome their hostility only if we show them that we are much stronger than they are and that we can do them great harm. Yet, such a policy leads to an unpleasant reliance on military might that can corrode our way of life, and can give a false sense of security. Enemies, after all, also have access to arms and missiles; living in a constant state of military confrontation is not happy or healthy.

We may learn from our forefather Jacob that confrontation with the enemy requires a three-fold strategy. We must turn to the Almighty and strengthen our spiritual lives. We must be ready to engage in diplomacy and concessions, as a reflection of our genuine wish to find ways to achieve peace and goodwill. We must have the military might to back up our prayers and our diplomacy.

For many centuries, Jews became accustomed to an attitude of passivity and defenselessness. They relied on prayers or on material gifts to those in power. In the modern period, Jews have added the strategy of political and military power. Our task today is to maintain a proper balance that includes all three dimensions.

By blending our spiritual, diplomatic, political, and military approaches, we can help "restore the crown of Israel's honor to its pristine glory."

Private Life and Public Exhibitionism

🖎 A recent scandal in our community relates to an article written by a student in an Orthodox women's college, published in a school publication. The author of the article tells of a sexual encounter—real or imagined. Defenders of the article argue for the right of freedom of expression. Critics complain that the article (published anonymously) reflects immoral behavior and should not have been included in a student publication of an Orthodox school. The media have enjoyed reporting on this incident, as they enjoy reporting on scandals in general.

Why would a student write such an article? Why would the editors of the publication agree to publish it?

Ostensibly, the student wrote the article to unburden herself of guilt. By describing her (real or imagined) experience in a public way, she must have gained some psychic relief. The editors chose to publish the article as a way of generating thought and discussion about an issue that seldom is discussed openly in an Orthodox school.

Seen in a wider context, it seems that a lot of people like to tell stories of their personal lives to large audiences. The media are filled with television shows where people tearfully confess their various sins; with salacious newspaper and magazine articles; with blogs and other social-media posts, where people reveal intimate details of their personal lives to be seen by any who choose to tune in. Exhibitionism seems to be fashionable among a large number of people. Modesty and personal discretion are not too popular in the modern media culture.

Many people do not seem to realize that there must be a boundary between private life and public life. It has been noted that not everything that is thought should be said; not everything that is said should be written; not everything that is written should be published. Modesty and personal discretion are important ingredients in life; one must be able to discern when to act/speak, and when silence is preferable. One must know and appreciate the value of privacy and personal dignity.

This week's Torah portion offers examples of serious mistakes in interpersonal relationships. Much agony could have been spared if the people involved would have maintained a proper boundary between private thoughts and public behavior and speech.

Jacob showed favoritism to Joseph and made him a special coat of many colors. Every parent knows (or should know) that showing favoritism to a child is an egregious error. It leads to jealousies and antagonisms among the children. Even if Jacob privately had a special love for Joseph, he could have/should have kept this to himself to the extent possible. By public shows of favoritism to Joseph, Jacob undermined the peace of his own family.

Joseph must surely have sensed that his brothers were jealous of him. But when he had dreams that implied his lordship over them, he went to them and related these dreams. Why didn't he just keep these dreams to himself? Why did he feel the necessity to tell the brothers his dreams, when this could only deepen their hostility to him?

If Jacob and Joseph had acted and spoken with more discretion, if they had kept their thoughts and dreams to themselves—the family would have been much happier and healthier.

One must know when to speak and when to refrain from speaking. One must have the intellectual and moral tact to know when and where it is appropriate to reveal one's inner thoughts, and when it is appropriate to be silent.

Maimonides discusses the issue of whether one should confess sins in public. In *Hilkhot Teshuva* 2:5, he notes that it is a great virtue for a penitent to confess his or her sins in public and reveal sins that had been committed against others. This is part of the process of repentance. It makes a person face up to his or her sins, and to be humbled by his or her errors. Maimonides then states that this rule applies only to sins committed against fellow human beings. "But sins between a person and God need not be publicized, and it is brazen to publicize them; rather, one should repent before God, blessed be He."

If one has committed crimes against others, one should admit these crimes and face the public censure that comes with this confession. If one has committed religious indiscretions that are a matter between him or her and God, then it is brazen to announce these sins in public. Rather, one should confess these transgressions privately, keeping them as a private matter between him or her and God.

The "tell-all" media climate encourages people to cross the line between the private and public aspects of their lives. It encourages people to compromise their dignity and self-respect.

When one has a private issue to discuss, one should discuss it privately with a trusted mentor or friend. If one feels guilty or unhappy about something, it is helpful to talk things out with someone who can help one to cope better with the situation. If one feels that a certain topic needs to be brought to the public's attention, one can find means of doing this without engaging in personal confessions.

Blurring the boundaries between private life and public exhibitionism is not simply a religious error; it is a mistake in the way we deal with our own humanity.

Thoughts on חנוכה

If I Had a Hammer

✍ The Shabbat of Hanukkah was observed among Sephardim of the Ottoman Empire as "*Shabbat Halbashah*," the Shabbat of providing clothing for the needy. Traditionally, the rabbi would deliver a sermon that day on the mitzvah of charity and lovingkindness. Beginning the following day, members of the community would bring clothing to the synagogue, and it would be distributed among the poor on Rosh Hodesh Tebet, the sixth day of Hanukkah.

A practical reason for this custom is that Hanukkah occurs just as winter approaches. It is imperative that the community provide clothes for members who lack adequate clothing to keep them warm during the cold season. Moreover, Hanukkah celebrates the sense of unity that prevailed among those Jews of antiquity who fought against the Syrian-Greek oppressors, and who re-dedicated the Temple in Jerusalem. Just as our ancestors recognized their responsibility to each other and to God, so must Jews of each generation recognize our commitment to each other and to God.

A Judeo-Spanish proverb states: "*el harto no cree al hambriento*"—one who is full does not believe one who is hungry. When one lives in relative prosperity, it is not always easy to feel empathy for those who lack basic necessities. People become complacent. Or they say: I worked for what I have, let the others work for what they lack. Why should I give my hard-earned money to help others? The one who is satisfied might not feel the genuine hunger pangs of the poor, and might not respond eagerly or compassionately enough.

In his story, "Gooseberries," Anton Chekhov writes:

> There ought to be behind the door of every happy, contented man someone standing with a hammer continually reminding him with a tap that there are unhappy people; that however happy he may be, life will show him her laws sooner or later, trouble will come for him—disease, poverty, losses, and no one will see or hear, just as now he neither sees nor hears others. But there is no man with a hammer. . . .

Shabbat Halbashah serves as a "hammer," as a reminder that we are all responsible for each other, that we need to provide for others just as they will need to provide for us if we should be in distress.

The lesson surely applies to providing material support for those in need. But I believe it can be extended to spiritual, intellectual, cultural, and communal life as well. The Jewish community sponsors a host of institutions dedicated to promoting Jewish life—synagogues, schools, cultural organizations, communal agencies, and so forth. These institutions attempt to look after our spiritual lives and to provide services and comfort to all of us. Just as we must be sensitive to the physical needs of the poor, so we must be sensitive to the spiritual needs of our entire community. It is easy to say: let others support these institutions, let others pay for these needed services, let others take responsibility for a flourishing Jewish communal life.

Shabbat Halbashah serves as a hammer, gently tapping on the wall, reminding us to become empathetic, involved, and sharing members of our community. There are so many challenges facing the Jewish community: Each of us needs to play an active role in strengthening and advancing our goals.

As we observe Hanukkah, let us remember to provide sustenance to those in physical need, and to provide sustenance for the spiritual needs of our entire community—since all of us need and benefit from the institutions that foster Jewish life at its best.

Hanukkah and Religious Freedom

Hanukkah is widely observed as a holiday that celebrates religious freedom. The persecuted Jews of ancient Israel waged battle against their Syrian/Hellenistic oppressors, and won the right to rededicate the Temple and to restore Jewish worship and religious practices.

Religious freedom is a wonderful thing. It allows us to worship God freely, without being coerced or intimidated by others.

Religious freedom is not a self-evident fact of life. As Jews, we have experienced many circumstances in which we did not enjoy this basic right. Medieval Iberia expelled Jews and Muslims, believing that only Catholics have the truth and that "infidels" must not be tolerated. Saudi Arabia of today does not tolerate non-Muslims to practice their religions freely. Indeed, throughout history (including our own times), various groups have not granted religious freedom to "outsiders." Only the faithful had rights in this world; and only the faithful would be blessed in the world to come. The infidels were deprived of rights in this world, and were doomed to perdition in the world to come.

The great nineteenth-century rabbi, Eliyahu Benamozegh of Livorno, pointed out an obvious—but startling—fact. In his book *Israel and Humanity*, he noted that historic Christianity and Islam claimed to be universal religions—and yet, they were not universal at all. They only made room for fellow believers; "infidels" were persecuted, even murdered. Those of other religions were not granted equal rights in this world, and were deemed to be unworthy of blessing in the world to come. Judaism—which is often depicted as a small, parochial tradition—is actually the religion that is the most universal. It teaches that all who accept the basic Noahide laws of morality are beloved by God. The righteous of all nations have a place in the world to come. While not condoning outright idolatry, Judaism leaves much theological space for non-Jews to achieve spiritual happiness and fulfillment. All humanity is created in the image of God.

When we light the Hanukkah candles, we need to remember the value of religious freedom. We also need to remind ourselves—and others—that religious freedom is a two-way street. It allows us to claim the right to practice our religion freely; but it also entails that we grant this same freedom to others who do not share our religious beliefs and practices.

Religious freedom is a problematic concept for those who are sure that they, and only they, have the absolute Truth. Such people tend to be extreme and intolerant. Since only they have the Truth, they have no patience for those who have other beliefs; indeed, they don't see the need to grant rights to others. They feel compelled to crush the "opposition," either by converting them, by coercing them, by oppressing them, or even by murdering them. For the single-minded bigots, religious freedom exists only to serve their interests and to guarantee their freedoms; but it doesn't involve a mutual commitment to religious freedom for others.

Even within the Jewish community, we have those who take this extreme view of religious freedom. They are happy to enjoy the benefits of freedom; but they disdain those Jews whose beliefs and observances are different from theirs.

Those who see themselves as the only Torah-True Jews do not think they should make religious space for others; on the contrary, they feel that the others should be brought into line with them even by means of coercion. They discredit those who are not in their camp. In Israel, where such extremists exert political power, they initiate coercive action and legislation that impinge on the freedom of others. Since they are convinced that they alone have Truth, they feel warranted in coercing others to follow in their ways. Their mentality is similar to extremists of other religions who find it difficult or impossible to let others enjoy religious freedom.

Religious freedom is not such a simple concept, after all. While it protects each of our rights to practice religion freely, it also demands that we respect the rights of others to do likewise. Religious freedom is the hallmark of a tolerant and wise nation and community. It is a lofty ideal to which all should aspire.

As we celebrate Hanukkah, let us seriously celebrate the value of religious freedom. Let us serve God with purity, with commitment, with spiritual heroism. And let us appreciate that all human beings also deserve the right of religious freedom. When extremists seek to deprive others of this freedom, all society suffers a loss of freedom and dignity.

The Hanukkah lights remind us that we can bring light into a dark world. We can hope that our lights will inspire others and bring them closer to the Almighty.

"Not by might, nor by power, but by My spirit said the Lord of hosts" (*Zekharia* 4:6).

Prudence in Good Times and Bad

🐦 Thanks to Joseph's interpretation of Pharaoh's dreams, the Egyptians were spared a terrible calamity. Joseph offered a plan whereby the Egyptians could store produce of the seven years of abundance, so that they would have food during the following seven years of famine.

What if Joseph had not been there to give this advice? Presumably, the Egyptians would have fully enjoyed the seven years of abundance, thinking that prosperity would never end. When the famine would then arrive, the people would have been unprepared for the economic downturn. They would soon have run out of food and would have suffered years of starvation.

Joseph's plan was good not just for the ancient Egyptians, but for all societies of all eras. Wise people know that economic life is marked by cycles of ups and downs, sometimes quite extreme cycles. There are periods of great prosperity and there are periods of dearth. There are bull markets, and there are bear markets. Prudent people always keep Joseph's plan in mind. When things are good, they don't get carried away with their good fortune. They save some of their funds and try to build up a financial reserve, so that they will be able to weather periods of economic downturn.

During periods of affluence, it is not easy to remember Joseph's plan. When things are going well, we have plenty of money; we feel generous; we spend freely. We don't often focus on the inevitable economic decline that will eventually hit us.

The *Jewish Forward* newspaper (December 16, 2011) reported on salaries received by top executives in Jewish not-for-profit organizations. A surprising number are being paid in the range of $400,000 to a high of $848,000 per year. These very high packages were probably offered at a time when the economy was booming and Boards felt comfortable being highly generous with Jewish charity dollars.

I subscribe to the notion that Jewish not-for-profits need to pay proper salaries to their employees. Unless proper compensation packages are offered, these institutions will not be able to attract the best and the brightest executives. Good executives are essential to the fulfillment of the missions of those organizations for whom they work.

However, I do question what constitutes "proper compensation." I recently read that President Obama's salary as President of the United States is $400,000 per year. With all respect to the executives in Jewish organizations, none of their jobs compares in difficulty and responsibility to that of the President of the United States.

The problem gets stickier when we realize that the top executives of our not-for-profit institutions have other lower level administrators on their staffs. If the top executives are making huge salaries, we can suppose that their vice-presidents and assistants are also making healthy amounts of income. This means that every time we make a contribution to these institutions, significant chunks of our donations go to support the executive team.

We understand the need to pay for overhead; otherwise the institutions could not function well. We understand the importance of paying respectable compensation packages. But it is difficult to get enthusiastic about making donations to institutions whose chief executives are being paid annual salaries of four, five, six, seven, eight hundred thousand dollars and more.

Perhaps one of the reasons salaries are so high is that the Boards of these institutions are often composed of very wealthy people. They may be earning millions of dollars a year and have vast estates; to them, $400,000 or $800,000 doesn't sound like all that much. Even baseball players get paid millions of dollars a year; so what's the problem with offering a half million or more dollars to our executives?

But what about those millions of people who don't earn astronomical amounts, and who are asked to make donations in order to support extravagant lifestyles for the executive staffs of the institutions who are soliciting their donations? And what if these millions of people lose confidence in the idealism of those executives who take huge salaries, even at a time when they are laying off workers? People might naturally ask: "Why should I be donating money to these institutions, when I'm struggling to pay my own bills, to pay my children's Day School tuitions, to put food on the table?"

During the prosperous years, these compensation packages (while a questionable use of charity dollars) do not seem so perturbing. After all, wealthy members of the Board contribute to cover these costs. The public feels economically well off and offers its contributions generously.

But when the "seven lean years" arrive, these compensation packages must surely raise eyebrows. It is unpleasant to receive requests for donations from institutions whose executives receive higher compensation than the President of the United States.

Joseph taught the ancient Egyptians the importance of prudence. When things are going well, we should not get carried away. We should stay focused on our long-range needs. We should build our financial reserves so that we will better be able to cope with eventual economic downturns.

We could use a Joseph today to help us plan properly for the long-range health and strength of our communal institutions. But until such a Joseph emerges, this responsibility devolves on each of us. Let us be wise; let us be prudent.

Halakhic Guidance for New Realities

🐾 When Jacob and family set out for the land of Egypt to re-unite with Joseph, the Torah informs us that Jacob sent Judah ahead "to show the way before him unto Goshen" (*Bereishith* 46:28). The Midrash offers an interpretation: Judah was sent ahead in order to establish a center for Torah study and "*hora-ah*"—a place for giving definitive halakhic rulings to guide the family in their new setting. This anachronistic interpretation (the Torah wasn't given to the Israelites until hundreds of years later!) reflects an interesting rabbinic insight.

I believe that this Midrash is indicating the vital importance of proper spiritual leadership—especially in new circumstances. Jacob had been able to provide religious leadership while the family lived in Canaan. But now that the family was moving away to settle in Egypt, Jacob was concerned about the spiritual health of his family in the new environment. He was already an old man; he may not have been confident of his ability to adapt to the new circumstances and meet the needs of the younger generations. So he sent Judah to establish a base for Torah study and *hora-ah*—instruction in practical religious living. Jacob understood that a new situation demanded new insights, new interpretations, new applications of old principles. He sent Judah ahead to set the spiritual framework for the Israelites.

Hora-ah—halakhic decision-making by our teachers—is an essential ingredient in religious life. The public needs to have clear answers and definitive guidance on matters affecting their religious observance. But the public also needs to have halakhic decision-makers who are not only versed in sacred texts, but who are fully aware of new realities and new circumstances.

Rabbi Haim David Halevy, late Sephardic Chief Rabbi of Tel Aviv, indicated that various rabbinic texts needed to be reevaluated in light of the newly established State of Israel. He argued that it was halakhically unsound to point to texts written during the many centuries of Jewish exile, and to apply those texts uncritically to problems facing a sovereign Jewish State. For rabbis to offer proper guidance to the Jewish State, they first need to recognize that they are living in a new situation, a new era; that the Jewish State has new responsibilities and challenges not explicitly discussed in the rabbinic literature that developed while Jews lacked their own State. Rabbis cannot make proper halakhic decisions relating to the State of Israel unless they first understand the nature of governmental responsibility for society—economics, military matters, diplomacy, international relations, democratic principles, and so forth.

A "ruling" was recently issued by over 40 rabbis in Israel that it is halakhically forbidden for Jews in Israel to sell homes or land to non-Jews. These rabbis cited texts from Maimonides and the *Shulhan Arukh*. This "ruling" is an example of narrow halakhic interpretation that ignores the new realities of maintaining Israel as a democratic State. The rabbis—in their concern for strengthening the Jewish population in Israel (especially in the North)—ignore the democratic principles upon which Israel was founded; foster discriminatory policies against non-Jewish Israeli citizens; shame Israel in the eyes of the democratic world; and justify anti-Jewish policies in territories and countries under non-Jewish control. These rabbis demonstrate a pre-modern mindset that does not factor in the real needs and responsibilities of a sovereign democratic Jewish State.

Fortunately, many—including the Prime Minister of Israel—have raised their voices in strong criticism of the statement by this group of rabbis. Rabbi Yuval Cherlow, the Rosh Yeshiva of the Yeshivat Hesder in Petah Tikvah, has argued that it is halakhically permitted to sell homes and land in Israel to non-Jews, and that this indeed is demanded by the democratic principles of Israel. If the rabbis are concerned about increasing the Jewish population in various areas of Israel, they should encourage Jews to move in—not forbid non-Jews from buying homes.

Our forefather Jacob understood that new times and new circumstances created new challenges for "showing the way" of Torah and halakha. We can't operate as though nothing has changed in the past hundred years. We can't provide meaningful and valid guidance if we are not fully aware of the broader implications and ramifications of our decisions. Narrow learning and narrow perspective lead to a stunted view of Torah and halakha—and ultimately undermine the credibility of those who claim to be halakhic decision-makers.

Let us remind ourselves of the fundamental Jewish teaching about Torah: "Her ways are ways of pleasantness, and all her pathways are peace."

The Ins and Outs of Synagogue Life

❧ In their fascinating book, *American Grace*, Professors David Campbell and Robert Putnam report on the state of religion in America. Based on comprehensive surveys and interviews across the country, they found that the overwhelming majority of Americans believe in God and identify themselves with a religious tradition. For religious Americans, this is pleasing news.

At the same time, the book also includes some unsettling information. The number of Americans who list themselves as "Nones"—i.e., those who do not identify with any religion—has become the fastest-growing religious demographic. Roughly 12 percent of Americans claim that they have no religious affiliation. Among younger Americans, that number rises to about 25 percent. Only a small percentage of those who list themselves as "Nones" are actually atheists. Most consider themselves to be spiritual human beings who believe in God or in some higher power, with only a small percentage who claim to be atheists.

The question arises: Why have these "Nones" opted out of formal religious affiliation?

Campbell and Putnam suggest that public discourse in America has mixed politics and religion so thoroughly, that many choose to opt out of both. Others have suggested that the secularized intelligentsia of America constantly speak disparagingly of religion and of God; this impacts especially on university students who are subject to indoctrination by left-leaning, anti-establishment, anti-religious professors.

Other factors may play a role in the alienation of a growing number of Americans from religious institutions: corruption of religious leaders; hypocrisy of religious spokespeople; self-righteous attitudes by this or that religious denomination; the bureaucracy of religious movements/institutions; church/synagogue politics and infighting; the expense of formal affiliation; the spiritual irrelevance of various forms of worship.

The issue of "Nones" relates to the Jewish community as to other religious groupings. We need to examine why Jews would willingly abandon their synagogues. Aside from reasons offered above for general disaffiliation, perhaps we can derive some insight from a rabbinic teaching relating to this week's Torah reading.

When Jacob and family began their sojourn to Egypt, the Torah reports that Jacob sent his son Judah ahead. The Midrash (*Bereishith Rabba* 95:3) suggests that Judah was tasked with setting up a meeting place where the family could gather to study Torah.

According to this Midrash, Jacob knew that the destiny of his family did not only depend on the food to be obtained in Egypt, but on the spiritual sustenance of the family's religious traditions. He sent Judah ahead, so that when the family arrived in Egypt they would immediately find a framework for the continuation of their spiritual lives.

The meeting place established by Judah was to provide the family with constant religious guidance. The purpose of that meeting place was to inspire, to encourage, to console—to bring people into a closer relationship with the Almighty. Those who gathered there would gain spiritual strength; they would maintain good morale and proper morals.

This model continues to be relevant today. We build synagogues as meeting places where we can all come together for Torah instruction and inspiration, for prayer and spiritual elevation. We want—and desperately need—our synagogues to be powerful bastions of religious ideas and values. We want our synagogues to raise our spirits and raise our understanding; we want our synagogues to inspire us to righteous living and social justice.

If a synagogue (or any religious institution) loses sight of its *raison d'être*, it becomes an artificial construct. Religious institutions can become so involved in the mundane aspects of running a "business" that their core ideas and mission are marginalized. People seem more concerned with the perpetuation of the synagogue organization than on the teachings for which the synagogue was established in the first place. When organized religion becomes overly "organized"—it runs the risk of losing its soul. When it loses its soul, it should not be surprised if people will opt out and become "Nones."

Each Jewish congregation would do well to think very carefully about its mission, its traditions, its responsibilities, its challenges. Although it is highly important to have meetings about repairing the synagogue's roof and planning the annual dinner, it is also highly important to have meetings to explore why we exist in the first place. How can we transform our synagogue by focusing on its role as a meeting place for Torah study and meaningful prayer? How can we transform our lives by engaging in acts of kindness, charity, and social justice? How can the synagogue be that central place where we can come to find enlightenment, inspiration, communal belonging?

For most of us, synagogue affiliation is rightly an important part of our lives. But for a growing number of "Nones," the synagogue is increasingly irrelevant. The vast majority of "Nones" seem to be spiritually alive and in search of religious meaning. If synagogues can re-focus on their core missions and can communicate their ideas and ideals to the wider community, we can hope that our synagogues will not only serve us better, but will also attract seekers who are looking for something authentic and meaningful.

Our forefather Jacob understood that his family needed a meeting place in order to maintain and enhance their spiritual lives. We must understand the need for our synagogues to play this role in our lives today.

Synagogues don't exist merely to perpetuate themselves; they exist to fill our spiritual needs, to foster our religious aspirations, to make us better human beings.

Thoughts on וידוי

Souls and Goals

🕮 Rabbi Dr. David de Sola Pool served Congregation Shearith Israel in New York City for a period spanning 63 years, from 1907 until his death in December 1970. In remembrance of the 40th year anniversary of his passing, I quote from an article he wrote in 1944, entitled: "Are We Disinheriting Our Own Children?"

> What parent would willingly disinherit a child, the child that looks to the parent with hero-worshipping trust? Yet tragically many are the parents in Jewry who are so preoccupied with trying to give their children a material inheritance that they disinherit their children of their spiritual heritage. They treat the child almost as if it were his lot to grow up to be a citizen of a world that is all body and mind, without soul. Our children have a right to a soul.

Dr. Pool lamented that parents are so busy making a living, they sometimes forget what is really important in life. They devote tremendous time and energy to material needs, but give scant attention to their own and their children's spiritual needs. Their children have the latest clothes, computers, technological inventions—but their homes don't reflect Jewish religious observances and traditions, don't manifest the joy and sanctity of Shabbat, don't echo with the sounds of Torah study and discussion. Even in those homes where religious observance may be higher, the observance may be a matter of rote and habit rather than a fulfillment of religious ideas and ideals.

If parents do not communicate a positive experience of Judaism to their children, they run the risk of disinheriting their children from their spiritual roots.

Many years ago, I met with an elderly member of our Congregation who was nearing his death. He had come to the United States from Europe as a young man; he worked hard; he married and had four children; he built a phenomenally successful business. He raised his children in luxury. He and his wife saw to it that their children went to the most elite private schools, attended the best colleges, drove the nicest cars. But they did not maintain a religious Jewish home; they did not give their children Jewish education beyond a Sunday school level. The father worked seven days a week in order to assure his family of a good, successful, and happy life. This congregant was basically a good man. He had a deep Jewish identity, and was generous to Jewish charities.

As he approached the end of his life, he called to speak with me. With tears in his eyes, he told me that he could not understand what had happened with his family. After all, he was a good Jew, a devoted member of the Jewish people. He worked so hard for so many years to create a prosperous life for his family. Now, as the sun was setting on his life, he realized that he had amassed a huge material fortune—but had lost his children to Judaism. All four had married non-Jewish spouses; one of them had converted to Christianity and was a deacon in his church.

In the well-known story, Faust sells his soul to the devil in order to achieve worldly success. At the end of his life, he realizes that the earthly success he had attained was essentially meaningless; he had traded his soul for empty and vain symbols of power. The story of Faust continues to resonate, because it repeats itself in so many lives. People lose sight of the ultimately important things, trading their souls for fleeting signs of material success. They not only lose their own souls; they disinherit the souls of their children.

The Torah tells us that our forefather Jacob, when he was about to die, called his children together. The Midrash suggests that Jacob was deeply concerned: Would his children carry on the faith and ideals that were so dear to him, that he had tried so hard to communicate to them? To reassure him, the children said in unison, Hear O Israel, the Lord is our God, the Lord is One. Jacob was so pleased to hear this united affirmation of faith, that he responded: Blessed be His name and glorious sovereignty forever and ever.

No matter how high or low our level of religious knowledge and observance is, we can all devote more and better time to the spiritual development of ourselves, our children, and our grandchildren. We all would like our children and grandchildren to affirm their Judaism and their Jewishness. We need to stay focused on this ultimate goal. We all have the right—and the deep need—for a soul.

Memory, History, and Us

℘ Some time ago, I was watching old home movies that were filmed during the early 1950s. On the screen I saw myself as a little boy. The movies were filled with laughing, dancing, singing relatives and friends—many of whom are no longer alive. I had the surrealistic experience of watching my parents—both long deceased—when I was actually much older than they were at the time when the movies were taken.

Looking at old movies or old photographs has a way of casting a spell on us. It transports us into the past. For a few short moments, we may vividly feel that we've returned to the past, that we are reliving an earlier time in our lives.

Studies of memory have demonstrated that we do not merely remember past events, but we also remember the feelings associated with those events. We smell freshly baked bread—and suddenly we are a child in our mother's kitchen. We hear a synagogue melody—and suddenly we are a little boy holding our father's hand in the synagogue, we are a little girl sidling up against our mother.

Our lives are deeply enriched by the memories of our past. We especially value those precious instants when we seem to be transported into the past, into the world of our memories.

This phenomenon has great relevance for our understanding of our relationship to history. As Jews, and as human beings, we are able to expand our memories far beyond our own personal experiences. By reading and studying, we enlarge our historical memories to include the generations that have preceded us. The more expansive our knowledge of the Jewish past, the more intense and the more vibrant should be our own Jewishness. We see the past not as something distant and impersonal, referring to others; but rather, we experience history as part of our own extended memory. It is personal and immediate. We empathize with and identify with our ancestors, almost as though we are with them.

This week's Torah reading includes Jacob's blessing of his grandchildren and concludes with the words: "and let my name be named in them, and the name of my fathers Abraham and Isaac; and let them grow into a multitude in the midst of the earth" (*Bereishith* 48:16). The medieval Italian Jewish commentator, Rabbi Ovadia Seforno, suggests that Jacob wanted his descendants to feel linked to their righteous ancestors, so that they would live their lives so as to be worthy progeny of Abraham, Isaac, and Jacob. They were to recall their ancestors not as abstract personalities, but as genuine presences in their lives.

For the Jewish people, history has always been experienced as a dimension of the present. As we go through life, we bring along our ancestors. We carry their names, we feel their presence.

Professor Yosef Hayim Yerushalmi, in his book *Zakhor*, makes a distinction between history and memory. History is an academic discipline dedicated to uncovering data from the past. It is cold, objective, dispassionate. On the other hand, memory is warm and personal. Professor Yerushalmi notes a paradox that while modern Jewry has experienced a phenomenal explosion in the field of Jewish history, the Jewish memory seems to have declined seriously. Jews may know more facts about Jewish history, but they may feel less connected to those facts.

We need to understand without any equivocation that Jewishness lives and is transmitted by means of memory, by feeling a living connection with our past. The study of history should lead us to expand our memories and our identification with our people's past; it should help us to feel that we are part of the long chain of Jewish tradition.

Home movies and old photographs are made of inanimate material. The people in the pictures cannot change. What gives life to the figures is our memory. Likewise, the data of Jewish history can only come alive if we animate them, if we treat them not as abstractions but as real and ongoing presences in our lives, if we can feel—at least at special moments—that we ourselves have re-entered the past.

Our continuity as a people is inextricably linked to our historical memory. We bring the past into the present; we project the present into the future. This is one of the great responsibilities of Jewish parents and grandparents—to imbue the younger generations with a sense of belonging to, and participating in, the history of our people.

This is also one of our great privileges and a source of our deepest fulfillment as Jews.

Thoughts on שמות

What Is Your Name?

🖎 When I was a student at Yeshiva College many years ago, I saw a passage scribbled onto a subway wall at the IRT 181st Street station. That passage had a big impact on me then, and continues to be important to me so many years later. The passage was a quotation from Alan Watts: "For when man no longer confuses himself with the definition of himself that others have given him, he is at once universal and unique."

It is so easy to confuse ourselves with definitions of ourselves given to us by others. People may stereotype us, may impose their standards on us, may treat us as objects rather than as autonomous human beings. They may judge us based on our religion, race, or political views; they may see us as "the other" without ever bothering to see who we really are. When we are constantly being dehumanized or stereotyped by others, it is all too possible for us to internalize the external definitions of ourselves imposed on us by friends and foes alike.

The Torah portion relates that Pharaoh feared the growing numbers of Israelites in Egypt, and he decided to enslave them and to have their male children murdered. Rabbi Hayyim Angel has pointed out that the Torah conspicuously avoids mentioning the names of any Israelites or Egyptians—except for Shifra and Puah—from the time Joseph died until the birth of Moses. (Pharaoh is a title, not a personal name.) People—both Egyptians and Israelites—had become nameless objects—oppressors and oppressed, masters and slaves. When humans are reduced to things, then both the oppressor and oppressed are dehumanized; they internalize false ideas about who they are and about their true worth as human beings.

To be universal and unique—to be who we really are—we need to develop a strong inner life that enables us to resist becoming victims of dehumanization. Dr. Bruno Bettelheim, who had been a Jewish prisoner in a German concentration camp, wrote that the prisoners feared not only for their physical lives; they feared that they would come to see themselves as the Nazis saw them—as animals. "The main problem is to remain alive and unchanged...the more absolute the tyranny, the more debilitated the subject."

A Midrash (*Tanhuma, Vayakhel*) teaches that each person has three names: the name given by parents, the name given by fellow human beings, and the name that one acquires for him/herself.

The name given by parents represents the parents' hopes for the child. The name may link the child to an ancestor; or may be something untraditional. This name reflects the parents' values and traditions. Each of us is shaped by the name our parents gave us. This is good and valuable for us, but should not be allowed to undermine our own individual freedom and choices. Parents should give us roots; but also wings.

The name given to us by fellow human beings represents our reputation in our community and wider society. The name might tend to idealize us or to demonize us; it might be true to who we are, or it might be a total misreading of who we are by people who do not know us or understand us. If we live our lives by the definitions given to us by others, we live a life of shadows and illusions.

These first two names are given to us by others. The third name, though, is what we acquire for ourselves. This name draws on what we've learned from parents and fellow human beings; but its ultimate source is our own individual minds and souls. Inside each of us is our own "name," our own real being. This is who we really are when we rise above externally imposed definitions of ourselves.

Throughout our lifetimes, we learn—we grow—we strive. Each of us is a work in progress. We derive strength and inspiration from many sources. We are accosted and dehumanized by unpleasant and hateful people. If we are to develop the full potential of our lives, we need to focus on the name we acquire for ourselves—our true selves. We need to foster the inner strength and wisdom to be universal and unique. We need to answer the question: What is your name?

For the Greater Glory of God

🦌 The great nineteenth-century English writer and art critic, John Ruskin, wrote an impressive work on Gothic architecture. In carefully studying the details of classic Gothic-style churches, he noticed a phenomenon of the deepest religious significance.

As could be expected, the craftsmen who worked on the churches' facades demonstrated remarkable skill. They obviously devoted tremendous effort and talent to make the churches' exteriors as beautiful as possible. Yet, Ruskin noticed that the craftsmen who worked on parts of the church buildings that were not visible to passers-by—high up on the roof, or behind walls, or eventually to be covered by ivy—were equally careful in producing magnificently beautiful designs. Even though these workers knew that no one would ever see their work, they nonetheless maintained the highest possible standard of workmanship. Ruskin was amazed. Why would workers be so diligent in creating art that would never be seen or admired by others?

The answer: These workers were not creating art to impress people. Rather, they were creating art as a sign of devotion to God. They were motivated by the purest love of God, by the desire to serve God with all of their ability and all of their emotion. They worked with such diligence not to gain accolades from human beings, but from a desire to serve the Lord anonymously and purely.

The greatest religious gestures do not stem from egotism or the desire to impress others; the greatest religious gestures arise when one manifests true love of God, humbly and quietly, without the slightest expectation of approbation from others.

When religious observance is tainted with egotism, the desire for power, the yearning for recognition—it is deficient. When religious devotion is expressed selflessly and modestly, it can rise to the greatest heights. This is true not only in one's private religious expression, but also in one's interpersonal relationships.

This week's Torah portion gives us a keen insight into the religious greatness of Aaron, the brother of Moses. It offers a model of genuine spirituality and humility.

At the dramatic scene of the burning bush, God appoints Moses to lead the Israelites out of their bondage in Egypt. Moses is reluctant to accept this responsibility and asks God to choose someone else. He claims that he is not articulate enough, perhaps reflecting a more general feeling that he was not up to the task.

God insists that Moses take on this responsibility. He tells Moses that his brother Aaron will be at his side, and will be able to speak on behalf of Moses. God informs Moses that Aaron will come to meet him, *"vera-akha, vesamah belibo,"* and he will see you and rejoice in his heart. These three Hebrew words have tremendous meaning, and tell us much about the greatness of Aaron and why he became the beloved High Priest of the people of Israel.

Aaron was older than Moses. Aaron had been living in Egypt all these years when Moses was living in peace as a shepherd in Midian. Aaron had to deal firsthand with the slavery of his people and obviously had a much clearer understanding of the situation than did Moses. One might have thought that Aaron was more entitled to have been chosen by God to be leader; he was older, more experienced, and more directly involved with the people of Israel. And yet, God chose Moses!

How would we imagine Aaron's reaction upon learning that God had chosen his younger brother, a shepherd in Midian, to be leader of Israel? We might have expected that Aaron would be jealous, angry, insulted, and resentful. But God tells Moses: Aaron will see you and rejoice in his heart! Not only was Aaron not upset, but he genuinely rejoiced in Moses' success. Aaron was not an egotist, he was content with his lot. He was not just superficially courteous to Moses, but he "rejoiced in his heart," sincerely and totally. Aaron had a unique capacity: the capacity to love, to rejoice fully in the success of others without feeling a grain of jealousy or ill-will.

It is not easy for people to rejoice in the success of others. People think: I should have received that honor, I am more deserving, I am more qualified. It is not easy for people to rise above egotism, jealousy, and resentfulness. To do this requires tremendous self-confidence, spiritual poise, serenity—and love. It requires the ability to transcend one's own ego, and celebrate in the virtues and successes of others. Aaron had these virtues.

The artwork of anonymous craftsmen of the gothic churches demonstrates love of God without ulterior motives. Aaron's piety shows the way to a religious life that fosters love and inner harmony in our interpersonal relationships. Purity in our religious devotion to God must be accompanied by purity in the way we conduct our lives. Our thoughts and deeds must be directed to the greater glory of God—in purity, humility, selflessness, and love.

Thoughts on וארא

Spiritual Slavery and Freedom

🐚 "The mitzvoth are the dictates of God, and we are bound to obey them as a servant obeys his master." This is the topic of a paper assigned to a cousin of mine, who is taking a class in Jewish studies. The class is studying various religious movements within Judaism, and the above statement was meant to characterize the Orthodox view. Obviously, the way the statement is phrased paints a narrow picture of Orthodoxy— implying that we are compelled to do mitzvoth unthinkingly, and we function essentially as mindless, mechanical slaves.

Although the Torah and rabbinic literature certainly contain sources that refer to the people of Israel as "*avadim*" (slaves) to the Almighty, the actual meaning of the term is far more nuanced than the English word "slave" connotes. For example, Moses is called God's "*eved*," but this is a term of high praise. It means that Moses had risen to the highest spiritual level possible for a human being. When the Israelites are told that they were no longer slaves to any human beings, but were only God's "*avadim*," this was a great moment of redemption and inner freedom for Israel. Yes, the mitzvoth are dictates of God; and yes, we are bound to obey them; but the relationship of Israel to God—as mediated through mitzvoth—is not meant to be one of blind subservience. We are not to see ourselves as victimized slaves who are compelled to slavishly fulfill the whims of our master.

What is the status of a slave? Haham Solomon Gaon, whose death anniversary we observed this past week, commented on the hard work and lack of spirit which overtook the Israelite slaves in Egypt.

> Hard work, when undertaken for the sake of achieving a certain aim can prove inspiring, but when such an aim is lacking in our endeavors, they then become a source of demoralization. The children of Israel in Egypt could not understand the meaning of the forthcoming redemption as announced by Moses because they had lost the spirit which had animated the undertakings of their forefathers. They were without courage, without faith, and this situation was aggravated by the fact that they had

to do work under cruel conditions and under aimless pressure which did not give them any sense of achievement. (*Haham Gaon Memorial Volume*, Sephardic House, 1997, p. 121)

Slavery is equated with powerlessness, futility, total subservience to cruel, unfeeling masters who have no regard for the slaves' value as independent human beings.

This is radically different from the "slavery" imposed on the Israelites by God. By being servants of God, the Israelites became free from domination by human beings; they found a clear direction and meaning in their lives. God did not impose mitzvoth on us in order to crush our freedom and autonomy, but rather to give us divine guidance on how best to live our lives. The mitzvoth are basic sources of freedom and spiritual blessings—not heavy, mindless burdens. As Maimonides explained, each of the mitzvoth was given by the all-wise God in order to perfect us. The mitzvoth were given with love and wisdom by our Creator who loves us and who wants us to find the highest fulfillment in our lives. The mitzvoth enable us to escape the ennui and futility that characterize so much of humanity.

I told my cousin that I would rephrase the title of the paper he was assigned: The mitzvoth are commandments of God, and we have the privilege of fulfilling them as a means of coming closer to God.

The *Pirkei Aboth* teaches that no one is as free as one who occupies him/herself with Torah. Those who truly experience Torah and mitzvoth are blessed with an incredible inner freedom, autonomy, and meaning in life. It is a supreme honor and privilege to be called "*eved Hashem*," a servant of God.

The great seventeenth-century figure, Dr. Isaac Cardoso, said it well: To those who despise Torah, six commandments seem like 613. To those who love Torah, 613 seem like only six. Whether Torah and mitzvoth are a blessing or a burden—this is very much in the eyes of the beholder. We are on the side of blessing.

The "Bystander Problem"

❧ A talmudic passage (*Sotah* 11a) offers an imaginary scenario relating to when Pharaoh was deciding to enslave the Israelites and murder their male babies. "Said Rabbi Hiyya son of Abba in the name of Rabbi Simai: Three were involved in that decision: Bil'am, Job, and Yitro." Bil'am, who advised in favor of these evil decrees, ultimately died a violent death. Job, who remained neutral, was later punished with horrible sufferings. Yitro, who opposed Pharaoh's decrees, had to flee, but was ultimately rewarded so that his descendants were great teachers of Torah.

The moral lesson of this teaching is that those who promote evil—like Bil'am—are eventually punished. Those who courageously resist evil—like Yitro—may suffer in the short run, but will ultimately be rewarded. Those—like Job—who remain neutral in the face of wickedness will endure horrible sufferings.

Bil'am went along with Pharaoh's decisions either because he actually agreed with Pharaoh, or because he thought it was in his own best interest not to resist the monarch. By being a "yes man," Bil'am would gain power and favors from Pharaoh. He had no qualms about becoming an accomplice to enslaving a whole nation and murdering their babies. Justice demands that Bil'am be punished for his moral turpitude.

Yitro resisted Pharaoh's decisions, even at personal risk. Yitro would not be party to wicked decrees. He stood up on behalf of the endangered Israelites and was compelled to flee from Pharaoh's wrath. Justice demands that Yitro be rewarded for his moral heroism.

But what about Job? What is the nature of his sin that made him deserving of terrible sufferings? After all, Job did not say that he agreed with Pharaoh; he did not validate Pharaoh's decrees. He simply stayed silent. He was prudent. He may have thought: "Pharaoh is going to do this regardless of what I say. Why should I endanger myself? Why should I incur his anger? Why should I stand up for the Israelites, or for righteousness, or for compassion? The safest thing for me is to remain neutral."

For his neutrality, Job was punished. Abstaining from moral responsibility is also taking a stand! When evil is not resisted directly, it is thereby allowed to flourish. As the nineteenth-century political thinker Edmund Burke said: "All that the forces of evil need to prevail is that enough good men do nothing." Evil flourishes in a moral vacuum. It cannot be extirpated without active resistance. Individuals and nations who "abstain" in the face of evil are accomplices of evil. Neutrality in the face of injustice and cruelty is not a morally acceptable position.

Psychologists have written extensively on the "bystander problem." Why do so many stand aside when they witness violence, cruelty, injustice? Why doesn't everyone feel a moral commitment to stand up on the side of right-eousness? Why are there so many Jobs and so few Yitros?

Job's neutrality—the "bystander problem"—might stem from perceived self-interest. Why should I get involved? Why should I take risks that might have negative consequences for me? Why should I antagonize those in power?

A main reason for the "bystander problem," though, seems to be that peo-ple do not assume personal responsibility. They rationalize: There are others who can intercede; there are others who are better able to help; somebody else will take responsibility, so it isn't necessary for me to get involved or to make personal sacrifices. It isn't that bystanders are necessarily immoral or heart-less; rather, they may simply not take things personally. They think: It isn't my issue; it isn't my responsibility; it's for others to solve.

Erich Fromm observed: "Most people fail in the art of living not because they are inherently bad or so without will that they cannot live a better life; they fail because they do not wake up and see when they stand at a fork in the road and have to decide" (*The Heart of Man*, p. 138).

This is the root of Job's sin: He did not wake up and realize he was at a fork in the road where he had to make a decision. That decision would define the nature of his character, his life itself. By remaining silent, he chose to be a "bystander," to let the forces of evil gain sway. He forfeited personal responsi-bility, not because he was a bad person but because he was a weak or self-cen-tered person. The sufferings of others did not awaken moral indignation within him. As a result, he himself ultimately underwent horrendous sufferings.

The talmudic lesson reminds us that we must not be part of the "bystander problem," but must take moral stands in the face of injustice, cor-ruption and wickedness. We must accept personal responsibility, and not assume that others will solve the problems for us.

The world is full of Pharaohs who promote wickedness and injustice. The world is full of Bil'ams who are only too happy to go along with the powerful Pharaohs. The world is very full of Jobs who stay silent and neutral in the face of evil. The world has a shortage of Yitros who realize that they stand at a fork in the road and have to decide, and have to take personal responsibility.

At the Threshold

🕮 In their new book, *American Grace*, Robert Putnam and David Campbell present a thought-provoking analysis of the role of religion in the United States. Based on a large nation-wide survey as well as exhaustive scholarly research, the authors provide keen insight into how religion divides and unites us. Although there are certainly clear rifts in our society based on religious beliefs, the overall tone of American life is actually quite tolerant and inclusive. The nation-wide study found that Americans feel warmest toward Jews, mainline Protestants, and Catholics. Jews actually are in first place in this regard, and the authors report that the "Jews are the best liked religious group in the country." This may come as a surprise to many Jews who see themselves as an unpopular or hated minority group.

The authors do not offer specific reasons for the popularity of Jews in America. They do suggest, though, that religious tolerance is fostered by the fact that Americans of different backgrounds often interact with each other. This personal interaction serves to break down negative stereotypes. By knowing people of various religions and races, working with them, establishing friendships with them—we come to realize how much we share in common. We come to respect others—and the groups of which they are part.

By extension, perhaps Jewish popularity in America can be understood as a result of the many positive interactions Jews have with their non-Jewish compatriots. In a positive stereotypical way, Jews are seen as people who value education, hard work, good citizenship, and strong family ties. Jews are well-represented in education, medicine, law, social work, public service, government, the arts, humanitarian organizations, and business. Jews are seen to be good people, good neighbors, and good citizens.

The flip side of the Jews' popularity is that non-Jews are happy to marry us! The rate of interfaith marriages in the United States among Americans in general is high and growing. The same is true among American Jews. The question arises: How can we participate actively and equally with non-Jewish

Americans, and yet retain our distinctive Jewish way of life—including the creation of Jewish marriages and Jewish families? We surely want to be respected and loved—but not loved out of existence!

The Torah portion of the week alludes to the significance of the threshold of the Israelites' homes, to distinguish themselves from the Egyptians. The threshold of the home was a defining marker. One of our ongoing mitzvoth is to place a mezuzah on the doorposts of our homes. The mezuzah contains a parchment with the first two paragraphs of the *Shema*. Thus, the very threshold of our homes has a significant marker separating the inner world of our homes from the outer world of general society.

The mezuzah serves as a reminder to us every time we leave or enter our home. It stands as silent testimony to the presence of God, to the importance of the mitzvoth, to the holiness that is to characterize a Jewish home.

American Jews need to pay close attention to the mezuzah. It instructs us on how we can maintain our distinctive religious traditions. When we cross the threshold from our homes into the public square, we glance at the mezuzah and remember who we are, what our religion teaches; we carry the sanctity of our traditions with us where ever we are. When we return home, we glance at the mezuzah and are reminded that we now re-enter our private, sacred space. When we learn to comfortably pass back and forth across the threshold, we learn that we can be devoted, faithful Jews—and at the same time, we can carry that faithfulness into our relationships with others. We can be pious Jews and good citizens. We can be devoted Jews and fine human beings.

Darkness that Leads to Light

❦ Rabbi Yitzhak Shemuel Reggio, a nineteenth-century Italian Torah commentator, offers an interesting insight concerning the plague of darkness. The Torah states that Egyptians spent three days in deep darkness while "all the children of Israel had light in their dwellings."

Rabbi Reggio opines that the plague of darkness did not befall the land of Egypt—but rather the eyes of the Egyptians. Egypt itself was full of light; but while the Israelites continued to enjoy that light, the eyes of the Egyptians were blanketed in darkness. If an Egyptian stood right next to an Israelite, the Egyptian would be unable to see—but the Israelite would see clearly.

Rabbi Reggio notes that after the plague of darkness, the Torah reports that "the man Moses was very great in the land of Egypt, in the eyes of Pharaoh's servants and in the eyes of the people." It seems that the Egyptians did not recognize the greatness of Moses until after they had experienced darkness. This plague somehow caused a transformation within them. They started to see things differently, more clearly. It took darkness to make them see the light!

For many years, the Egyptians did not think twice about their enslavement of the Israelites. This was a "normal" fact of life, not to be questioned. They did not see that anything was morally wrong with the status quo. They had grown so accustomed to their pattern of thinking, that they did not question the validity of their assumptions and their lifestyle. When they were plunged into absolute darkness, they began to realize how wrong they had been. They came to understand that their assumptions and patterns of behavior were immoral. When they "saw the light," they then recognized the greatness of Moses. He was, after all, telling the truth! He—not Pharaoh—was the agent of truth.

The transformation within the minds of the Egyptians may also be evidenced by the Torah's later statement that the children of Israel found favor in the eyes of the Egyptians, so that the Egyptians gave them presents. The Egyptians no longer saw the Israelites as slaves, as objects to be exploited; rather, they saw the Israelites as fellow human beings who had been cruelly mistreated. Egyptians felt empathy toward the Israelites, whom they had previously treated so callously and viciously. They wanted to give them presents, to demonstrate human solidarity.

Rabbi Reggio's insight might be extended to relate to human life in general. People live with assumptions, values, and patterns of behavior typical of their societies. They do not necessarily self-reflect on whether these assumptions are true or ethical. It is highly difficult to rise above one's milieu and judge one's reality in a dispassionate, honest manner.

Professor Daniel Kahneman, the Israeli Nobel Prize winner in Economics, has coined the phrase "illusion of validity." He points out that we tend to think that our own opinions and intuitions are correct. We tend to overlook hard data that contradict our worldview and to dismiss arguments that don't coincide with our own conception of things. We operate under the illusion that our ideas, insights, intuitions are valid; we don't let facts or opposing views get in our way.

The illusion of validity leads to innumerable errors, to wrong judgments, to unnecessary confrontations. If we could be more open and honest, self-reflective, willing to entertain new ideas and to correct erroneous assumptions—we would find ourselves in a better, happier, and more humane world.

The ancient Egyptians had the illusion of validity, believing that their murderous, slavery-ridden society was fine. They did not question their lifestyle, opinions, or worldview. It took the plague of darkness to make them think more carefully about the nature of their society—and the nature of their own humanity. Once they "saw the light," they were able to make positive adjustments. Although Pharaoh and his army continued to foster the pre-darkness views, the people as a whole seem to have re-oriented their way of thinking and acting.

The plague of darkness might symbolize the need for each of us to periodically clear our minds, re-evaluate our assumptions, and see where we might have fallen victim to the illusion of validity. In the darkness and quiet of our inner selves, we can try to shed light on our opinions, values, attitudes, and behaviors. We can try to rise above ourselves, as honestly and objectively as possible.

An old proverb has it that "no one is so blind as the one who refuses to see." We might offer an addendum to this proverb: "No one sees so clearly as the one who has first experienced darkness."

Thoughts on בשלח

Worries about Our Worrying

✍ *Q.* What is the text of an Emergency Alert sent out by a Jewish Organization?

A. Start worrying! Details to follow.

This joke reflects an ongoing reality of Jewish life. There always seems to be something to worry about, some crisis that is about to erupt, some threat to our survival. Even when we don't yet know the details, we are called upon to get into the worrying mode.

The late Professor Simon Rawidowicz wrote a fascinating essay entitled "Israel—the Ever-Dying People." He points out that in each generation, going back many centuries, Jews thought that Jewish history was coming to an end. They worried about destruction at the hand of vicious enemies; they worried about exiles and expulsions; they worried about spiritual decline; they worried about assimilation. It seems that since the time of Abraham, we've been worrying about our imminent demise. Although we have been "ever-dying," Professor Rawidowicz reminds us that after 3,500 years we are still alive!

Perhaps our very awareness of the fragility of our existence has given us an added tenacity to survive, to find ways of solving problems. The nineteenth-century rabbi, Israel Salanter, once quipped: "When people come to a wall that they can't go through, they stop. When Jews come to a wall that they can't go through—they go through."

This week's Torah reading includes the dramatic episode of the Israelites crossing the Red Sea. When they reached the shore of the sea, they faced an existential crisis. Behind them, the Egyptian troops were coming to destroy them. In front of them was the Red Sea. They were trapped, with no obvious solution to their dilemma.

The Midrash tells of various reactions among the Israelites as they pondered their imminent destruction. Some said: We should have stayed in Egypt! Others said: The situation is hopeless; we and our families will perish. Woe unto us.

The common denominator of these approaches is that they led to psychological and emotional paralysis. Crying over what they could have done or should have done did not address their current crisis; it stifled their ability to cope. Declaring the situation to be hopeless led to despair. They came to a wall—and they stopped.

The Midrash tells that Nahshon ben Aminadav, head of the tribe of Judah, walked into the Red Sea. When the water reached his neck, then the sea miraculously split—and the Israelites were saved. Nahshon is described as a great hero because he took things into his own hands; he acted decisively; he risked his own life.

Yet Nahshon's heroism was not the result of a sudden burst of desperation. Rather, we can imagine that Nahshon deliberated carefully before entering the sea. He might have thought: God performed so many miracles for us in Egypt; God obviously has unlimited power; if God wanted us to be liberated from Egyptian servitude and to be brought into the Promised Land, surely God can and will make good on His promises to us. Armed with this reasoning, Nahshon entered the Red Sea. He was confident God would redeem His people. Nahshon came to a wall—and he went through; and he brought the rest of the people through as well.

When we receive Emergency Alerts from Jewish organizations telling us to start worrying because we are facing enormous threats, we should worry. But we should worry in the right way. Worrying that stems from regret that we should have or could have done things differently—such worrying is negative and self-defeating. The past is over, and we need to confront the crisis as it faces us now. We don't have the option of returning to the past to undo decisions. (Hopefully, we can learn from these past decisions when we get through the current crisis, and contemplate how to make future decisions.) Likewise, it is not productive to sink into self-pity and passive despair. Indeed, despair feeds on itself and infects others with a spirit of helplessness.

We should worry like Nahshon worried. We should not minimize the dangers and the risks; but we should deliberate on what is at stake and how we can overcome the difficulty. We should have confidence that if God has brought us this far, He will keep His promises to us and bring us ultimate redemption. We should be ready to act decisively, to think "out of the box," to maintain forward momentum.

On April 17, 1818, Mordecai Manuel Noah—one of the great American Jews of his time—delivered an address at the dedication ceremony of Shearith Israel's second synagogue building, on Mill Street in lower Manhattan. He closed his talk with a prayer: "May we prove ever worthy of His blessing; may

He look down from His heavenly abode, and send us peace and comfort; may He instill in our minds a love of country, of friends, and of all mankind. Be just, therefore, and fear not. That God who brought us out of the land of Egypt, who walked before us like 'a cloud by day and a pillar of fire by night,' will never desert His people Israel."

For Ourselves and for Others

𝕎 A major theme in Jewish liturgy and religious observance is *"zekher litsiyat mitsrayim"*—in remembrance of the exodus from Egypt. The exodus was a central event that has profoundly impacted on the destiny of Israel. It ties together vital ideas: the providence of God; the election and nationhood of Israel; the victory of good over evil; the importance of prayer and song in expressing gratitude to the Almighty.

Rabbi Nissim Gerondi, a leading sage of fifteenth-century Spain, taught that the slavery experience was intended to purify Israel, to impress upon us the evils of oppression. We learned that we were to be kind to the stranger, for we ourselves were strangers in the land of Egypt. From this firsthand experience, we were to learn an unflinching commitment to righteousness to our fellow human beings. If Jews throughout the ages have been at the forefront of compassion and social justice, much of the credit belongs to our commitment to *"zekher litsiyat mitsrayim."*

This commitment extends not only to fellow religionists, but to humanity as a whole. A striking example occurred in New York on March 8, 1847.

Hazan Jacques Judah Lyons of Congregation Shearith Israel in New York City took the lead in organizing a community event to raise funds for Irish famine relief. Members of New York's Jewish community gathered at Shearith Israel, where Hazan Lyons gave an inspiring appeal to help the starving Irish. He recognized that the Jewish community had plenty of needs of its own. "We are told that we have a large number of our own poor and destitute to take care of, that the charity which we dispense should be bestowed in this quarter...that self-preservation is a law and principle of our nature."

At the same time, Hazan Lyons rejected this attitude. Yes, we must care for our own; but this does not preclude our offering help to those beyond our community who are also in need of assistance. He spoke of a connecting link between us and the Irish sufferers:

> . . . that connecting link is strong enough and long enough to withstand all attempts to make the separation [between us and them] complete and irreparable. . . . Forged as it was by religion, virtue, and charity, it is indestructible, it is all powerful. That link, my brethren, is HUMANITY! Its appeal to the heart surmounts every obstacle. Clime, color, sect are barriers which impede not its progress thither.

As Jews, we must care for our fellow Jews. As human beings, we must care for our fellow human beings. This is a large challenge, and not always easily balanced.

Maimonides (*Hilkhot Matanot Aniyim* 7:13) provided an order of priority in our charitable giving. One's relatives take priority over others. The poor of one's household have priority over the poor of the town; the poor of one's town have priority over the poor of other towns. A general rule is that the poor of the land of Israel are given the same priority as the poor of one's own town.

Although it is a priority to help those closest to us, this does not exempt us from helping a wider range of humanity. As Jews who remember our servitude in Egypt, we cannot be callous to the needs of others, to the cries of strangers.

One of the problems confronting contemporary American Jewish philanthropy is that Jews may have become too "universal"—offering vast amounts of charity to non-Jewish causes, while not providing enough for the specifically Jewish needs. American Jews surely support many Jewish causes here, in Israel, and throughout the world. But vast amounts of Jewish philanthropy are devoted to universities, cultural institutions, non-Jewish charities, humanitarian causes. While these are worthy causes, our philanthropic dollars should reflect at least an equal commitment to the Jewish people.

If we do not look out for ourselves, who will? But if we only look out for ourselves, then we have missed the key lesson of "*zekher litsiyat mitsrayim*"—the lesson that has molded us into a compassionate, sensitive, and kind people.

Thoughts on יִתְרוֹ

The Ten Suggestions?

🕊 Modern western civilization trains us to value independence, autonomy, freedom of choice. We have an aversion to being told what to do by authoritarian figures; rather, we like to make decisions based on our own judgment. We are open to advice and suggestions; but we are less than enthusiastic about being bossed around.

If a Revelation at Mount Sinai were to take place again in our times, we would probably prefer to receive the Ten Suggestions rather than the Ten Commandments. We can take or leave suggestions; commandments—especially from an authority like God—seem to leave us with little personal choice.

Because of popular discomfort with "commandments," the word *mitzvah* (which means commandment) is often translated as "good deed" or "act of kindness."

But for a religious Jew, commandments are viewed in a very positive light. They are not external burdens imposed on us, but avenues of connection with God. By living according to God's own guidance for us, we actually achieve a higher level of inner freedom. We are freed from extraneous concerns and worries; we can focus on what is really important in our lives, on our spiritual and moral development. When we fulfill a commandment, we feel the presence of the loving and all-wise Commander. Doing a mitzvah properly is liberating.

Dr. Barry Schwartz, in his book *The Paradox of Choice*, powerfully demonstrates how moderns are less happy because of the wealth of choices available to us. We demand autonomy and freedom to make choices—but at some point, things spin out of control. Instead of liberating us, our multitude of choices can paralyze us. People find it increasingly difficult to make decisions because they have too many options from which to choose. Even in matters of marriage, people find it problematic to make a decision—perhaps there's someone else out there who is better, richer, smarter. The happiness index in the United States has shown steady decline, even as material prosperity and number of choices have grown.

Happiness is not equated with the choices available to us, but rather on our ability to make the right choices. Dr. Schwartz suggests that people would be happier if they were not "maximizers" who insisted on getting the "best" of every choice they make. Rather, people should be "satisficers"—they should make decisions based on fewer choices and know when to be satisfied with their decisions.

Mitzvoth are a God-given road map to becoming "satisficers." We are trained to know which foods we may eat, and which foods we may not eat; which relationships are proper, and which relationships are not proper; which conduct is moral, and which conduct is immoral. By eliminating many useless and unproductive options, the mitzvoth direct us in the path of inner strength and freedom to make satisfying choices. Life is seen not as a grand competition to get the "best," but as an adventure in becoming our own best by coming closer to the ways of God.

By studying and observing mitzvoth—commandments—we put our lives into context with God. This is not an insignificant achievement. When given the choice to follow God's commandments or human beings' suggestions, we would be wise to choose the mitzvoth.

Bringing the Revelation to the World

❧ The people of Israel witnessed the singular Revelation of God at Mount Sinai, an experience that was to change the course of history. No other people before or since has had such a direct public communication from God.

A Midrash teaches that the words of the Revelation actually split into 70 languages, indicating that the Torah contains a message for the 70 nations of the world, i.e., humanity as a whole. The Israelites were chosen to be God's messengers, to deliver the teachings of Torah to the world. The nations were to see the Israelites as sources of divine truth so that they would say: "Surely this great nation is a wise and understanding people" (*Devarim* 4:6). The Talmud reports the opinion of Rabbi Eliezer that the Jews were exiled from their land in order to gather converts in the lands of their dispersion (*Pesahim* 87b).

Jews are expected to be great communicators, to bring important ideas to the nations of the world. To fulfill our responsibilities, we must recognize that we are part of the human family, that we must understand the languages and ideas of the nations, and that we must be able to enter into meaningful discussion with others. The Torah presents us with a vast agenda. This agenda can be met only through engagement and involvement with humanity. It would be incredible to think that God's expectation at Mount Sinai was that the Jewish people would live in isolation from the civilizations of the world, that we would be confined to physical and mental ghettos.

Yet, engagement with the civilizations of the world entails risks. If we learn the languages and cultures of other nations, we might assimilate into their patterns. Instead of bringing them closer to the ideals of Torah, we might ourselves be drawn away from the Torah way of life. The "outside world" presents dangers to our spiritual lives. Nonetheless, we are called upon to be a light unto the nations. In spite of the risks involved, we must have confidence that the Torah can successfully confront every civilization, that we can heroically maintain our own way of life while at the same time sharing in the life of humanity as a whole. We are to be a "wise and understanding people" actively participating in human civilization; we are not to be a reclusive, narrow people, afraid of the world, afraid of our own weaknesses.

Modern civilization surely poses spiritual dangers to the Jewish people. Some argue that it is best for Jews to give up on the world and simply worry about ourselves. Let us insulate ourselves from the "outside world" to the extent possible. Let us wall ourselves into spiritual ghettos.

It was recently reported that some rabbis, including the Sephardic Chief Rabbi of Israel, signed a letter forbidding the use of the Internet. They warned about the "spiritual dangers" and the availability of immoral content on the Internet. These rabbis claim that it is a Torah obligation to avoid using the Internet. If one's livelihood depends on it, one must be sure that the best possible filtering software is used to sift out all the sinful content on the Internet. Rabbi Moshe Shafir, editor of *Yom Leyom*, the newspaper of the Shas party, has described the Intenet as "a bad devil" subjecting its users to the worst religious sins a Jew could ever commit. He calls upon readers to "throw away this device of impurity and abomination, and obey the outstanding rabbis of the generation [who forbid using the Internet]."

Surely, the Internet has content that undermines religious values and ideals. Surely, every effort must be made to filter out the objectionable material. But is it realistic or religiously mandatory to avoid using the Internet?

The rabbis who forbid the Internet and think of it as a "bad devil" are essentially asking Jews to disconnect themselves from the major means of communication among the people of the world. They seem to overlook the vast amount of positive material on the Internet, including a tremendous number of Torah websites that have given religious knowledge and strength to so many thousands of people.

These rabbis want to march us back into the pre-modern era, thinking that if we only close our eyes and plug our ears, all the evils of the modern world will somehow vanish. Is their ruling going to make the Jews appear to be "a wise and understanding people" in the eyes of the nations? Or will it simply consign us to occupy the backwaters of human civilization, living as an isolated sect with no message to and no engagement with humanity?

It is proper to be concerned about the dangers of the Internet and other modern technological advances, and it is proper to provide filters and safeguards that protect us from improper material. But it is absurd to call on us to "throw away this device of impurity" when it is a powerful link between us and the rest of the world, when so much good can be accomplished through it. The Internet, as other modern technologies, is "neutral"—and can be used for good and for ill. The correct strategy is not to outlaw the Internet, but to instruct people on how to take advantage of its immense powers and how to avoid its negative elements.

At the Revelation at Mount Sinai, the Almighty surely expected something great from the people of Israel. He surely expected us to be His messengers in bringing the ideas and ideals of Torah to the nations of the world. He surely expected us to be viewed as "a wise and understanding people" who maintain exemplary righteousness. He expected us to have the spiritual strength and stamina to hold fast to our values while interacting constructively with the nations of the world.

משפטים

You Shall Not Oppress the Proselyte

🐾 The Torah commands emphatically: You shall not oppress the stranger. Rabbinic tradition has interpreted this commandment to refer to the sin of causing pain to converts to Judaism. Indeed, one who oppresses a proselyte is guilty of committing 36 (and some say 46) sins.

Since proselytes have made the choice to join the Jewish people and to accept the Torah, they are to be treated with great respect and sensitivity. To be faithful to the teachings of Torah necessarily entails being solicitous of the wellbeing of converts. To trample on the feelings of proselytes is to trample on the Torah.

To our chagrin and horror, it seems that this mitzvah has been violated—and continues to be violated—by the very rabbis who are supposed to be safeguarding Torah traditions. It seems to have become fashionable in some Orthodox rabbinic circles to follow the narrowest, most stringent and xenophobic opinions relating to the acceptance of converts. Instead of following the sensible and accessible teachings of Talmud, Rambam, and *Shulhan Arukh*, these extremists have imposed requirements that make conversion excessively difficult, and often very unpleasant for would-be converts. (Please read my article on conversion, in the *Min haMuvhar* section of jewishideas.org)

The problem is exacerbated by rabbis who cast doubts on halakhic conversions, if those conversions don't meet their extreme standards. Several years ago, Israel's Chief Rabbis cast doubt on conversions performed by Orthodox rabbis in the Diaspora, and indicated that they would not accept such conversions unless the proselytes went through a process approved by them. Thus, thousands of halakhic proselytes and their families have been caused terrible and unnecessary pain. Their Jewish identities are challenged or simply rejected.

A battle has arisen in Israel over the status of conversions performed by Israeli rabbis serving in the military. Thousands of converts and their families have had their Jewishness challenged and undermined by Hareidi rabbis. Recently, Israel's Chief Rabbi ruled that these conversions are all valid. No sooner had he uttered this ruling than did other Hareidi rabbis lambast him, and claim that his ruling has no validity. The very rabbis who should be worried about the sin of oppressing the proselytes are the most public and egregious violators of this cardinal Torah principle.

Is it good for the Jewish people and the State of Israel to be held hostage to the most extreme and rejectionist rabbis? Do we really want such rabbis to have the authority to decide who is and who is not Jewish?

While it would have been nice if the Chief Rabbinate in Israel had promoted a humane, compassionate, and inclusive program for conversion according to halakha—they obviously have not succeeded at this. On the contrary, they have ceded their authority to an increasingly vocal and extreme right-wing Hareidi rabbinate.

The status quo is intolerable for the State of Israel and for the Jewish people worldwide. The solution is for the government of Israel to "privatize" conversions—take this area out of the legal authority of the Chief Rabbinate. Thus, each person who wishes to convert should be allowed the freedom to study with the rabbi of his/her choice. The local rabbi will have a better understanding of each convert's situation than a bureaucratic Bet Din structure. Once a person is halakhically converted by recognized rabbis, that person is to be considered Jewish by the State of Israel. That person's conversion is not subject to retroactive annulment. That person is a Jew forever, without ever having to worry about having his/her Jewishness called into question by the Jewish State.

If segments of the community do not wish to accept such converts, that is their own sin and their own responsibility. They can follow the most extreme views in terms of their own personal choices; but those extreme views cannot be imposed on the State of Israel and on the rest of the Jewish people.

The oppression of proselytes is a sin of the greatest magnitude. Those who foster this oppression are violating the very halakha they purport to defend. The current wave of extremism brings shame on Torah, brings shame on halakha, brings shame on the high ideals of our religious tradition.

Sports and Sportsmanship

℘ At a recent basketball game between two yeshiva Day Schools, a parent of one of the players behaved very badly. He shouted abusive comments at members of the opposing team. He screamed a threat against one of the players.

This parent is an Orthodox rabbi, well known in his community; but he obviously was unable to control his rage and his overbearing competitiveness. Like so many other parents, he allowed his unbridled emotions to interfere with basic decency, good sportsmanship, and proper interpersonal relationships. His behavior shamed his son, shamed himself, and shamed the Torah.

Sports can and should be a framework for developing good values—teamwork, self-improvement, physical fitness. If managed properly, gym classes and athletic programs can be a tremendous boost in the moral and physical development of children.

Too often, though, these programs allow—and even encourage—the wrong values. They permit a few aggressive players to dominate play, and don't focus on developing the skills and self-confidence of all the students. They are more concerned with winning games than with making all players feel like winners. They overlook rough play and egregious fouls if they think that will help the team win games.

Too many parents, who should know better, encourage these negative features. They invest so much emotion into winning games that they seem to forget that much more important issues are at stake. They set exactly the wrong example for their children. They put exactly the wrong kind of pressure on gym teachers and coaches. Their egotistical drive to win games should not be allowed to undermine the values of good sportsmanship, teamwork, and respect for all players.

I attended Franklin High School in Seattle (there was no Jewish high school there in those days), and was blessed to have outstanding teachers—including gym teachers. I recall Mr. Luft, the school's football coach, and a man who produced a lot of winning teams.

In gym class, he set strict rules. For example, when we played basketball no shot could be made until at least three players on the team handled the ball first. No one was allowed to dribble more than twice. A third dribble meant the ball had to be turned over to the other team. We all abided by these rules, and all of us got a chance to be included in the game, to handle the ball, to shoot baskets.

The goal wasn't to "win at all costs"—but rather to help each player gain skills, experience, and self-confidence. This framework taught the need for teamwork, for inclusivity. Mr. Luft understood that an athletic program was intended to help each student reach his potential. He taught not only sports, but—even more importantly—sportsmanship.

This week's Torah portion reminds us that we are all responsible for one another. We need to be sure that we do not ignore or oppress those who are in positions of weakness, that we foster an inclusive and compassionate world-view. We need to think beyond competitiveness and beyond "winning at all costs"—and we need to focus on the development of morality and decency.

Since children generally enjoy physical activity, gym classes and athletic programs can and should be a tremendous asset for religious education. Children can receive life lessons in ethical behavior, sportsmanlike conduct, and consideration for the feelings of others—all while having a wonderful time playing in the gym. If Mr. Luft could instill these values in our public high school gym classes, surely our yeshivot and Day Schools should be able to instill these values in our children in their gym classes. And surely the school administrations and faculties—and parent bodies—should set the proper tone for their schools and communities.

Sports aren't just about games; they are about life. Good sportsmanship isn't just an extra frill; it is the essence of sports education. *Middot* aren't only to be learned in the classroom; they are to be learned in the gym and on the basketball court.

And parents should be cheering—not jeering—from the sidelines.

Thoughts on תרומה

Thinking to be Thoughtful

✌ My wife and I were recently having a quiet dinner in a local kosher restaurant. Before long, a young family was seated at a table across from us. As veteran grandparents, we are used to children making a bit of noise. No problem.

Soon, though, the father took out a camera and started taking photographs, and more photographs, and more photographs. His camera had a flash, and with each photo the flash filled the restaurant and the reflection bounced off the mirrored walls. Aside from being very disturbing to us (and the other patrons of the restaurant), the flashes were painful to our eyes. When our patience finally ran out, we politely asked the father if he could take photographs later, or without the flash.

We thought that a person who received such a complaint would have apologized for having caused us (and others) unpleasantness. However, the father responded to us in a rude manner, as though we were at fault, as though we had no right to intrude on his freedom, as though he had every right to take photographs no matter how disturbing this was to others. After his outburst, he must have realized he was in the wrong, and he put away the camera; but he did not apologize. On the contrary, he glowered at us angrily.

This week's Torah portion describes the construction work in the ancient Tabernacle, the sanctuary of the Israelites as they traveled in the wilderness. Hovering over the holy ark were two cherubim. "And the cherubim shall spread out their wings on high, screening the ark-cover with their wings, and with their faces one to another; toward the ark-cover shall the faces of the cherubim be" (*Shemot* 25:20).

The faces of the cherubim not only had to be toward the ark—but toward each other. A rabbinic interpretation teaches: to face divinity, we need to face each other. If we are to honor God, we are to honor each other. We need to look into each other's eyes, to see our shared humanity, to deal with each other with compassion and thoughtfulness.

Too often, people behave in a self-centered fashion, without considering the feelings of others, without thinking how their behavior may cause pain or discomfort to others. Their spiritual vision extends to their own immediate needs and wants; they will do what they choose regardless of how this may impact on others.

Good manners are not a frill, but are essential elements in a religious and righteous life. Good manners demonstrate self-respect and respect for others. Politeness is a sign of kindness and thoughtfulness.

Rudeness is a religious and social deficiency. Thoughtfulness is a religious and social virtue. Let us think carefully so that we act thoughtfully.

Somebody Else Is Not Available

⁊ Over the years, I have been deeply and favorably impressed by individuals who have come forward with suggestions for the betterment of our synagogue, our Institute, our community. These individuals not only offered constructive advice, but they volunteered to give time and money to implement their suggestions. Their ideas and suggestions emerged from their minds, hearts, and souls; they were committed to improve things and to be part of the constructive work that needed to be done.

Over the years, I have been deeply and unfavorably impressed by other individuals who have come forward with suggestions for the betterment of our synagogue, our Institute, our community. These individuals did not volunteer to give time and money to implement their suggestions. On the contrary, they expected "the rabbi" or "the synagogue" or "the community" or "the rabbinate" to expend time and money—however much—without their having to do anything more than make suggestions. Even worse, when their suggestions were not and could not be implemented, they expressed frustration and anger.

Jewish communities are always involved in serious projects—providing religious services, erecting or repairing buildings, improving schools, implementing new programs, providing for the needy, and so forth. Everything costs time and money. Not every idea or suggestion is good; not every project is wise. People can differ widely on the priorities list of things to be done. However, we work together and come to consensus; and then we proceed. For the Jewish community to achieve worthy goals, each individual needs to feel a personal stake, and needs to help to the extent of one's means and abilities. No one of us can do everything; but not one of us should do nothing.

In this week's Torah portion, we read of the contributions that were to be made for the building of the Mishkan, the holy sanctuary in the wilderness. People were asked to contribute according to the generosity of their hearts. The Torah's description includes two factors: 1) contributing; 2) a generous heart. If one contributes reluctantly or begrudgingly, there is a deficiency in the quality of the gift. If one shows generosity of heart—but doesn't actually contribute according to one's means—this is an even greater deficiency. A proper gift entails the right quality—generosity of heart—and the actual contribution. Good-heartedness and good intentions that are not accompanied by actual giving—are vacuous. Giving without good-heartedness is not the ideal.

My father-in-law, Rabbi Paul E. Schuchalter, of blessed memory, once ran an "obituary" in his synagogue bulletin. The "obituary" lamented the passing of Somebody Else. It praised Mr. Else as the most popular person in the synagogue. Whenever there was a fund drive, everyone immediately turned to Somebody Else. Whenever volunteers were needed, people recommended Somebody Else. Whenever congregants were called upon to attend minyan or adult education classes, they knew they could always rely on Somebody Else. The "obituary" concluded with the sad observation that with the passing of Somebody Else, members would no longer be able to rely on his readiness to participate in the life of the congregation. It was now up to all members of the Congregation to no longer depend on Somebody Else, but to depend on themselves.

In the late 1880s, Rabbi Moshe Yaakov Ottolenghi was an important educator in Salonika. He offered a homiletic interpretation of the Mishnah that states: "On the eve of the Sabbath near to dusk, a man must say three things in his home: Have you taken the tithe? Have you prepared the Eruv? Light the Sabbath lamp."

He explained this passage as follows: As a person comes near the time of death (eve of the Sabbath near to dusk), one needs to review one's life. Did he/she give tithes, i.e., did he/she contribute appropriately to needy people and charitable causes? Did he/she prepare the Eruv, i.e. did the person serve as an *Areiv*—a guarantor—for the wellbeing of his fellow human beings? Did the person take responsibility and feel a personal stake in the lives of others? If the person can answer yes to these questions—i.e., he/she did contribute appropriately and he/she was invested personally in the wellbeing of others and the community—then "light the Sabbath lamp"—one can present his/her soul before the Almighty with illumination and brightness.

Rabbi Ottolenghi stressed the need for contributing, and for contributing with a generous and sincere heart. Both elements are essential to a proper religious person.

We cannot rely on Somebody Else, on "the rabbis," on "the community" on "the synagogue" to do what needs to be done. Vacuous complaints and empty demands achieve nothing.

Each of us has a role to play. Each can give of our talents and resources to the best of our ability. Each can take personal responsibility and realize that Somebody Else isn't available to do the work that needs to be done.

Thoughts on תצוה

Remembering Abraham Lincoln

☞ Until 1968, American's celebrated February 12 as Abraham Lincoln's birthday and February 22 as George Washington's birthday. These commemorations were then replaced with Presidents' Day on the third Monday of February. This was widely perceived as a downgrading of American veneration of Lincoln and Washington. With the growing pressures for egalitarianism and multiculturalism, it was to be expected that great national heroes be cut down to size. After all, they were flawed human beings, not much better or different from ourselves.

In his perceptive book, *Abraham Lincoln in the Post-Heroic Era*, Dr. Barry Schwartz traces the dramatic drop in Lincoln's prestige, especially since the 1960s. He writes:

> Ours is an age ready to live without triumphal doctrine, an age in which absolutes are local and private rather than national, a post-heroic age in which national greatness is the epitome of the naive and outmoded. (p. 191)

In the post-heroic era, it has become fashionable to focus on the flaws of American society and the evils of American history. Our "heroes" have now tended to be athletes and entertainers rather than singularly great political figures. Indeed, to identify a public figure as "great" is to invite a barrage of criticism from the politically correct opposition, stressing that person's numerous sins and shortcomings.

Those of us who spent our childhoods before the mid- to late 1960s are still the biggest fans of Lincoln. Those whose childhoods were in the late 1960s and later were less likely to study about the great Abraham Lincoln that we knew: the common man born in a log cabin who went on to become one of America's great Presidents; the man of homespun wit and wisdom; the President who saved the Union; the President who emancipated the slaves; the President who was deeply religious in his own special way. As children, we learned not just to respect Lincoln, but to see in him a quality of excellence to which we ought to aspire. Lincoln's greatness was an inspiration; he represented the greatness of America and the American dream.

This week's Torah portion tells of the eternal lamp that was to be lit with pure olive oil in the Mishkan, the wilderness sanctuary of the Israelites. The eternal lights in our synagogues derive from this ancient practice of our ancestors. The significance of the lamp—symbolizing the Divine Presence—is that it was "eternal"—always to be lit. It was not a large torch or bonfire; it was not part of a huge powerful structure: it was a small, quiet light; its virtue was in its steadiness. It was always lit, always giving light and inspiration.

Perhaps we ought to think of greatness in terms of the eternal light. Greatness does not entail having all the virtues and strengths; greatness does not depend on external pomp and glory. Greatness, like the eternal light, needs to be steady, to give light, to inspire from generation to generation.

It is futile to argue that Abraham Lincoln—or any human being—was absolutely perfect and without shortcomings. However, this does not negate the possibility of human greatness, any more than it would be to negate the greatness of the eternal light because it was not a larger, stronger light. A great human being is one whose life offers a steady light and inspiration to the generations, whose words and deeds have had profound positive impact on others, whose existence has helped transform our world into a better place.

Abraham Lincoln was a great man with a lasting legacy to his country and to the world. His spirit is well captured in the closing words of his second inaugural address, delivered on March 4, 1865:

> With malice toward none; with charity for all; with firmness in the right, as God gives us to see the right, let us strive on to finish the work we are in; to bind up the nation's wounds; to care for him who shall have borne the battle, and for his widow, and his orphan—to do all which may achieve and cherish a just, and a lasting peace, among ourselves, and with all nations.

Happy birthday, President Lincoln. And thank you; thank you very much for who you were and what you did and what you mean to us.

In Search of a Real Tzaddik/ Tzaddeket

🖋 An ad in a recent issue of our local Jewish newspaper announced that "a Tzaddik" was coming to town, and that he would be speaking at a certain time and place. The ad included a picture of the "Tzaddik"—a man with a long beard and black hat, with his eyes gazing soulfully heavenward.

Several months ago, I received a copy of a synagogue bulletin that also featured a picture of a "Tzaddik" who was to visit the synagogue. This "Tzaddik" had the appropriate beard and black hat, along with long sidelocks, and of course, his eyes were gazing soulfully heavenward.

Indeed, during the past year or so I've noticed a number of ads and fliers announcing the forthcoming visits of "Tzadikkim," all of whom were bearded men, dressed in black, with eyes gazing soulfully heavenward.

Whenever I see such ads, I wonder: What genuine Tzaddik would be brazen enough to make his righteousness public? Which real Tzaddik would allow himself to be marketed in such a way? Wouldn't a real Tzaddik be a humble person who would be deeply embarrassed to pass himself off as a Tzaddik, who would be mortified to be pictured in ads that imply that he has holy powers? And are all true Tzaddikim men with beards, black hats, and "spiritual" eyes?

Obviously, there is a demand among elements of the Jewish public for "Tzaddikim." People want to believe that there are individuals who have reached a profound level of holiness and who can somehow impart their spiritual powers to benefit those who listen to them. Regrettably, we have read of various "Tzaddikim" who have been found to be charlatans and outright criminals. Instead of praying for their supporters, they have preyed on their supporters.

I fully believe there are Tzaddikim and Tzaddikot in our world; but I also believe that these very righteous and pious people are humble and private. They don't pose as saints, and they don't let others market them as holy people with great spiritual powers. They don't seek to make money by commercializing their righteousness.

In this week's Parasha, we read of the *ner tamid*, the eternal light that was to be lit in the Mishkan. Our synagogues have adopted this symbol and have placed a *ner tamid* in front of the holy ark. The *ner tamid* is not an ostentatious torch, but is a humble steady light. It reflects spiritual power by its very gentleness and constancy, not by shouting out its holiness and not by trying to call attention to itself. The *ner tamid* suggests basic qualities of spirituality—humility, quietness, constancy.

Alan Watts, a popular writer on Eastern religion, offered a keen insight:

> The most spiritual people are the most human. They are natural and easy in manner; they give themselves no airs: they interest themselves in ordinary everyday matters, and are not forever talking and thinking about religion. For them, there is no difference between spirituality and usual life. . .". (*The Supreme Identity*, p. 128)

Each of us has a thirst for connection with the Almighty. Each of us feels spiritual uplift when we are in the presence of truly good and pious people. But we ought to be very suspicious of those who presumptuously present themselves as being "Tzadikkim," or who seek to raise funds from us as a means of our gaining blessings from the "Tzadikkim." It is not by accident that Jewish folk tradition refers to the 36 Tzadikkim Nistarim—hidden saints—upon whom the world depends. The truly righteous are "hidden," and even they themselves are too modest to imagine that they are among this group of Tzadikkim.

We each should want to be in the presence of genuine Tzaddikim. The proper thing is not to look for such Tzaddikim in newspaper ads or fliers, and not in cult-like gatherings. The proper thing is for each of us to strive to be a Tzaddik or Tzaddeket, to live as fully and deeply with a spirit of righteousness, humility, and constancy.

Thoughts on פורים

Gladness and Joy

✍ With the victory of the Jews over their enemies, the Megillah informs us that "the Jews had light and gladness (*simha*) and joy (*sasson*) and honor." What is the difference between *simha* and *sasson*, and how does this impact on our understanding of this verse's message?

Simha: This refers to physical contentment. When the Torah commands us to have *simha* on the Festivals, the Talmud interprets this to mean that we should eat meat and drink wine. *Simha* is enjoyed when we have a good meal. The seven wedding blessings refer to how God provided gladness (*simha*) to Adam and Eve in the Garden of Eden. This, too, can be understood to refer to physical contentment and wellbeing. Adam and Eve were provided with the wonderful climate and foods of paradise.

Sasson: This refers to emotional, spiritual joy. The prophet Isaiah likens God's joy in Israel to the joy of a bride and groom. The joy (*mesos/sasson*) of bride and groom entails a profound sense of feeling complete, of having found a beloved partner with whom to face the adventure of life. Whereas *simha* is "me-oriented," *sasson* is "other-oriented." Whereas *simha* is a feeling of contentment, *sasson* is a feeling that life has meaning.

So the verse in the Megillah might be understood as follows. Upon winning their freedom from oppression, the Jews felt "light"; the darkness and gloom was removed from their lives. Then they felt gladness, *simha*. They were pleased that they were physically safe. Then they felt joy, *sasson*. They attained a higher spiritual satisfaction; they understood that their salvation had divine meaning, that their lives had greater purpose. Once they attained that level of understanding, then they experienced "honor"—honor in the form of self-respect as well as honor from others who recognized the transformation which had occurred to the Jews.

A recent edition of ABC National News had a piece on happiness in America. Drawing on the results of Gallup Polls, the report described various factors that Americans described as conducing to happiness. The polls found that the ethnic groups that are the "happiest" are Jews and Asian Americans!

I won't offer explanations relating to Asian Americans, but I will venture a suggestion about why Jews consider themselves so happy.

On the *simha* level, Jews are among the most educated, hardest working, and most affluent groups of Americans. While this might explain contentment, it doesn't explain real happiness. For the *sasson* factor, the Jews have an important asset: the cultural tradition of striving, of trying to change the world for the better, of social justice and responsibility. *Sasson*—real joy— comes by being concerned with the lives of others. American Jews—whether religiously observant or not—share this tradition of helping others, giving charity, volunteering for social causes, and so forth. I think this is a major factor in the American Jews' happiness. It is a combination of *simha* and *sasson*. Once we have attained both of these aspects, we then move on to "honor," where we can take pride in our achievements, and where we can be recognized by others for the important values we represent.

The Megillah tells us that the Purim holiday was established as a celebration for Jews of all generations. Mordecai and Esther called on Jews to give each other gifts of food, and to give charity to the needy. What an impressive way to establish a holiday of victory! It wasn't just about eating and drinking and having a good celebratory party. Rather, Jews were instructed to share with others, to support the poor—to remember that true happiness involves concern and involvement in the lives of others.

The message of Purim, then, may be seen as a progressive development in our perspective on life. First, we need to clear the darkness of hatred and violence from our midst; then we need to care for the material wellbeing of our families and communities; then we need to recognize the true spiritual joy that comes with a sense of purpose and meaning in life; then we achieve the level of self-respect, and respect in the eyes of others for the values and traditions we represent.

A Purim Miracle

🕊 Esther the Jew marries King Ahashverosh. Her Uncle Mordecai tells her not to reveal that she is Jewish. The Jews throughout the 127 provinces of the Empire know Esther is Jewish. But not one of them gives away the secret. Ahashverosh, Haman, and the entire royal court are kept in the dark about the Queen's true identity.

This, commented Rabbi Haim David Halevy (late Sephardic Chief Rabbi of Tel Aviv), was an amazing phenomenon, a veritable miracle. Not one Jew in the entire empire betrayed the secret. The Jewish people were united, discreet, and disciplined to an extraordinary degree.

Let us imagine how this story would play out if it occurred today.

Jewish reporters would fiercely try to outscoop each other to report about a Jewish Queen.

Wikileaks would put an image of Esther's birth certificate on the Internet, with the indication that she was born Jewish.

The Hareidim would demonstrate worldwide at the travesty of a Jewish woman marrying a non-Jewish king, a wicked one at that.

The Chief Rabbinate of Israel would issue a statement that Esther's Jewishness was in question, and that she would need a *"giyyur le-humra"* (a conversion to be on the safe side) if she wanted to be considered Jewish for purposes of *aliya*.

The Zionists would point to Esther and say: you see, the Jews of the Diaspora are assimilating; they all should make *aliya* before they totally disappear.

The zealous Litvaks would say: Esther is merely a Persian Jewess and doesn't have our fine Ashkenazic pedigree. We wouldn't want our sons to marry such a woman.

Chabad would send another *shaliah* to Shushan, to re-enforce the staff already there at the Chabad House. Cholent (Persian style) would be dished out each Shabbat morning along with prayers for the Queen's prompt release from bondage in the palace.

The Sephardi Federations around the globe would glow with quiet satisfaction that one of their own made the big time.

The peaceniks would say: This whole crisis could have been avoided if Mordecai simply bowed to Haman and would not have been so stubborn. If Jews simply gave everything away, we wouldn't have to worry about anti-Semitism.

The kabbalists would manufacture a new batch of red strings for bracelets, and sell them at a suitable price to those who wanted to provide mystical salvation to Esther and the Jewish people.

The secularists would blame the fanaticism of the religious community; the religious would blame the secularists for their innumerable sins, which surely brought on God's wrath.

Jewish newspapers would be filled with spicy attacks and accusations, op-ed pieces, and letters to the editor. Everyone would have an opinion, invariably wrong. All the commotion within the Jewish community would catch the attention of the non-Jewish media.

It would not take too long for Queen Esther's hidden identity to be revealed. Esther would have then been ejected from the throne; Haman would have had full sway; the Jews would have had no powerful person to intercede on their behalf. The Purim story would have ended in disaster. The joyous holiday of Purim would never have come to be.

The Jews of the ancient Persian Empire demonstrated remarkable intelligence and restraint. They understood what was at stake and they rose to the occasion with admirable self-control. They surely had differing opinions and ideologies among themselves; but when faced with national crisis, they knew enough to set their differences aside, to refrain from destructive gossip and back-biting.

While we modern Jews cannot hope to achieve the unity and self-control of the ancient Persian Jewish community, we can strive to act and speak with discretion, courtesy, and respect for the views of others. We can avoid vitriolic attacks on those with whom we disagree. We can focus on the really big issues which confront the Jewish people, and think how each of us can be constructive members of our community. We can know when to speak and when to remain silent. We can know when action is necessary and helpful, and when action is counter-productive and misguided.

Rabbi Halevy thought it was miraculous that the Jews of ancient Persia acted so wisely and so discreetly. Perhaps it is too much to expect such miraculous behavior from us. But perhaps—with intelligence, compassion, discretion, and respectfulness—we can be part of a new Purim miracle for our generation.

Thoughts on כי תשא

On Taming Our Inner "Cats"

An ancient Greek parable tells of a cat that was magically transformed into a Princess. The Princess was elegant, well-mannered, and always with a ready smile on her face. Everyone seemed to be enchanted by her nobility.

And then, one day, as the Princess greeted a group of admirers, a mouse happened to run into the room. In an instant, the Princess was transformed back into cat-like behavior. The illusion was over. Everyone realized she was not really a Princess after all, but was a cat who was posing as a Princess.

The parable points to a basic issue confronting each human being. Civilization attempts to fashion us into noble, idealistic, and moral beings. At the same time, we have within us our cat-like qualities and emotions—jealousy, greed, vindictiveness, pride, and anger. Human life is an ongoing effort to maintain ourselves as noble people, and to keep our inner "cat" under control. The more we can internalize the noble values, the more we can truly transform ourselves into good people. The less control we have over our inner "cat," the greater is the gap between our superficial veneer and our real selves.

This week's Torah portion includes the attributes by which God revealed Himself to Moses. The Talmud teaches that we are to emulate these attributes in our own behavior, that is, to be merciful and gracious, long-suffering and abundant in goodness and truth. To attain these qualities requires constant effort and self-awareness. It is all too possible to adopt these qualities on a superficial level, but not to transform them into our real natures. We can pretend to be kind and compassionate, but have hearts that are selfish, envious, and cruel. We can put on an act of being merciful and gracious, but these qualities will not suppress the inner "cat" when we are faced with temptation.

It is important to focus on one of the 13 attributes that sometimes gets forgotten: truth. To be true means to have our external behavior and internal emotions in line with each other. When we are not "true," then we are pretenders and frauds, religious imposters. We may appear to be a Prince or Princess, but deep down we are still a cat.

In his Laws of Repentance, Maimonides writes of sins for which people generally do not repent. Why not? Because they do not realize that they've sinned. They rationalize their behavior, so as to convince themselves that they've done nothing wrong. If one thinks he/she is a Prince or Princess, and refuses to acknowledge the inner "cat," then such a person is not likely to repent, change, or improve.

Such people may fool others. They certainly may fool themselves. But they do not fool the God of Truth.

Standing Tall and Strong for Israel and the Jewish People

🖋 Some years ago, I read about a German Jew who established a "Jewish Nazi Society" during the 1930s. While Jews throughout Germany (and Europe in general) were facing horrible anti-Jewish persecutions, this Jewish man internalized the vicious anti-Semitic propaganda to such an extent that he also became a Jew-hater. Perhaps he thought that by identifying as a Nazi, he would be spared personally from the anti-Jewish persecutions. He wanted to be considered as "a good Jew" in the eyes of the Nazis, rather than be accounted among the "bad" Jews whom the Nazis were tormenting.

I don't know what ultimately happened to the members of the Jewish Nazi Society, but I doubt that they were spared by the Nazi hate machine. The Nazis hated Jews for having Jewish blood, regardless of their beliefs or political leanings. Jewish Nazis were just as despicable to Nazis as any other Jews. The Jewish Nazis were despised by Jews for their treachery; and despised by Nazis for their Jewishness.

These thoughts came to mind as I contemplated the phenomenon of Jews in our time who struggle to undermine Israel, and who identify themselves with those who strive to destroy the Jewish State. These individuals seem to suffer from the same psychological problems as members of the Jewish Nazi Society in Germany.

Israel is constantly barraged by its enemies—through terrorism, economic boycotts, political isolation, anti-Israel propaganda, threats of war and nuclear destruction. To the enemies of Israel, the Jewish State is the object of blind, unmitigated hatred. The enemies use every possible forum to malign Israel and deny its legitimacy.

This unceasing war against Israel is resisted courageously by the Jewish State, by Jewish supporters of Israel, by millions of non-Jewish supporters of Israel. It is bizarre and morally repugnant that the one tiny Jewish country in the world has to suffer so much abuse. It is a matter of honor to stand up for Israel and to remind the world of the right of the Jews to their own homeland. We need to counter the attacks against Israel in every forum. We need to speak truth to combat the unceasing stream of lies heaped up against Israel.

Does this mean that we must agree with and condone everything that Israel does? Of course not. Israelis themselves are vocal in their criticisms of aspects of Israeli life and government policies. As long as criticisms are voiced with love, they should be welcome. They help shake the status quo and move things in a better direction. But criticism must be balanced with an appreciation of the amazingly impressive positive aspects of the Jewish State.

While fair and loving critics are vital to Israel's welfare, haters are destructive. Haters do not seek to improve Israel—they seek to destroy it. Their goal is not to encourage a vibrant, flourishing Jewish State—their goal is to eliminate the Jewish State. The hatred is so blind and so intense, that it is oblivious to facts and figures. For haters, Israel is guilty just by existing. It is particularly regrettable when people of Jewish ancestry align themselves with the haters. In some perverse way, they may think this separates them from the fate of Israel and the Jewish people—they think they will be viewed as "the good Jews" in contrast with the Zionists who are viewed as "the bad Jews." But such Jews are despised by Jews as traitors, and are despised (or mocked) by the haters of Israel—because after all, these hating Jews are still Jews!

The enemies are happy to use such people for propaganda purposes; but if they were ever to succeed in their wicked designs, these hating Jews would not fare well. Their treachery to Israel and their fellow Jews would not make them beloved by the enemies of Jews and Israel.

We have read recently of Jewish haters/self-haters who have participated in—and even spearheaded—anti-Israel boycotts. We have read of Israeli professors/left-wing intellectuals who have participated in anti-Israel programs on college campuses throughout the world. We have read columns by Jewish journalists that are so blatantly unfair to Israel that it makes us shudder.

The great sixteenth-century kabbalist and biblical commentator, Rabbi Moshe Alsheikh, offered a homiletic interpretation of the first verse in this week's Torah portion. When the Israelites are to choose a leader (*ki tissa et rosh benei yisrael*), they should choose one who is totally devoted to Israel, who is willing to give his life on behalf of the Lord and on behalf of the people (*ish kofer nafsho*). It is destructive to have half-hearted or self-serving people in positions of authority. Total commitment is an essential component of leadership.

But this interpretation applies not only to the officially designated leadership; it applies to each Jew. Each of us is an ambassador of our people; each of us represents the history, culture, and traditions of the millennial Jewish experience; each of us is part of the Jewish destiny. To play our roles as proud and courageous Jews, we need to overcome inferiority complexes and reject "politically correct" pressures; we need to stand tall and stand strong, with the wholeness of our being, on behalf of the God of Israel, the Torah of Israel, and the People of Israel.

Thoughts on וַיַּקְהֵל

Wisdom of the Heart

🐚 Carl Sandburg once observed: "We know that when a nation goes down and never comes back, when a society or civilization perishes, one condition may always be found. They forgot where they came from. They lost sight of what brought them along. The hard beginnings were forgotten and the struggles farther along" (*Remembrance Rock*, 1948, pp. 18–19).

Sandburg was pointing to a significant feature of a living civilization: It remembers its beginnings, and it sees itself as an organic part of the past. The ancestors have an ongoing vote, albeit not veto power. When this connection with the past is lost, the civilization unravels and declines.

In contemporary life, these words of Sandburg have increasing significance. We live in the "me generation," when ego gratification seems more important than upholding tradition. Advertisers constantly emphasize that products are "new," "improved," with an "updated formula." Nothing is more passe than the past, than the old. Even in matters of literature, art, and religion—society seems bent on discovering new forms and chasing after new fads, while sneering at "old-fashioned" traditional styles. People aren't interested in where they came from, but in where they are now and where they may be tomorrow. The more these tendencies set into a society, the clearer it is that the society is in decline. It becomes like a tree that rejects its own roots, not realizing that its life and future depend on those roots.

The Talmud (*Berakhot* 55a) states that God only gives wisdom to one who has wisdom. Shouldn't God be giving wisdom to those who lack it, rather than to those who already have it? We may understand this talmudic passage in light of *Parashat Vayakhel*.

In describing the building of the Mishkan, the wilderness sanctuary of the ancient Israelites, the Torah states that God called upon those who were "wise of heart" to do the work. This refers to a special kind of wisdom, not merely a high I.Q. God appointed those who had an aesthetic sense, who were receptive and imaginative, whose hearts were in tune with the history and destiny of their people. God gave wisdom—and gives wisdom—to those who are receptive to receiving wisdom in this special way. Those who lack "wise hearts" are simply not receptive to this wisdom.

This quality of having a "wise heart" is vital to the wellbeing of every society, and certainly of every sacred endeavor. It is a repudiation of egotism and an affirmation of loyalty to the greater glory of God. It is sensitivity to the historical context of the people, and commitment for organic development. It is rejection of the quick-fix attitude that cares more for self-gratification than for the greater good of the society.

Let us pray that we be worthy of having a wise heart, so that we and our children, and our children's children will all be faithful to God and true to the Torah and Jewish traditions.

Thoughts on פקודי

Synagogue Jews

❧ What role does the synagogue play in people's lives? Here are several models.

THE "HOSPITAL" SYNAGOGUE: This refers to people who come to the synagogue in emergencies—at a time of crisis, illness, death of a loved one. Normally, they avoid the synagogue; but they turn to it in moments of need. The synagogue is akin to a hospital—a place they generally avoid, and only attend in dire situations.

THE "MUSEUM" SYNAGOGUE: This refers to those who visit the synagogue for the nostalgic qualities it offers. They enjoy experiencing the old relics of religion, and feel culturally enriched by their visits. They attend on holidays or other special occasions, as a social/cultural obligation. The synagogue is akin to a museum, a building that houses old things and old memories.

THE "ENTERTAINMENT HALL" SYNAGOGUE: This refers to those who attend synagogue because they have a good time there; they meet friends; they hear nice music; they listen to a sermon; they enjoy the kiddush following services. They want the synagogue to entertain them, to come up with new melodies and new programs. If the synagogue ceases to entertain them, they stop attending, or they go to another synagogue that they find more entertaining.

While each of the above models has its role, the following model is the most important.

THE "SACRED SPACE" SYNAGOGUE: This refers to those who are seeking communion with the eternal, ineffable God. They come to synagogue often, and in a spirit of yearning. When they enter the sanctuary, they feel the power of the "sacred space." They sit humbly, quietly, thoughtfully. They absorb the atmosphere; they savor their words of prayer; they lose themselves in meditation. They have not come to synagogue because of an emergency crisis; nor to experience the museum-like qualities; nor to be entertained. They have come for something far different: they have come to commune with God, to understand themselves, and transcend themselves.

The Torah portions of recent weeks have focused on the building of the Mishkan, the wilderness sanctuary of the ancient Israelites. God commanded the building of the sanctuary so that "I may dwell among them." A sanctuary is a sacred space: it is sacred by virtue of our sanctifying it, and our receptivity to having God dwell among us. When we enter a synagogue, we should do so reverently, humbly, thoughtfully. The synagogue is not a hospital, or a museum, or an entertainment hall. It is a sacred space. "Happy are those who dwell in the house of the Lord." Having the proper mindset is essential to a meaningful synagogue experience.

If we understand what it is to be in a sacred space, we begin to understand what it means to have God dwell among us—and within us.

וַיַּקְהֵל-פְקוּדֵי Thoughts on

A Spiritual Revolution Underway

🕊 (This week's Torah portion opens with Moshe calling together the people of Israel. A *kahal*, congregation, is composed of individuals who share a common background, destiny, ideology. Often, a *kahal* is centered in a particular location. But a *kahal* can also be composed of individuals who may be in different locations, but who share ideas and ideals. This week's Angel for Shabbat column is based on an address I delivered at the annual dinner of Yeshivat Chovevei Torah, held on Sunday night March 11, 2012. It relates not just to the large *kahal* that attended the dinner, but to the worldwide *kahal* of Jews who believe in an intellectually vibrant, compassionate, and inclusive Orthodox Judaism.)

Washington Irving, one of the leading American authors of the early nineteenth century, wrote a popular story "Rip Van Winkle," familiar to all of us. Rip is famous for having slept for 20 years! As he made his way to a quiet spot in the Catskill Mountains, he passed the village inn on which he saw a picture of King George III. When he returned to the village after his 20-year "nap," he passed the same inn; but now instead of seeing a picture of King George III, he saw a picture of President George Washington.

Rip Van Winkle had slept through a revolution.

How does one manage to sleep through a revolution? This might be the result of apathy, aversion to risk, fear, lack of vision. It is not easy to be alert to the challenges of a revolution. It is simpler to stand aside, or go into hiding, or fall asleep.

The Midrash teaches that only 1/5 of the Israelites actually left the servitude in Egypt during the Exodus. The vast majority were unable to grasp the significance of freedom, or were daunted by leaving familiar surroundings—however oppressive—to march into an unknown wilderness on the way to a new land. The Torah tells us that the Israelites left Egypt *"ki goreshu miMitzrayim,"* because they were expelled from Egypt. Rabbi Haim David Halevy, late Sephardic Chief Rabbi of Tel Aviv, asked: Why did the Israelites have to be expelled from Egypt? Wouldn't they naturally and eagerly wish to leave Egypt to attain their freedom? Rabbi Halevy answered: There is a strong human tendency that resists change, that prefers the status quo. The Israelites were reluctant to leave Egypt to enter an unknown dimension of freedom and responsibility—so they literally had to be expelled from their slavery. Freedom is not easy to attain or to maintain.

What is the process of a revolution? How do people ultimately overcome their apathy and fear, so that they actually become ready to take risks for the sake of their higher ideals?

First, people have a feeling of malaise. They sense that something is very wrong; they feel that there is injustice that must be corrected. Then, they begin to formulate these feelings into ideas; they articulate their grievances and their dreams. Finally, they move to action. They form coalitions, build institutions, create infrastructure for change.

There is a quiet revolution going on in the Jewish world right now. We are part of it. We are not sleeping through this revolution.

There is malaise, a strong feeling that things need to be changed dramatically. Within the Orthodox world, there has been a sharp turn to the right, with a frightening and dangerous increase in authoritarianism, obscurantism, and intellectual narrowness. Within the Jewish community at large, there has been a sharp turn to the left—alienation from traditional Judaism, increased secularization.

Much of the "middle" has fallen asleep. It has allowed halakhic authority to slip almost entirely into the hands of Hareidi elements. It has not done enough to offer a dynamic, creative, intellectually alive Orthodoxy that could attract many thinking Jews who have opted out of Torah and mitzvoth.

But we have a group of "revolutionaries" who work steadily to re-energize Orthodoxy, to re-generate its intellectual vibrancy, to create an Orthodoxy that is compassionate, inclusive, open, awake, engaged; that is alive with energy, spirituality, beauty; that sees Judaism as a world religion with a message for all humanity, not as a self-contained sect. There are voices articulating a grand vision of Orthodoxy, an Orthodoxy that is intellectually and spiritually attractive and meaningful.

Yeshivat Chovevei Torah is as the center of this revolution. The Institute for Jewish Ideas and Ideals is at the center of this revolution. Various like-minded individuals and groups here, in Israel, and around the world are at the center of this revolution. It is a long, difficult, uphill grind. There are so many obstacles— apathy, cynicism, and outright opposition. Just as the ancient Israelites needed to be prodded into choosing freedom, so our communities today need to be reminded to choose freedom and individual responsibility, to eschew authoritarianism and sectarianism, to work for a grand vision of Judaism for ourselves, our children and grandchildren—and for the generations to come.

Yeshivat Chovevei Torah is blessed with an administration, faculty, and student body who are committed to Torah tradition with this grand vision in mind. The students of YCT are intellectually alive, idealistic, and committed to an Orthodox Judaism that has a message for the entire Jewish community and for society at large. This is an institution that trains and encourages students to think for themselves, to study deeply—and to go out and change the world! YCT is at the center of a revolution in Jewish life; and all of us who are awake to this revolution, who participate in it as best we can, will ultimately be rewarded with victory.

The Me'am Lo'ez, the classic Ladino Torah commentary, draws on Midrashim relating to the giving of the *Luhot* on Mount Sinai. The first set was given amidst great fanfare—thunder and lightning and the blasts of the shofar. Hundreds of thousands of Israelites were gathered at the foot of the mountain to witness this amazing event. And yet, when Moses brought these *Luhot* to the Israelites, he found them dancing around a golden calf. He cast down the *Luhot* and shattered them.

Moses then ascended the mountain a second time. There was no fanfare, no great commotion. God told Moses to carve out the two stone tablets by the sweat of his own brow. This second set of *Luhot*—created by the quiet effort of a lone man atop a mountain—became the spiritual foundation of our people. This teaches that the valuable and permanent things in life are often attained individually, quietly, all alone atop a mountain, by the sweat of our own brow.

Each of us sometimes feels that we are alone atop a mountain, struggling without anyone noticing or caring. We worry that what we are doing will bear no fruit, that we will continue to deal with golden calves and idolatries and lapses of faith. The world is complicated, and the Jewish world even moreso.

Rabbi Nahman of Braslav taught that the whole world is a narrow bridge. There are dangers that confront us. There are risks. There are opponents who want to bring us down. But, taught Rabbi Nahman, the essential thing is not to be afraid. *Kol haOlam kulo gesher tsar me'od; vehaIkar lo lefahed kelal.*

There is a revolution underway, and we are all part of it. There is so much to do and so many obstacles in the way. It is easy to lose heart, to stand aside, to go to sleep. But let us remember what is at stake and let us seize this historic moment.

The essential thing is not to be afraid, not to be afraid at all.

Thoughts on וַיִּקְרָא

Religion and Superstition

✍ During the past week, I received an email from an organization in Israel seeking donations for which donors would merit success, happy marriage, and good health. The organization offered to have a Torah scholar pray at the Kotel from the Fast of Esther through the seventh day of Passover. They assured donors that this is a "very powerful time for hidden blessings to be revealed."

Not long after getting this spam, I received in the mail a glitzy brochure from another organization seeking donations so that the "*gedolei haDor*" will pray on our behalf at the Kotel. The brochure features photos of sages with long white beards, who assure us that by supporting this charity we will gain wonderful rewards.

These are recent examples of the ongoing process of cheapening Jewish prayer, and of undermining the spiritual foundations of the Jewish people. The above charities, and many others as well, prey on the gullibility and fears of the public. They claim to have direct access to God—through their "Torah scholars" and "*gedolei haDor*"— that the rest of us lack. They claim that these prayers at the Kotel will be effective, whereas our own prayers anywhere else will not be as effective. Charlatans abound who promise miracles, if only we will give them ample donations. They will write us amulets, bless red strings, send us holy water or food, pray for us at the Kotel.

There is, of course, a long history of charlatanism and shamanism in religion—including Judaism. There have always been those who claim to have the keys to God's inner chambers, and that—for a price—they would intercede on behalf of those who turned to them.

Superstitious practices and beliefs, even if dressed in holy garb, are inimical to the purity of religion. They blur the line between religion and superstition, degrading and disgracing true religion.

As we approach the Purim holiday, we recall that Esther requested that the Jews fast during their hour of distress. Rabbinic tradition has understood this as a call to prayer and repentance. Esther did not ask Jews to send donations to holy people at the Kotel; or to pay for prayers by supposed saints and scholars. No, she called on each Jew to reach out to God from the depths of his/her heart. And the Jews were redeemed.

Let us each turn to the Almighty in sincere and pure prayer. This is the special privilege and responsibility that Judaism offers us: to stand before the Master of the Universe directly. The Torah of God is pure; we must not allow it to be defiled by misguided superstitious beliefs and practices.

Synagogues, Empty and Full

℘ National polls conducted by the Gallup Organization report that, of all religious groupings in the United States, Jews are least likely to attend public worship at least once a week. The only group scoring lower than Jews consists of atheists, agnostics, and those with no religious affiliation!

Less than 15 percent of the Jewish community attends synagogue services weekly. When the Gallup poll is adjusted to exclude Orthodox Jews who attend synagogue more regularly, it turns out that less than five percent of all other Jews attend weekly synagogue services.

Many reasons are offered to explain this disturbing alienation of American Jews from their synagogues: increasing secularization; decreasing religious observance; the high cost of synagogue affiliation; low levels of Hebrew proficiency among most American Jews; the lack of spirituality in many synagogues . . . and many other such explanations.

People who do not attend synagogue seem to feel no lack in their lives. Indeed, a recent Gallup poll found that Jews have the greatest sense of personal wellbeing among all American religious denominations. Masses of Jews do not connect to weekly worship—and yet they feel good about their lives.

Yet, a significant and growing number of Jews is attending synagogue more often, more enthusiastically, and more meaningfully. Many of these are Orthodox Jews, for whom religious worship is a basic necessity of spiritual life. It would be unthinkable for observant Jews to absent themselves from public prayer. Others are spiritual seekers who want religious fellowship in their confrontation with the Almighty. They may or may not be Orthodox Jews, but they have a religious craving that seeks to flourish within a community. It's not enough to have private moments of spiritual reflection; a communal structure provides a strong, steady framework for spiritual growth.

While we certainly must address reasons why so many Jews are disconnected from regular worship, we should pay attention to why so many Jews are increasingly seeking communal settings in which to express their religious devotion.

A good synagogue is not merely a place to recite one's prayers. A good synagogue is a community. It brings together like-minded people who want to come before God as a Jewish community; who want to study Torah together; who want to share their lives with others; who want to strengthen, console, help each other. A good synagogue is a community that includes old and young, men and women—that engages the minds, hearts, and souls of congregants. A good synagogue is deeply rooted in Jewish tradition, and deeply committed to the Jewish future.

Dr. David Pelcovitz recently lectured at Congregation Shearith Israel in New York City. He reported on something he had learned about growing date trees! A farmer explained that a date tree that grows alone generally does not produce sweet dates. Rather, date trees do best when in a grove. The root systems of the trees form a network that strengthens each tree. Date trees that grow in groves, near other date trees, produce sweet dates. The trees are healthier and more productive.

The Psalmist wrote: "a righteous person flourishes like a date tree." The analogy is clear: a righteous person—like a date tree—is able to flourish when one has a network, when one is strengthened by and gives strength to others. An individual's spirituality is enhanced and sweetened by ongoing interrelationships with a community of spiritual seekers.

The Torah portion of the week focuses on the rituals and worship in the Mishkan among the ancient Israelites. It underscores the value of personal spiritual development within the context of a communal setting. We come before God not merely as lone individuals, but as members of a community. We are concerned not merely with our own personal spirituality, but with being part of a religious community that draws on its traditions, that serves all its members, that creates a healthy and meaningful framework for future generations.

So many Jews—for so many reasons—have disconnected themselves from regular synagogue worship. Our hope is that they find their way back to the synagogue. Our responsibility is to invite them back, listen to them, share with them. By re-connecting with synagogue communities, they not only strengthen and sweeten their own lives, but they add strength and sweetness to our synagogues and to our future generations.

Thoughts on שבת הגדול

Ice, Fire, and the Search for the Middle Path

🖎 The Jerusalem Talmud (*Hagigah* 2:1) teaches that the way of Torah is a narrow path. On the right is fire, and on the left is icy snow. If one veers from the path, one risks being destroyed by either the fire or the ice. The Torah way of life is balanced, harmonious, and sensible. It imbues life with depth, meaning, and true happiness. But it is not easy to stay on the path.

Veering to the left freezes the soul of Judaism. When one abandons the warmth of traditional Jewish belief and observance, one falls prey to the ice of skepticism, materialism, hedonism. One confronts what Viktor Frankl has called an "existential vacuum," or what Peter Berger has termed "spiritual homelessness."

Veering to the right causes one to become embroiled in religious fanaticism, excessive zeal. This tendency generates a spirit of isolationism, self-righteousness, authoritarianism, reducing religious life to a self-imposed spiritual ghetto.

The *Jerusalem Post* reported a survey indicating that about two-thirds of Israeli Jews will participate in a Seder for Passover this year; about 80 percent of new *olim* will do likewise. This means that one-third of Israeli Jews and 20 percent of new *olim* will **not** be at a Seder. For this huge number of Jews, participation at a Seder means little or nothing. They do not feel a religious—or even a national or cultural—impulse to celebrate Pessah with a Seder. If this is so in Israel, it is all the more so in the Diaspora. This is the way of ice, the freezing of the soul of Judaism.

On the other hand, we witness the patterns within Orthodoxy where stringencies upon stringencies are added to Passover observance. Food items need multiple *hashgahot* to appease various segments of the community. Religiously observant people don't eat in the homes of other religiously observant people who do not keep up with all the latest *humrot*. This is the way of fire, the burning of the soul of Judaism and turning the Torah life into a cultic framework.

How do we stay on the healthy, balanced, middle path of Torah? Why do the forces of ice and fire grow so strong, as the middle path seems to grow weaker and less confident? Modern Orthodoxy stands for the middle path. It strives to maintain devotion to Torah and halakha, while avoiding the extremes of the right and left. Yet, Modern Orthodoxy finds that its children are being pulled toward both extremes. Some move to the right, thinking that this is a "more religious" approach. Some move to the left, surrendering to the prevailing secular values of society. Why does Modern Orthodoxy feel imperiled?

It is difficult, even uninspiring, to fight for moderation, balance, compassion, and inclusiveness. It is so much easier to take extreme positions, where one can argue from the vantage point of ice or fire, rather than to be "lukewarm." At a time when the vision of Modern Orthodoxy is so desperately needed, Modern Orthodoxy seems to have lost its voice, its confidence, its ability to steer intelligently between the way of ice and the way of fire.

All Jews—whether Orthodox or not—need to hear a principled and articulate expression of the middle path of Judaism, that veers neither to the right nor to the left. Happily, there are some Modern Orthodox voices that are rising to the challenge. Let us all listen carefully. The future of Judaism and the Jewish people are at stake.

שבת הגדול/צו Thoughts on

When Wickedness Parades as Justice

🐚 U.S. Supreme Court Justice Robert Jackson took leave from the Court to serve as the United States' chief prosecutor at the Nuremberg trials of Nazi war criminals. He wrote that "the most odious of all oppressions are those which mask as justice." He sharply criticized the role of judges and legal systems to legitimize tyranny and oppression.

Judge Jackson understood that the atrocities of the Nazis were all purported to be "legal." Laws were passed depriving Jews of all rights. Laws were passed to round up, imprison, and murder Jews. All those who participated in these heinous actions were following the law of the land!

The problem, though, was that the law itself was starkly immoral; the government that promulgated murderous laws was itself evil; the "legal system" that allowed such "laws" to be passed and implemented was the epitome of injustice, cruelty, and wickedness. Moral people should have denounced such "laws" and should have resisted the "legal system." If enough good people had risen against the tyrannical laws and the murderous Nazi regime, millions of lives would have been saved.

In our times, we also witness tendencies to legitimize wicked and immoral behavior by means of declaring such evil to be "legal." The United Nations is perhaps the world's most nefarious example of this tendency. The UN routinely passes resolutions condemning Israel—not because these condemnations relate to moral and sound judgment, but because a malicious cabal of Israel-hating nations muster the majority to pass anti-Israel resolutions. There isn't even the faintest element of fairness to these resolutions, not the slightest effort to understand Israel's position, not a word of condemnation of groups and nations who attack Israel in every way they can. The UN espouses resolutions and policies that are dressed in the garb of "international law" when in fact these resolutions and policies are classic examples of immorality, injustice, and corruption of the value of law.

It's not just the UN that tends to cloak immorality in the dress of justice. There are groups of anti-Israel and anti-Semitic people who seek to undermine Israel; they insidiously pose as being interested in human rights, as guardians of international law. Yet, they operate with malice toward Israel and perpetrate the vilest propaganda against her; they support boycotts of Israel; they constantly rebuke Israel for any real or imagined shortcoming. Many seemingly good-hearted people get swept up in the "politically correct" anti-Israel bashing. They are gullible in the extreme, and don't have the time or moral courage to try to find out actual facts. These people will condemn Israel for causing pain to Arabs in Gaza, but will never raise a word of protest when thousands of missiles are fired into Israel from Gaza. They will condemn Israel's intransigence, but will never call to account Arab and Muslim leaders who unashamedly call for the destruction of Israel. Thinking that they are standing for "human rights" and for "international law," these people are in fact accomplices in immorally seeking to deprive Jews of their rights. They foster "laws" and "resolutions" and "policies" that are in essence criminal, unjust, immoral.

In Psalm 81, we read: "*lo yihye bekha el zar,*" let there be no strange god among you." The Talmud (*Shabbat* 105b) offers a more literal and more profound interpretation of this phrase—you shall not have within yourself a strange god. According to this interpretation, the verse is not warning us against worshiping external idols. Rather, it is telling us to look within ourselves for strange gods, for evil inclinations, for false divinities. It is demanding that we introspect, that we maintain truth, that we reject the false gods that mislead us into false beliefs and corrupt behaviors.

This is a message of utmost importance for all people. None of us should allow "false gods" to fester within us, to blind our eyes to our moral responsibilities. All humans must strive to root out the evil inclination that leads to discriminatory attitudes, to corrupt laws and resolutions, to following along with the "politically correct" but morally bankrupt anti-Israel chorus. We must remember the words of Justice Jackson that "the most odious of all oppressions are those which mask as justice."

This coming Shabbat is known as *Shabbat haGadol*—the great Shabbat recalling the Israelites' preparation for their redemption from Egypt. Just as the ancient Israelites were redeemed from their cruel oppressors, so we pray that today's Israelites will be redeemed from their oppressors. We pray that all humans will strive honestly and sincerely to remove the "strange gods" of hatred, hypocrisy, and malice from within themselves.

Our rabbis taught: In the month of Nissan our ancestors were redeemed, and in the month of Nissan we will be redeemed in the future.

פסח

Passover Symbols—Symbols for Our Lives

🕮 Here are a few thoughts about the main symbols of the Passover Seder plate.

Matzah:

Matzah is a basic, no-frills item. It is flour and water, without leavening. It stands for our basic selves, unpretentious, not inflated with vanity or pride. Matzah reminds us that we need to remember who we are; that we need not (and should not) participate in the rat race of one-upmanship; that we cannot let our own internal happiness be dependent on how others judge us. Matzah is what it is, without apology, without need to impress others, without worrying if other foods are fancier or more elegant.

Because of its sheer simplicity and honesty, Matzah symbolizes freedom. When we really know who we are, we gain a fine sense of our own freedom. We can be strong unto ourselves; we can rise above the fray; we can stop playing games of who has more, who has better, who has control. When we are free within, we have the confidence to live our own lives, not the counterfeit lives that others would impose on us.

Pessah:

The Pessah offering in the ancient Temple in Jerusalem was to be eaten in groups of family and friends; the paschal lamb was not to be prepared for only one person. If Matzah symbolizes the inner strength of the individual, the Pessah offering reminds us that we are part of a family, part of a larger community. For us to grow as meaningful human beings, we need to see beyond our individual selves. We remember our family origins—our parents and grandparents, our earlier generations. We link ourselves to our traditions and see ourselves as part of a grand dramatic unfolding of family history. We recognize that we are also links in that chain of family tradition, with responsibilities to family and friends—and to generations yet unborn.

Maror:

The Maror, bitter herbs, reminds us that the world includes many people whose lives are filled with suffering, pain, and bitterness. As we are grateful to the Almighty for the blessings He has showered upon us, we cannot forget the bitter tears that are shed by hungry children, by helpless parents, by lonely and frail elderly people. We cannot forget the immeasurable pain inflicted by wars, by terrorism, by cruelty, by disease, by poverty.

As we sit around the Seder table, the Matzah reminds us of our basic individuality; the shankbone (symbolizing the Pessah offering) reminds us of our link to family and friends; the Maror reminds us that our happiness and fulfillment also depend on our concern for those who are less fortunate, those whose lives are embittered.

The Maror also reminds us that no one gets through life without experiencing times of sadness and pain. At those times, we need family and friends to come to our aid, to comfort us; and when others are grieving, they need us to console them and help them.

Matzah, Pessah, and Maror, then, have ongoing messages for how we can lead better, happier, and more meaningful lives. Together, they contribute to our inner freedom, our family continuity, and our commitment to make this a better world.

The Not-So-Simple Child

🪶 The Passover Haggadah presents a dramatic format for dealing with questions relating to religious observance. It presents four children, representing different attitudes toward Jewish belief and ritual, along with the framework for how to answer each of the questioners.

The *rasha* (wicked child) is antagonistic to Jewish tradition. He/she does not feel part of it, and asks: What's the point of all this ritual? Why do you do these things? The Haggadah realizes that there is little to be gained by entering into argument with such a person, or to try to convince the *rasha* through logical discussion. Rather, the Haggadah provides a different kind of response: I do these things because God brought ME out of Egypt. I will not debate with you; but I will tell you why this is so meaningful to me. Through my personal testimony, perhaps you will get a sense of why Jewish belief and observance are so significant and meaningful.

The child "who does not know how to ask" (every child knows how to ask questions!) is one who is so uninterested in Judaism that he/she isn't even curious enough to ask a question. The response is identical to the response given to the *rasha*—I give my personal testimony of why being Jewish is so important and meaningful, of what the laws and traditions mean to me. If I can give an enthusiastic and sincere story of my own commitment, perhaps the child's interest will be aroused.

The *hakham* (wise child) asks about the laws. He/she accepts Judaism and wants to know every detail of the halakha. The response is: We teach this child all the laws and customs.

The *tam* (simple or naive child) asks: What is this? We answer: Because with a mighty hand God took us out of Egypt. There seems to be a disconnect here. How is this response relevant to the question? How does it help the child understand what is transpiring at the Seder, or the broader issue of what is the meaning/purpose of religious observance altogether?

I think we need to re-examine the question and answer relating to the *tam*. Although *tam* is usually translated as "simple" or "naive," the word also has a much different meaning. It means pure, unblemished, whole. Our forefather Jacob is described as being *tam* and so is Job. Noah is called *tamim*, from the same root. The *tam* of the Haggadah isn't simple at all, but is actually the most profound of the four children.

The *tam* accepts Jewish belief and ritual, but his/her question isn't about what to do—but about why. The *tam*, in search of wholeness, is not satisfied with an intellectual discussion of the laws and customs. The *tam* wants to understand how these laws and customs increase one's closeness to God, how they enhance spirituality. The *tam* is saying: yes, I'll do what the religion requires, but I need something more. I need to know the inner spirit of what the religion demands of me.

The response is: If you are seeking the inner meaning and you want to deepen your spirituality, then you need to understand: God is great; God is a presence in our lives; God's mighty hand took us out of Egypt; God's mighty hand continues to play a role in our lives today. The laws and traditions of Judaism aim at one thing: to bring us closer to God. Every time we perform a mitzvah, we bring God into our consciousness and into our lives. The more connected we are with God's presence, the deeper and more meaningful are our lives. If we will develop our spiritual natures, we will be better, happier, and wiser people. God's mighty hand is reaching out to us every moment of every day.

The Kotzker Rebbe once said: When a person needs to cry, when a person wants to cry—but cannot cry: that is the most heart-rending cry of all. When a person feels the deep need to cry out, but is emotionally stifled—the person's life is not "whole." I would paraphrase the Kotzker Rebbe's words: When a person needs to feel close to God, when a person wants to feel close to God—but cannot feel close to God: that is the most heart-rending feeling of all.

This is the dilemma raised by the *tam* : We are living at a time of spiritual malaise, of "existential vacuum," of "spiritual homelessness." I want to feel close to God—but I feel distant from God. How can I come closer? How can I achieve spiritual wholeness?

The answer: Remember always that God is a presence in our lives. Every mitzvah is an entry point to a deeper spiritual awareness. Take time to think quietly and alone. You can open your heart and emotion and intellect. You can cry out. You can feel God's closeness. If you will open yourself to spiritual growth, you will find the redemption and wisdom that you seek.

For us to be able to respond to the four types of "children," we ourselves need to have the commitment, knowledge, sincerity, and integrity to give authentic answers. We need to understand the nature of the questions—and the questioners. We need to make our case honestly and powerfully. We need to explain the laws and traditions. Perhaps most importantly, we need to know how to respond to the *tam*—the person seeking religious wholeness, spiritual fulfillment, intellectual purity.

We need to reflect not only on "what," but on "why."

A Tribute to a Small Group of Jews from 1730: Thoughts for the Closing Days of Passover

❦ What was happening in the Jewish world around the year 1730?

Rabbi Israel Baal Shem Tov (1698–1760) was precipitating the development of a new movement in Judaism—Hasidism. This movement took root in the Ukraine, and spread widely among Ashkenazim of Eastern Europe.

Rabbi Yaacov Huli published the first volume of the *Me'am Lo'ez* in Constantinople in 1730. The *Me'am Lo'ez* is a Ladino biblical commentary that became a classic among Sephardim of the Ladino-speaking world.

Rabbi Hayyim Benattar (1696–1743) was a spiritual influence among Moroccan Jews, and had a profound impact on world Jewry through his Torah commentary, *Ohr haHayyim*.

The Gaon of Vilna (1720–1796) was a child genius, growing into one of the most venerable sages of the Jewish people. His mastery of Talmud and halakha were legendary; he was an arch-opponent of Hasidism.

Moses Mendelsohn (1729–1786) was to become a founding figure in Jewish Enlightenment. Born in Dessau, Germany, he was the foremost Western European Jewish thinker of his time who sought to put traditional Judaism into a philosophically sophisticated framework.

While these individuals represent powerful trends affecting many thousands of Jews throughout the world, something happened in 1730 that surely received very little worldwide attention at the time.

In 1730, Congregation Shearith Israel of New York City dedicated its first synagogue building—the first synagogue building erected in North America—on the seventh day of Passover. Shearith Israel, founded in 1654, was the first Jewish congregation on this continent. Until 1730, the community was quite small and met for worship in rented quarters. By 1730, the congregation felt able—with the support of Sephardic congregations of Amsterdam, London, Curacao, and Suriname—to build its own building.

In 1730, the dedication of Shearith Israel's synagogue on Mill Street would have attracted little notice from the great Jewish communities of Europe, the Middle East, and North Africa. New York was a remote and tiny Jewish community, far from the pulsating Jewish life of the "old world." New York could not boast of a Baal Shem Tov, or a Yaacov Huli, or a Hayyim Benattar or a

Gaon of Vilna, or a Moses Mendelsohn . . . or of a substantial Jewish community that could influence the larger Jewish world.

Yet, perhaps to the ultimate surprise of those great "old world" communities, Shearith Israel became the foundation stone of the American Jewish community. Its members struggled for and won civil rights for Jews in America; they fought in the American Revolution and shared in the birth and development of the United States. That little synagogue building, dedicated on Passover in 1730, is a symbol of the religious devotion, idealism, and commitment that characterized early American Jewry. Although that first building no longer stands, many of the furnishings of the Mill Street synagogue grace Shearith Israel's chapel in its current synagogue building on 70th Street and Central Park West (dedicated in 1897).

Shearith Israel was established by Sephardic Jews of the Western Sephardic tradition. Its "mother" Congregation was the famous Portuguese Synagogue in Amsterdam. While the synagogue custom was—and continues to be—that of the Western Sephardim, Shearith Israel, even from its earliest years, included Sephardim and Ashkenazim alike. It was—and continues to be—a remarkable Jewish institution with a diverse membership of Jews of many backgrounds and various levels of religious knowledge and observance.

Since the late seventeenth century, the Western Sephardic tradition has eliminated kabbalistic texts and practices from the synagogue service, preferring a more rational and classical synagogue service. This tradition has emphasized order and dignity, a fine sense of aesthetics, a commitment to social justice and involvement in general society, an embracing of Jewish and general knowledge.

Although the dedication of Shearith Israel's synagogue building on Passover 1730 must have seemed a relatively insignificant event in the Jewish world, it turned out to be of tremendous historic significance. This pioneer congregation, with its first synagogue building on North American soil, was the harbinger of an American Jewish community that was to grow into the largest and most influential Jewish Diaspora center in modern Jewish history.

As we celebrate the closing days of the Passover festival this year, it is appropriate that we remember the spiritual heroism of the members of New York's tiny Jewish community who dedicated this continent's first synagogue building on the seventh day of Passover in 1730. It is appropriate to remember that events that may seem small at the time, can become landmark turning points in history.

שמיני

Computers, Holiness, and the Power of Change

🐚 In 1980, our synagogue office became computerized. Each of our staff members was given a computer on which to do our work. My computer sat in my office in an unopened box for about a year. A member of the synagogue Board visited me one day and saw the box. He asked why I wasn't using the computer.

I answered: I don't need it. I have a secretary. I have an electric typewriter. Why should I get started with this newfangled contraption? He immediately asked to use my phone, and he called a friend who was a computer teacher. For the next two days, she came to my office and taught me how to use the computer. After those two days, I became "addicted" to the computer, and don't know how I could live without it.

This episode came to mind recently, when I had a discussion with a computer expert from Los Angeles who has many older clients who did not have computers during their childhoods. He told me that one of the biggest problems is getting these people to overcome their psychological resistance to entering the world of computers.

Why did I leave my computer box unopened for a year? Why do people resist learning new computer programs?

The problem does not stem from intellectual or physical inability. Once we learn to use computers, we do fine. The problem is different: It entails overcoming a psychological barrier. A new way of doing things tends to threaten the way we've always done things in the past; it threatens our comfort level, our feeling of being in control. We suddenly become dependent on technicians, who seem to speak in a language we can't fully understand. The world is changing rapidly, and we are becoming dinosaurs. Stop the world, I want to get off!

But once we overcome these psychological barriers, we can enter the new age and learn the necessary skills, and actually find satisfaction and joy in our progress. The determining factor is: Do we have the right mindset? Do we have the will to change? Do we have the inner strength to start from scratch, as though we're back in first grade?

This dilemma, in a different form, is raised in this week's Torah reading. God tells us: "Sanctify yourselves and be holy; for I am holy." Rashi points out that "sanctify yourselves" means we need to develop the right attitude; "be holy" can be fulfilled only after we want to sanctify ourselves.

Just as some people have psychological barriers about computers and other technology, some have psychological barriers about religion. They prefer to leave the "box of religion" unopened, because it may challenge their comfort level. They are nervous about religious faith, about commitment to mitzvoth, about changing their lifestyles. Or, they may already be religiously observant, but they are uneasy about getting more deeply involved, more intensely learned; they don't know where this will lead. They don't want to upset the status quo.

The Torah is aware of these concerns; so it teaches us first to sanctify ourselves, to develop an open and receptive attitude, to reach a proper comfort level in our spiritual growth. Once we have made this internal shift in the way we approach life, we can then go to the next step: be holy. We can grow in our religious knowledge and commitment without being blocked by self-imposed psychological barriers.

People crave spirituality, but are afraid of spirituality. They don't know how to express it. Or they fear that it will lead them to change in new, untested directions. The Torah assures us: Don't be afraid. We can overcome our resistances and our anxieties. We just need to start by sanctifying ourselves, by teaching ourselves to be receptive, by changing our attitudes. If we can overcome these internal psychological barriers, we can then move on in a more productive, more creative, and happier way.

People fail in life not because they don't have the power to change and to grow; but because they inwardly resist change and growth. People succeed in life because they have the strength to learn, to grow, to see life as an unfolding adventure that should be lived with courage and vitality.

Confronting Tragedy

❦ In this week's Torah portion, we read of the tragic deaths of two of Aaron's sons. When he learned the sad news, "Aaron was silent," *vaYidom Aharon.* Commentators have offered various explanations of Aaron's silence. He may have been speechless due to shock; he may have had angry thoughts in his heart, but he controlled himself from uttering them; he may have been silent as a sign of acceptance of God's judgment.

Within biblical tradition, there are a number of phrases relating to confrontation with tragedy.

"*Min haMetsar Karati Y-ah,*" I call out to God from distress. When in pain, it is natural to cry out to God, to shed tears, to lament our sufferings and our losses. To cry out when we are in distress is a first step in the grieving process.

"*Tefillah leHabakuk haNavi al Shigyonoth.*" Dr. David de Sola Pool has translated this passage: "A prayer of Habakuk the prophet, in perplexity." After crying out at our initial grief, we move to another level of mourning. We are perplexed. We want to know why this tragedy has happened? We want to understand how to reconcile this disaster with our belief in God's goodness. We are in a state of emotional and spiritual confusion.

"*Mima-amakim keratikha Ado-nai.*" I call out to God from the depths of my being. This introduces the next stage in confronting tragedy. It is a profound recognition, from the deepest recesses of our being, that we turn to—and depend upon—God. It is a depth of understanding that transcends tears, words, perplexity. It is a depth of understanding and acceptance that places our lives in complete context with the Almighty. We may be heart-broken; we may be perplexed; we may be angry—but at the very root of who we are, we feel the solace of being in God's presence. When we reach this deepest level of understanding, we find that we don't have words or sounds that can articulate this inner clarity. We fall silent.

"And Aaron was silent." Aaron was on a very high spiritual plane. While he surely felt the anguish of "*Min haMetsar,*" and experienced the perplexity of "*Shigyonoth,*" he experienced the tragedy "*Mima-amakim,*" from the very depths of his being. His silence reflected a profound inner wisdom that was too deep for tears and too deep for words.

"May happiness multiply in Israel, and may sadness be driven away."

Thoughts on תזריע

Talmudic Logic

🖎 *Question:* Why do Jews answer a question with another question?
Answer: Why shouldn't Jews answer a question with another question?

There's something about the Jewish mystique that likes questions. Every question seems to generate another question; every answer engenders another question. How did we get to be so question-oriented?

One answer might be our long history of Talmud study. The Talmud is a veritable treasure house of questions. It analyzes every statement from different angles. It asks: Why does the text use this word, but not that word? What are the implications? Why did this rabbi hold that opinion, and why did the other rabbi disagree? Does the statement in one place contradict a statement in another place? How can we resolve the contradictions?

A recent article in the Israeli newspaper, *Yediot Aharonot,* discussed a fascinating phenomenon in South Korea, the home of nearly 50 million people. Intellectual leaders in South Korea wondered why Jews have excelled so incredibly—winning a high proportion of Nobel Prizes, major national and international awards in the sciences, math, literature, medicine, and so forth. They concluded that the secret of the Jewish "genius" is the Talmud! Because Jews study Talmud, they become analytical, logical, and they ask a lot of questions. They search for truth, and analyze every detail along the way.

The Talmud has been translated into Korean, and many thousands of South Korean children are now studying Talmud. Many Korean homes have sets of Talmud, so that adults can study along with their children. There are more—a great many more—South Koreans studying Talmud than there are Jews studying Talmud!

While I am all in favor of Talmud study and I agree that this study is intellectually enriching, I think Talmud study in itself will not generate more Nobel Prize winners for South Korea, or Israel, or anywhere else. First, one can sharpen analytic skills by studying math or logic or analytical philosophy. Second, many Jewish "geniuses" who have made impressive intellectual achievements have never opened a volume of Talmud in their lives!

It is not the Talmud itself that can make us wise, but the "talmudic method" that is the key. Over the centuries, this method of asking questions, and more questions, and then more questions—has become ingrained in the Jewish psyche. Whether or not a Jew has studied Talmud, the talmudic method is the tradition that he/she has inherited from parents and grandparents. This method is applied to all areas of intellectual inquiry, and this method reaps vast results.

The "talmudic method" goes further than logical analysis of data and opinions. One of the six divisions of the Talmud is *Toharoth*—dealing with laws relating to ritual purity and impurity, including, for example, topics in this week's Torah portion. Ritual purity and impurity cannot be detected in a microscope, and are not derivable by logic or math. They relate to another dimension of reality, a dimension that transcends what we see and what we can quantify. They are intellectual abstractions.

Thus, the talmudic method—and the Torah itself—pushes us to think beyond the obvious. It teaches us to consider abstract concepts that reflect different dimensions of reality. In studying the laws of ritual purity, we enter a different zone of awareness and sensitivity. Although these laws seem so strange to many moderns, they actually are important elements in the development of the "Jewish mystique." They teach us to look beyond the apparent, to imagine different realities, to envision things that can't be seen with our eyes.

I am not sure if the South Koreans will plumb the depths of the talmudic method; but it is to their credit that they are trying.

Question: Should we Jews devote more time and energy to studying Talmud and teaching it to our children?

Answer: Shouldn't we be at least as interested in Talmud as the South Koreans?

Thoughts on מצרע

Jobs, Careers, and Callings

🐚 The priests of old (the Kohanim) had high-prestige positions, serving as spiritual leaders of the people of Israel. They received priestly gifts and seem to have lived comfortable lives.

Yet, when we read this week's Torah portion, we see that the Kohanim had some unpleasant responsibilities. They had to examine the wounds of lepers and arrange for their purification. They had to check clothing and houses that were struck by a leprosy-type plague. If we also consider that the tasks of the Kohanim included the daily slaughtering of animals in the Tabernacle (and later in the Temple in Jerusalem), we realize that the Kohanim did not always have an easy go of things.

Let us imagine how three Kohanim would have described their duties.

Kohen A: I have a miserable job, but I have no choice in the matter. I'm a Kohen, so this is my lot. I toil at many unpleasant tasks; but I need to do these things to make a living. I have a job.

Kohen B: My work has its ups and downs. Although I don't enjoy all aspects of my responsibilities, I do my best. I want to gain the respect of my peers and the public at large. Perhaps if I work hard enough, I will rise in the priestly ranks, and maybe even become the High Priest. I have a career.

Kohen C: I am privileged to be a servant of the Lord and to fulfill His commandments. When I bring sacrifices I feel I am helping people to come closer to God. When I examine the wounds of lepers, I have the opportunity to help the forlorn and downtrodden and to bring them purification. I am blessed to have these special opportunities. I have a calling.

What is the difference between these three Kohanim? They all perform the same duties and have the same responsibilities. The difference isn't objective, but subjective. The difference is in how they interpret their lives and their duties.

Kohen A sees himself as a victim trapped in a bad job. He derives little satisfaction from his work, and probably looks forward to the day when he can retire. He has to work, because he needs to feed himself and his family.

Kohen B is not enthusiastic about his work, but sees it as a framework for personal advancement. If he works hard and well, he may advance to a higher position. Even if he doesn't like all aspects of his work, he has the inner satisfaction of feeling a challenge to rise in the ranks.

Kohen C focuses on the good he can do in his position—how he can help people come closer to God and to achieve spiritual purification. He views the unpleasant tasks as positive opportunities to serve God and the community. He feels a special joy in having been chosen to do his work.

While Kohen A is probably unhappy most of his working days, and while Kohen B is modestly pleased with himself— Kohen C is by far the happiest. He is the only one who interprets his work not as a job or a career—but as a calling. He sees ultimate value in his responsibilities, even in those things that seem so tedious and messy.

Now, let us apply the lessons of these three Kohanim to ourselves.

We all need to work for a living. We all have aspects of our work that are pleasing, and aspects that are not so pleasing. Some of us are miserable at our work, some are moderately satisfied, and some are really happy. The difference is not necessarily in the kind of work we do: but in our attitude toward our work.

Some people have jobs. They work for their paycheck. They need to earn a living and support themselves and their families. But they don't particularly like their work. They don't see any ultimate value in it, or much personal fulfillment in it. They may spend 30 or 40 years at a job they really don't like and don't enjoy. But they feel trapped. They have no choice. They have to work, and this is their job.

Some people have careers. They work for a company that gives incentives for increased pay, and higher-prestige positions. They don't necessarily see ultimate value in their work, but it's a living and provides a certain degree of excitement and upward mobility. They work for 30 or 40 years at it, and can't figure out exactly what they accomplished in their years, except for receiving paychecks and rising to higher ranks in the company. What difference did it all make?

Some people have callings. They work not for themselves and not for their companies—but for some higher vision of what life is supposed to be. They seek meaning and fulfillment in life. They are idealists who can view the simplest and most menial tasks as an entryway to personal redemption. They genuinely want to help others, to do their share to create a better society and a better world, to fulfill the expectations that the Almighty has for them.

In the final analysis, all of us can be in the category of Kohen C—if only we will set our minds to it, if only we will see our lives in larger brushstrokes, if only we can imagine that what we do really has ultimate value. We are not just cogs in a wheel who perform tasks for pay. We are not just go-getters who strive to get ahead of others on the treadmill. No, we are human beings seeking personal meaning and fulfillment in our lives.

Whatever kind of work we do, we can see it as a job, or a career—or a calling. A shift in vision, a shift in attitude—and we can become different and better and happier people.

Wandering, Focusing—
and Creativity

❧ What did the Israelites do during their 40 years of wandering in the wilderness?

They didn't need to work for their food, clothing, or shelter. They didn't have businesses to run. They didn't have homes to repair or gardens to tend. They didn't have theaters for entertainment or arenas for sporting events. They didn't have televisions or internet connections or Facebook. They didn't have a formal school system for their children, or summer camps, or vacation homes.

We may assume that the Israelites—men, women, and children—spent part of their days studying Torah. But what else did they have to do? How did they deal with what must have been overwhelming boredom? What did the Almighty have in mind when He imposed 40 years of wandering on them?

Actually, this extended period of wandering and boredom may have proven to be one of the best things that happened to the Israelites of those times—with a lesson for us today.

Wandering is an essential ingredient in the development of imagination and creativity. When we let our minds roam, we often come up with fresh ideas and insights. If we are constantly busy with our work and with our electronic devices, our minds become constricted. We are subject to an unending barrage of images and information—we have no time to let our minds drift, to daydream, to transcend the ever-present stimuli that shower us unremittingly. Our great sages over the generations practiced *hitbodedut*—isolation of oneself from the hurly-burly of life by means of meditation, wandering, going to unfamiliar places.

I suspect—although the Torah does not inform us of these details—that the Israelites experienced tremendous boredom when they began their sojourn in the wilderness. But then, they must have realized that they needed to create structure for their lives. They must have developed groups and classes for the children. Storytellers and singers must have emerged. They needed to draw on their imaginations and creativity in order to make life happy, meaningful, and fulfilling. They learned to improvise and to think "out of the box."

When I was a little boy, I would sometimes complain to my mother: "I'm bored." My mother wisely responded: "That's wonderful. It's good to be bored.

Now use your imagination and see how you can break through your boredom." Boredom is a jumping board for ingenuity and innovation.

During those years of wandering, the Israelites also received a number of very detailed commandments. They were told to build a Mishkan and were given precise measurements, types of materials and fabrics, even the color of the fabrics to be used. They were given a highly ritualized system of offerings and sacrifices. They were given precise rules about which animals they may and may not consume. In this week's Torah portion, we read of the technical laws relating to ritual purity. Why did the Israelites need so many specific laws with so many meticulous details?

Why would the Almighty demand rigorous adherence to such precise rules? Couldn't the Israelites worship just as well in a Mishkan that they built according to their own desires? Why did the Almighty delineate the exact materials and colors, rather than just let the people do what they chose on their own? What was the point in giving such specific rules about sacrifices, and food consumption, purity, and impurity?

I believe that the stress on details underscores the second ingredient in creativity. It isn't enough simply to wander in an unstructured manner. The mind needs to be tuned in to specific details, to be able to observe things very carefully. God was teaching the Israelites not to view things in an undifferentiated way, but to focus intently on specific materials, colors, sizes, animal characteristics, unusual blemishes on one's skin. The emphasis on these details provided the broader lesson of the importance of focusing on the details of objects, on our surroundings, on all those things that constitute the world we live in.

The Israelites' 40 years in the wilderness served as the religious and creative foundation of our people. From that experience, we learn the essential importance of wandering and imagining, of letting our minds roam and invent. We also learn the vital need for focusing on details, and taking the time to see things as they really are in their uniqueness.

What did the Israelites do during their 40 years of wandering in the wilderness? They became a dynamic, creative, focused and imaginative people. They set the foundations for the future development and creativity of the people of Israel for all eras to come, including our own.

Thoughts on קדושים

Seeking Correct Diagnosis and Treatment

א Receiving an incorrect medical diagnosis can be very serious, even fatal. If one's condition is not accurately determined, the prescribed treatment (or non-treatment) can cause needless suffering.

Receiving an incorrect spiritual diagnosis can also prove to be dangerous. If one does not know the root of one's problem, one cannot properly address it.

Sociologists point out that the Jewish community faces a number of problems: assimilation and intermarriage; non-attendance at synagogue services; low levels of Jewish education among large numbers of Jews; low birth rates, and so forth. Modernity has posed—and continues to pose—serious challenges. In a website asking "Will your grandchildren be Jewish?" data is presented demonstrating that for most non-observant Jews, the answer is NO.

During the nineteenth century, Jews were confronted with the problem: How can we make/keep Judaism attractive to Jews who live most of their lives in the secular world? The diagnosis given by some was: Let's water down Judaism so that it demands less of Jews. If it's easier, it will be more attractive. Movements were formed that did away with many of the ritual commandments of Judaism; that removed much Hebrew from the prayer services; that styled synagogue services to be more "modern." This pattern continued through the twentieth century, and continues in various manifestations today.

This diagnosis has proven to be wrong. Few Jews became more religious, or more devoted to Judaism. Few attended services more often, certainly not even once a week. The sociological data of the past generations is available: Those Jews who chose "easy" forms of Judaism not only did not become more religious themselves, but their children and grandchildren generally moved further away from Judaism.

Because of generally low rates of synagogue affiliation and attendance in synagogues today, synagogue leaders wonder: What can be done to improve the situation? What is the right diagnosis? If we don't diagnose the problem correctly, our treatment may prove to be useless or even detrimental.

Various diagnoses are given: make services more "relevant"; introduce different music; be more "spiritual"; get more people to participate; provide free kiddush, and so forth.

Although these suggestions may have merit, they all deal with superficial matters and don't get to the root of the issue. They offer short-term band-aids, and don't offer a real cure that can bring healing and strength to the Jewish religious organism.

This week's Torah portion teaches us to be holy, because God is holy. It teaches us that life needs to be placed into a spiritual context, so that we understand that God is at the center of our being. Religious life—holiness—is attained not by increasing our egotism, but by humbly seeking to serve God and humanity in a spirit of selfless devotion.

At the root of the spiritual malady of modern religion, including Judaism, is a loss of this sense of holiness. People are generally far more concerned with advancing their own secular lives than in serving the Lord. Yet, if religion is not taken with full seriousness and commitment, it is doomed to fritter itself away.

The duty of religious leadership today is to focus on the real challenge to our spiritual health—the loss of holiness, the loss of the sense of the sacred. Offering this program or that innovation to gratify peoples' egos and comforts will not be of long-lasting value.

The "diagnosis" is: a loss of the holy. The "cure" is: to take Judaism more seriously, to reconnect with the Almighty, to infuse life with the fullness of Torah learning and observance. We don't want gimmicks or short-term and short-sighted suggestions that aim at inflating our egos; we want serious, long-term, visionary suggestions that aim at sustaining our souls and our spirits.

Many people don't want to hear the diagnosis, and certainly don't want to accept the suggested treatment. They prefer short cuts, easy and gratifying modes of feeling Jewish. Holiness isn't on their agenda. Devotion to Torah and halakha is not their priority. They ask for a feel-good religion that makes few demands. They do not realize that this approach is not only superficial for themselves, but it undermines the Jewishness of their children and grandchildren.

Judaism has flourished these past 3,500 years because a core of Jews in each generation has seen the Torah as a Tree of Life, has lived according to its teachings and laws, has lived in search of the holy. Judaism will flourish for the next centuries and millennia because of a core of Jews in our generation and future generations who take Judaism seriously; whose mission is to serve God with all their hearts, all their souls, and all their might. Sorry, no short cuts!

The Image and the Reality

❦ Some years ago, the *Jerusalem Post* published results of a poll of Israelis dealing with attitudes toward Orthodox Jews. Respondents generally identified Orthodox Jews with religious coercion, distinctive clothing, political infighting, and with Hareidim who do not serve in the Israeli military and do not carry their weight in the Israeli economy. Only 19 percent of respondents identified Orthodox Jews as people committed to Torah and mitzvoth!

Surely, such polls are merely snapshots of how respondents feel at a certain moment. If these same respondents were asked more detailed questions, they might have come up with more positive descriptions of Orthodox Jews. They may have remembered nice, thoughtful Orthodox Jewish neighbors or business associates; or kind Orthodox Jews who helped them when they were in need. There are definitely many wonderful Orthodox Jews in Israel, as well as throughout the world.

Yet, the results of that poll are troubling. Indeed, I think it is fair to say that attitudes toward the Orthodox have worsened considerably over the past few years. The Israeli Chief Rabbinate is associated with extreme and unpopular positions on various issues. The Orthodox religious bureaucracy causes distress to many who wish to convert, marry, or divorce. The Hareidi element has become increasingly coercive. The political infighting of the "religious" political parties is troubling.

If the general public has negative or incomplete views of Orthodoxy, then Orthodoxy itself bears much of the blame. If the popular image of Orthodox Jewry conjures up religious coercion, political manipulation, and self-righteous isolationism, then Orthodoxy is failing in its mission.

This week's Torah portion reminds us of the commandments to sanctify God's name and to avoid desecrating God's name. We are taught to conduct our lives in such a way that we reflect honor on God. Like it or not, each of us is an ambassador of God and Torah. We are responsible not just for living upright and moral lives, but also for projecting an image of righteousness and kindness to society at large. If only 19 percent of poll respondents identify Orthodox Jews with Torah and mitzvoth, while 81 percent identify Orthodox Jews with negative features—we are definitely not fulfilling these mitzvoth properly.

The Talmud (*Yoma* 86a) quotes the sage, Abayei, who interpreted the verse "And you shall love the Lord your God" to mean that "the Name of Heaven should be beloved because of you." Our words and deeds should inspire people to come closer to God and Torah, not repel them from God and Torah.

The Talmud continues: "If someone studies Torah and Mishnah, and attends on the disciples of the wise, is honest in business, and speaks pleasantly to persons, what do people then say concerning him? 'Happy the father who taught him Torah, happy the teacher who taught him Torah; woe unto people who have not studied the Torah; for this one has studied the Torah— look how fine his ways are, how righteous his deeds!'...But if someone studies Torah and Mishnah, attends on the disciples of the wise, but is dishonest in business, and discourteous in his relations with people, what do people say about him? 'Woe unto him who studied the Torah, woe unto his father who taught him Torah; woe unto his teacher who taught him Torah!' This man studied the Torah—look how corrupt are his deeds, how ugly his ways."

It seems to be a growing fashion within Orthodoxy to assume more and more stringencies in religious observance. Yet, this religious zeal seems to be confined to details of ritual law without a concomitant zeal for broader moral/ethical laws.

The Orthodox world will not draw the masses of Jews to Torah by means of coercion, political infighting, or bureaucratic control. It will not cause the Name of God to be beloved by adopting ever more ritual stringencies and policies of isolationism.

If we are indeed to fulfill the commandments of sanctifying God's name and avoiding the desecration of God's name, we will need to adopt great stringencies in these halakhic categories. We will need to be meticulous in our words and deeds so as to ensure that we reflect piety, righteousness, sweetness, and compassion. We will need to speak gently and thoughtfully, and to avoid religious coercion at all costs. We will need to show that Torah-observant Jews conduct business, politics, education, and everything else with the highest and most rigorous standards of morality.

Until the entire population views Orthodox Jews in a positive light, we are failing in our religious responsibilities. Let us raise a religious voice that sanctifies God's name. Let us be sure that the grand image of Torah life is reflected in the reality of how we conduct our lives.

יום העצמאות Thoughts on

Happy Are You, O Israel

꩜ Between 2005 and 2009, researchers at the Gallup World Poll surveyed thousands of respondents in 155 countries to find out the "happiness" levels in each country. They asked people to reflect on their overall satisfaction with their lives. Do they feel free? Are they making a living? Do they feel intellectually engaged? Are they relatively free of pain? Do they feel that they are respected by others?

The top five countries on the happiness scale, based on the percentage of citizens who say they are thriving, are Denmark, Finland, Norway, Sweden, and the Netherlands. These are prosperous countries, not involved in wars, out of the center of the world's problems. Costa Rica and New Zealand come next.

In eighth place, there is a tie among four countries: Canada, Australia, Switzerland—and ISRAEL.

Yes, Israel. This tiny country—surrounded by enemies, threatened constantly by terrorism and war, subject to an Arab economic boycott, frequently maligned by the media, torn within by ethnic and religious strife—is among the world's happiest countries!

To gain perspective, the United States is ranked 14; France is 44; Saudi Arabia is 58; Russia is 73; Japan is 81; China is 125.

62 percent of Israeli respondents described themselves as thriving; 35 percent as struggling; and 3 percent as suffering. With these figures, Israel is tied for eighth place among the 155 nations surveyed.

Given its many problems, why is Israel so happy? Why is it among the happiest, most thriving, most creative countries of the world?

I believe the answer is: the grand human spirit of the people of Israel. Israelis—in spite of many differences among themselves—recognize that they are part of an incredible, dynamic adventure. Israel is the only example in the history of humanity of an ancient nation exiled from its land, forced to live (often under horrific conditions) as a minority group scattered throughout the

132

world—who after nearly 2,000 years returned to its ancestral land, revived its ancient language, and re-established its historic culture. Israelis—and all members of the Jewish people—understand that we are living in a unique period of history. Israelis are happy not only because they are thriving intellectually, culturally, scientifically, militarily; but because they understand that their lives mean something, that they are pioneers in restoring the honor and strength of the Jewish people after centuries of powerlessness and disgrace.

Happiness doesn't mean having no troubles and no problems. Happiness means believing that life has meaning and direction, that one's life counts, that one is building for the future.

The Jewish people, throughout the ages, has demonstrated an astounding optimism, an unflinching faith in the future. In spite of all the difficulties we have faced, we have never given up on our mission to be a light unto the nations.

The Talmud (*Berakhot* 4b) quotes the opinion of Rabbi Yohanan who taught: Who has a place in the world to come? One who recites the "*geulah*" (prayer for redemption) connected to the Amidah prayer of the evening service. I think this passage can be understood as follows: Who is the one who will have ultimate redemption? It is one who can dream of redemption even at "night," even at times when everything seems dark and bleak. This is the eternal genius of the Jewish people—to dream of and work for redemption—regardless of how difficult the external circumstances appear.

As we prepare to celebrate *Yom Ha'Atsma'ut*—Israel Independence Day—let us take tremendous pride in how much Israel has accomplished since its establishment in 1948. Let us rejoice that Israel is one of the happiest, most creative, most advanced countries of the world. Let us pray for true peace and redemption—happiness for all Israel and for all humanity.

Happy *Yom Ha'Atsma'ut*.

Thinking Ahead, Far Ahead

In this week's Torah portion, we read: "And you shall count for yourself (*usfartem lakhem*—second-person plural)" seven weeks of the Omer. In next week's Torah portion, we read: And you shall count for yourself (*vesafarta lekha*—second-person singular)" seven Sabbath years. Why is the plural used when counting the weeks, and the singular used when counting years?

An answer: The commandment to count seven weeks is addressed to the public at large. The Torah assumes that people can keep focused on a mitzvah for seven weeks. However, when it comes to counting years for the sabbatical cycle, the Torah addresses itself to the sages of the great court—to individuals, not to the general public. Most people cannot stay focused for such a long span of time as a 50-year cycle. This commandment was aimed at those specially gifted individuals who are so wise and so visionary that they can think ahead and plan for the 50-year cycles.

It is understood that not everyone can dream great dreams, can stay clearly focused on the long span of the future. Yet, that is exactly what religious leadership is called upon to do. I would suggest that this is what every Jew is expected to aspire to do—even if it is known in advance that most of us will fall short.

Religious leadership needs to be in the hands of those who are great dreamers and visionaries, those who see the long view of Jewish history and destiny, those who are tirelessly committed to serving God and humanity with love, kindness, compassion, wisdom.

Our society has an overwhelming tendency toward short-term planning. Companies' stocks go up or down based on quarterly profit reports; company executives face tremendous pressure to show immediate results. People want instant information—via internet, iPhones, Facebook, and other media. The news is fed in quick, catchy sound bites. The media need to produce news, to attract advertisers and revenues. Few journalists have the time, inclination, or luxury to actually study events in historical context, or to offer reasoned projections for the coming decades. Politicians and public personalities communicate by short Twitter comments, or with slogans. They don't give us thorough analysis of the issues; they don't provide depth of context or logical projections for the future. They want to get re-elected. They can't worry about 10 years from now or 50 years from now. And the electorate is equally impatient, concerned with the moment or the few months or years ahead.

This tendency has had a profound impact on religious life. People are demanding short term spiritual satisfaction. Sects and small religious groupings are multiplying at a rapid pace; each group attempts to satisfy a particular "market niche" among the public. Few seem to be thinking about the long-term viability of religion, or what constitutes a "healthy" religious organization. Rather, success is often measured by the prevailing business model: How many customers do we have? How much income did we bring in?

Who is thinking about our souls? Who is investing the time and thought to foster a religious life that is deep and strong, that can withstand popular pressures and market demands? Who is reminding us that when it comes to the human spirit, instant gratification is not the path to long-term growth and development?

The nineteenth-century historian, Henry Adams, offered a distinction between a politician and a statesman. A politician listens to what the public is saying and then formulates policies in line with popular opinion. In contrast, a statesman formulates carefully thought-out policies, and then tries to persuade the public to adopt them. A politician seeks popularity and expediency, and is a slave of public opinion; a statesman seeks what is best—even if not popular—for the wellbeing of society, and attempts to shape public opinion accordingly. A politician speaks and acts for the moment; a statesman speaks and acts for the long-range good of the society.

Religious life, along with all other aspects of life, requires that we all try to be statesmen rather than politicians; that we all seek to think carefully about the past, about our current context, and about the future. The strategy of short-term gratification is not one upon which to build a healthy society.

The Torah highlights the uniqueness of those individuals who can think beyond the framework of weeks, and who can envision terms of 50-year cycles. This is a challenge for each of us. We need to be thinking ahead, far ahead.

Being True to Oneself and to Others

🕊 A while ago, I attended a conference that attracted a number of rabbis and academics. At lunch, I found myself sitting next to a gentleman whose name tag indicated that he was a "Professor." Given his title, I assumed he taught in a university and I asked him what was his field.

He replied that he taught remedial English in a local Junior High School. Although this is certainly a worthy position, I had never heard of a Junior High School teacher claiming the title "Professor." This struck me as an example of occupational inflation—an attempt to puff up one's credentials and self-importance. It was what Matthew Arnold would have called "the grand gesture, without the grand thing."

When people assume inflated titles and when they trump up their credentials, this indicates their own feelings of inadequacy. They assume that no one will respect them if they were truthful about themselves—so they fabricate fancy titles and honors in the hope of impressing the public with their worth.

In fact, such behavior does just the opposite. While some people may fall for the false titles and credentials, most people can see right through the ruse. Instead of gaining respect for the pretenders, they lose respect. What thinking person would want to honor someone who needs to stoop to title inflation, who tries to create a false and fraudulent self-image in the hope of impressing others?

No one is so worthy as the one who does not need to pretend about his/her worthiness. No one is more believable than someone who is honest, truthful, and realistic about him/herself.

In this week's Torah portion, we read: "And you shall not wrong one another" (*Vayikra* 25:17). A Hasidic Rebbe, Reb Bunim, offered an insightful interpretation of this verse by changing the first letter of the Hebrew word "*amito*" from an *ayin* to an *aleph*. According to his reading, the verse means: "And you shall not do injustice to your own truthfulness." A person needs to have an honest self-evaluation, and should not compromise his/her integrity by compromising his/her truthfulness and trustworthiness.

In a society driven by competition and desire for prestige and power, it happens often enough that people lose sight of this basic teaching. They want to advance; they want to be respected. In the process, they forget who they are. They inflate themselves into something untruthful; they insist that others accept their false self-evaluation; they do injustice to their own truthfulness and trustworthiness. They fool some of the people some of the time. In the long run, though, they do not fool anyone—least of all their own selves. How immensely sad!

We each are who we are; we each strive to be better, to grow, to become wiser. We need to take the time to understand who we are—our strengths and our weaknesses. We need to stay true to ourselves, and to others. If we lack honesty and truthfulness, we lack vital ingredients of a good, happy life.

To grow as truthful human beings, we must avoid trying to pass ourselves off for something we are not. Occupation "inflation" does not make us greater, but lesser. Puffed up egos do not make us more important, but less worthy.

"It has been told to you, O human being, what is good, and what the Lord does require of you: only to do justly, and to love mercy, and to walk humbly with your God" (*Micah* 6:8).

בְּחֻקֹּתַי

Walk, Not Talk

🙠 A man who lives near our synagogue recently attended an evening service in order to say *Kaddish* in memory of his father. Although we almost always have a minyan present, that night we had a problem. The weather was bad, some of our "regulars" were out of town—we only had eight men at services.

Our guest was agitated and angry. He had come to say *Kaddish*, but we were not able to provide him this opportunity. He stomped angrily out of the synagogue, indignant that we did not have a minyan when he needed one.

Yes, it is a pity that we missed minyan that night.

But who was this man who was so angry at us? He was a neighbor of the synagogue who has lived nearby for many years. However, he is not a member of the synagogue and has not contributed even one cent to the synagogue for all these years. He never attends the synagogue, except when he needs to say *Kaddish*. Although he has done nothing to strengthen the synagogue or to bolster our minyan (except when he needs to say *Kaddish*), he expects the synagogue to be there to serve him at his convenience; he expects 10 men to be at services whenever he deigns to show up.

He feels that he has a right to benefit from the synagogue, even though he does nothing to help the synagogue maintain itself. He was indignant that 10 men didn't show up for him to say *Kaddish*, even though he never shows up to help make minyan for others. He feels entitled to take, but doesn't feel responsible to give.

This week's Torah portion begins with the words: "If you walk in My statutes." The Torah might have said: If you observe My statutes, or if you keep My statutes." Why does it use the word "walk"?

Rabbi Hayyim Palache, a sage of nineteenth-century Izmir, explained that when the Torah commands us to "walk" in God's ways, it means that we are to be active participants. We are not supposed to wait for opportunities to fulfill mitzvoth, but we are urged to "walk," to actively seek ways of doing that which is right and good.

To walk in God's statutes means that we actively take part in religious life, that we happily and eagerly accept responsibility to do our share as part of the community. It means that we pay our way, and do our best, and participate as well as we can.

Some people somehow think that they are entitled to benefit from synagogues or other communal institutions, even though they do not participate in maintaining those institutions. Who exactly is supposed to pay the bills? Who exactly is supposed to attend daily services and make minyan every morning and evening? These people don't really care, as long as the responsibility doesn't devolve on their shoulders. Let others provide!

The Torah portion reminds us to walk in God's statutes, to participate actively, happily, and responsibly in maintaining a vibrant Jewish religious life. Those who shirk the responsibility and privilege of walking in God's ways deprive themselves of the satisfaction and self-respect that come with ethical, righteous, religious living.

Synagogues and communal institutions don't exist just through wishful thinking. Minyanim don't happen just from good intentions. If we each do not do our share, we have no right to expect others to pick up the slack for us.

Let us walk in God's statutes. It's an important key to personal happiness and communal strength. What is needed is "walk," not "talk."

Human Dignity, not Bureaucratic Indignity

🐾 In his essay "The Community" (*Tradition*, 17:2), Rabbi Joseph B. Soloveitchik underscored the dignity of each individual: "To recognize a person is not just to identify him physically. It is more than that: it is an act of identifying him existentially, as a person who has a job to do, that only he can do properly. To recognize a person means to affirm that he is irreplaceable. To hurt a person means to tell him that he is expendable, that there is no need for him. The halakha equated the act of publicly embarrassing a person with murder."

In our technological and bureaucratic world, it is easy to lose sight of the dignity of the individual. We are often reduced to identification numbers, or to long lists of clients/patients/customers, where our particular personalities are of little account. We are shuffled through the system along with thousands of other faceless people.

Rabbi Soloveitchik pointed out that we need to be careful to stay alert to the humanity of those with whom we deal. This is true not only in general interpersonal relationships, but also in matters of halakha.

Historically, when people had halakhic questions or issues, they brought them to their local synagogue rabbi. The rabbi knew them, knew their families, knew the context of their lives. Since there was a personal bond between the individual and the rabbi, there was also honest communication.

In recent years, the halakhic world has undergone increasing bureaucratization. An Israeli rabbi recently lectured a group of American rabbis, telling us that Jews in Israel often lack a strong personal tie to their rabbi. The rabbi is appointed by the *Rabbanut*, and the rabbi frequently doesn't even live in the community he is supposed to serve. He is a religious functionary paid by the government. He gets paid whether or not he develops close relationships with members of the community.

When the rabbinate becomes a bureaucratic system, it invariably becomes like other bureaucracies. It becomes more distant from the public; it sees people as case numbers; it needs to "process" cases, rather than spend the time and effort to really understand the people who come before them.

The centralization of the rabbinate—whether in Israel or the Diaspora—ultimately depersonalizes the halakhic system. We have *dayyanim* passing judgment in cases of conversion, Jewish status, *agunah*, and so forth, who have no personal connection with the people whose lives are radically affected by their decisions. We have *posekim* who argue the fine points of halakha based on their halakhic tomes—but who don't look into the eyes and don't hear the voices of the very people they are supposed to serve. Rabbis issue rulings on conversions—even if they have seldom or never actually worked with a convert, or experienced the spiritual or personal struggles of the convert. Rabbinic courts "process cases" of marriage and divorce, without knowing much about the inner lives of those whose lives are being powerfully transformed.

Halakha works best when it is most human and humane. It is most meaningful when the rabbis and the laypeople know each other and understand each other. When local rabbis feel unable to solve the issues that are brought to them, they can turn to other rabbis for guidance. When technical matters such as divorces are required, the local rabbi should be there to help his congregants through the process.

In an increasingly depersonalized world, the religious community needs to keep focused on the dignity of the individual.

This week's Torah portion describes a census that took place among the Israelites in the wilderness. A census can be the ultimate depersonalization process: It is interested in a head count, not on the nature of the people whose heads are being counted. At the same time, the Torah goes out of its way to insist that those being counted should not be treated as numbers. They were to be counted "by their families, by their fathers' houses, according to the number of names." Even in this bureaucratic procedure, each individual was to be seen as part of a family and was to be counted by name. Each was a real human being, and the Torah did not want the census takers to forget this essential fact.

Religious life demands keen sensitivity to the uniqueness of each person. Halakha functions best when our full humanity is recognized and respected. The halakhic system must foster human dignity, not bureaucratic indignity.

Confronting the Wilderness

❧ The people of Israel began their experience as a free nation—in the wilderness of Sinai! After their long servitude in Egypt, they might have hoped for a quick transition to a beautiful land flowing with milk and honey; they might have experienced a tremendous surge of optimism on their redemption from slavery.

But instead of a quick and happy transition, they found themselves in a wilderness. In this less than hospitable environment, they had plenty of time to mull over their troubles and fears: How long would it take for them to reach the promised land? What obstacles and dangers awaited them? How many wars would need to be waged? The wilderness is an ideal place for despair and brooding, for serious loss of morale.

The Spanish thinker, Ortega y Gasset, in his book *The Revolt of the Masses*, suggested that feeling lost and forsaken is an essential ingredient in proper human development. "And this is the simple truth—that to live is to feel oneself lost—he who accepts it has already begun to find himself, to be on firm ground....He who does not really feel himself lost, is without remission; that is to say, he never finds himself, never comes up against his own reality" (p. 157).

The wilderness was the formative framework for the development of the Israelites—as individuals and as a nation. By feeling "lost" they came up against "their own reality." They had to mobilize their inner resources; they had to strengthen their spirits; they had to think creatively.

This week's Torah portion provides insight into how the Israelite's coped with their wilderness experience. They took a census. They organized themselves into tribal divisions, appointing leaders over each tribe. Instead of lamenting their fate, they took meaningful steps to evaluate their strength and to form themselves into governable legions. The Torah emphasizes that they counted the people "by name," i.e., they focused on the individuality and uniqueness of each person, and did not simply lump people together in an impersonal way.

The wilderness experience of the Israelites has continued meaning for us today. When we feel lost, when we feel despair...this is a time for us to grow. The feeling of being in a wilderness is a challenge to us, an opportunity to discover who we really are. When we are complacent and self-satisfied, we lack the stimulus to push ourselves to the limits of our capacities. Like the ancient Israelites, we need to count our friends and allies—upon whom can we depend? Who can really be trusted to stand with us in time of crisis? We need to take specific actions to enable us to cope with real and perceived challenges. We need to see ourselves and others as "names"—not as impersonal ciphers.

But first of all, we need to draw on our own inner strengths. Instead of being frightened or demoralized by the wildernesses we face in life, we need to think quietly and clearly about what we can do to address the challenges before us.

Until we come up "against our own reality," we do not live our lives to their fullest.

Thoughts on שבועות

A New Revelation?

🐦 On Shavuoth, we commemorate the awesome Revelation at Mount Sinai, when the Almighty presented the Ten Commandments to the people of Israel. All of the Israelite men, women, and children experienced that solemn moment, marking an everlasting covenant between God and the Israelite nation.

Let us imagine that God would invite us to a second Revelation at Sinai, asking all the Jews of the world to attend.

— The Hareidim would say: We cannot be in the same domain as the non-religious or less religious Jews. We are pure, and we will not have contact with those of lesser purity.

— The Secularists would say: We cannot attend because we do not want to be bound by any commandments. We are citizens of the world and don't want the particular responsibilities of being Jewish.

— The non-Orthodox would say: We can't attend unless the event is egalitarian; and unless there is no expectation that we accept any commandments. We are open to suggestions, but not to commandments.

— The Modern Orthodox would insist that the Revelation also include divine words relating to science, philosophy, and the modern world.

— Hassidim would demand that they be placed near their own rebbes, and not anywhere else.

— Each Sephardic and Ashkenazic ethnic group would insist on having its own *hazzan*, its own *minhag*, its own pronunciation of Hebrew.

— Unaffiliated Jews would turn up out of curiosity; the Kabbalah Center would set up booths on the outskirts selling books and red strings.

— Alienated and ignorant Jews would complain: This event is boring; we need a rock band or other entertainment to make it attractive.

The hypothetical second Revelation might not be such a happy and congenial event, after all. And yet, it should be a tremendous unifying experience for the Jewish people.

The Talmud (*Eruvin* 21b) teaches that King Solomon instituted two practices, and a heavenly voice approved of both. One practice is the washing of hands before meals; the other is the setting up of *eruvin* (boundary enclosures). Washing hands relates to personal purification. After we wash, we remain silent until reciting the blessing over bread. During that period of time, we are in a uniquely private domain, involving only us and the Almighty. Interpersonal relationships are excluded. The *eruv*, though, provides a method of including others in our domain. It is a symbolic way of turning a public area into a private area by considering all of us as one extended family and community.

For us to be a whole, united Jewish people, we need to draw on both of these wise practices established by King Solomon. We need to concentrate on personal purity, on fostering a direct and powerful relationship with God. We need the humility to accept God's commandments, and to delight in them. At the same time, we need the "*eruv*" philosophy that attempts to include as many as possible within our domain. It is a philosophy of inclusion, not exclusion; it is a way of extending boundaries and demonstrating concern for our neighbors—even those with whom we may disagree.

Shavuoth is the festival on which we recall the Revelation at Mt. Sinai. It is also a good time to plan for a hypothetical second gathering of Israelites at Sinai—and to think carefully how we can envision such an event as an opportunity to bring all of us together.

For the Jewish people to find its spiritual balance, we will need to work on personal spiritual development and purity; and also on strategies that are grand enough to allow all of us to stand together in the presence of God.

Two Communities, One Destiny

❧ (This article appeared in the Israeli newspaper, *Haaretz*, May 23, 2012.)

"Something there is that does not love a wall." So wrote the great American poet, Robert Frost. Walls divide us, separate us, block us from free contact with each other. At the same time, we can't live without walls. We need boundaries to maintain our individual selves, our communities, our nations. Just as we feel the need to resent walls, we also need to appreciate their value.

But where to draw boundaries and where to build walls are matters of great controversy.

The Jewish people is a case in point. Who belongs within the boundaries and who doesn't? Who is Jewish and who is not Jewish? Historically, a Jew is defined as someone born of a Jewish mother, or someone who converts to Judaism. Someone born of a Jewish mother is within the walls. Someone who wishes to convert must find a way to gain entry through the walls.

For the Hareidim, and the Hareidi-dominated Chief Rabbinate of Israel, the walls are built to exclude and disenfranchise would-be converts, unless they wish to fully adopt an Orthodox lifestyle. Obstacles are placed in the way of those who wish to join the Jewish people; stringencies are added. In the Hareidi view, one is Jewish according to the strictest interpretation of halakha, Jewish law, or one is not Jewish at all. There is no middle ground.

For the non-Orthodox, the walls are generally set at a much lower level. The goal is to include as many as possible who wish to cast their fates with the Jewish people. The strictures of halakha are set aside or minimized. In their view, once a person has undergone conversion—whether in conformity to Orthodox halakha or not—he or she is fully Jewish.

And then we have the dilemma of the Modern Orthodox community. The Modern Orthodox are deeply committed to halakha, which has requirements for conversion and for those who would perform conversions. The halakha has boundaries. There is a wall, but it need not be as restrictive or oppressive as that erected by the Hareidi rabbinic establishment.

Indeed, the halakha provides a meaningful and accessible entry into Judaism and the Jewish people. The Talmud, Maimonides, the *Shulhan Arukh*—and so many other halakhic sources—are far more inclusive and compassionate than the prevailing views and policies within the Orthodox rabbinate today.

But what is the status of those who have converted under non-Orthodox/non-halakhic auspices? Can or should the Modern Orthodox community accept such individuals as fellow Jews?

The answer—keenly reflecting the dilemma—is no and yes.

No, such individuals have not followed the halakhic route; halakha, for all its kindness, has boundaries.

Yes, such individuals have abandoned their former religions and have willingly chosen to be part of the Jewish people. They cannot be considered simply as "non-Jews." While they haven't entirely entered the boundaries of the Jewish people according to halakha, they also no longer belong within the boundaries of their previous faiths.

We need to confront a serious reality. Many thousands of people identify themselves as Jews—even though they are not Jewish according to halakha. They may be children of Jewish fathers and non-Jewish mothers; or they may be non-halakhic converts to Judaism; or they may be individuals who have adopted Judaism/Jewishness in their own way. These individuals are deeply committed to Judaism/Jewishness, and rightly feel quite offended if their Jewish status is denied or belittled.

The "halakhic establishment," though, tends to see such people simply as non-Jews. I know a person who had a Conservative conversion, who later went to an Orthodox Bet Din to arrange for an Orthodox conversion. A rabbi on the Bet Din, upon learning of her Conservative conversion, told her: "You are not Jewish. You can go to McDonald's and eat a cheeseburger." Although this is a particularly grotesque example, it reflects a widespread attitude within the "halakhic community." If you are a non-Orthodox convert, you simply are not Jewish.

The reality is that we have an Orthodox community deeply committed to its standards of halakha; and we have a large community of people who think of themselves as being Jewish, although they have not met the criteria of halakha even according to the most lenient halakhic opinions.

There is a boundary. There is a wall. No one should pretend the wall does not exist. There are, in fact, two communities of Jews: halakhic Jews, and non-halakhic Jews. We are all one people. We all share one destiny. But because of the halakhic wall between us, we can't marry each other unless one side or the other agrees to change the boundary line.

The wall between the two communities of Jews would be less painful if the Orthodox rabbinic authorities presented a more appealing and inclusive halakhic road to conversion; and if it fostered a sense of respect and shared destiny with non-halakhic Jews. It is also necessary for non-halakhic Jews to take seriously the commitment of Orthodoxy to classic halakha, and not to assume that the conversion issue is merely a political power struggle. By studying the halakhic sources, they would gain deeper insight into the matters at stake.

At a time when the Jewish people face so many challenges, it is essential for all Jews to seek ways of forging a shared destiny in spite of the halakhic boundary lines that separate us. We can respect and appreciate each other's Jewish commitments, even if we differ on where those boundary lines belong.

In fact, we are two Jewish communities. Still, we must never forget that we are all part of one Jewish people.

Imagining Peace

🖋 "May the Lord lift up His countenance toward you, and grant you peace." (*Bemidbar* 6:26)

When bombs are exploding and tanks are rolling, it is difficult to imagine peace. When children are taught to hate and suicide/homicide murderers are called "freedom fighters," it is difficult to imagine peace. When all sides list their grievances and do not listen to the grievances of others, it is difficult to imagine peace.

But if we do not try to imagine peace, peace will not come. So let us imagine, in spite of all the "facts on the ground," that peace must be achieved. What voices can guide us? What words can be a salve to our wounds? How can we put the dream of peace into real terms?

In 1919, Rabbi Benzion Uziel, then a young rabbi, spoke to a conference of rabbis in Jerusalem. He stated: "Israel, the nation of peace, does not want and never will want to be built on the ruins of others....Let all the nations hear our blessing of peace, and let them return to us a hand for true peace, so that they may be blessed with the blessing of peace." In 1939, when Rabbi Uziel became Sephardic Chief Rabbi of Israel, he delivered his inaugural address in Hebrew, and then added words in Arabic. He appealed to the Arab community: "We reach our hands out to you in peace, pure and trustworthy. . . . Make peace with us and we will make peace with you. Together all of us will benefit from the blessing of God on His land; with quiet and peace, with love and fellowship, with goodwill and pure heart we will find the way of peace."

Rabbi Uziel's words reflected the wishes of the tiny Jewish community in the land of Israel in those times. His words still reflect the wishes of the Jewish community of Israel today. Hawks and doves alike would like nothing better than genuine, secure peace. They would like Israeli society to be free and happy, without the specter of warfare and terrorism, without the constant threat and reality of Arab military, economic, and political attacks. They would like to live in harmony with their Arab neighbors—and to trust that their Arab neighbors will want to live in harmony with them.

But Rabbi Uziel's words need to be stated and restated by the leaders of Israel. The idea of reaching a mutually rewarding peace must be put into words, must be repeated, must be believed and taught. Will words create peace? Not immediately. But they will set the foundations of peace. The words will help transform the dream of peace into a framework for peace.

In 1919, at the Paris peace conference following World War I, the Emir Feisal, one of the great Arab leaders of the time, made the following comments about the Jewish desire to return to their ancient homeland in Israel: "We Arabs...look with the deepest sympathy on the Zionist movement....We will wish the Jews a most hearty welcome home. . . . I look forward, and my people with me look forward, to a future in which we will help you and you will help us, so that the countries in which we are mutually interested may once again take their places in the community of civilized peoples of the world."

I do not know if any Arab leaders today can say these words with sincerity. Yet, if Arab leaders—especially Palestinian leaders—could find the strength to say these words, the dream of peace might be brought closer to reality. Israel wants most what the Arab world has for the most part not given: a sign of acceptance, a sign of welcome, a sign that Jews have a right to live in peace and tranquility in the land of Israel. The people of Israel need to hear what Emir Feisal said: Welcome home; we will help you, and you will help us. Together we will raise our peoples to great cultural and economic heights.

We need to hear these words. The people of Israel and the Arab nations need to hear these words. If we are to imagine peace, we must articulate the words that can point us to peace. If we all start saying—and believing, and teaching our children these words—we will be on our way.

But who has the courage to speak as Rabbi Uziel and as Emir Feisal did? We are waiting. Israelis and Palestinians are waiting. Jews and Muslims and Christians are waiting. The world is waiting. Let us hear these words, let us begin to understand.

Religious Enlightenment

🕊 Some time ago, I attended a Bar Mitzvah at a prominent Modern Orthodox synagogue. The Bar Mitzvah boy attends a Modern Orthodox Day School, as do most of his many friends who attended synagogue that Shabbat morning. Among the adult guests were many individuals who are active in their Modern Orthodox synagogues.

I left synagogue that morning with a feeling of frustration, even sadness. What should have been a festive occasion and a celebration of Judaism at its best . . . was instead a glaring example of something amiss in the Modern Orthodox world.

Although almost all of the children were students in Orthodox Day Schools, their behavior in synagogue was lamentable. They talked throughout the services, as though prayer had no meaning to them. A number of the girls were dressed in mini-skirts and sleeveless blouses, as though they were attending a disco rather than a holy place of worship.

The behavior of the adults was not any better. People talked, joked, laughed, and carried on as though they were in a café or at a social event. Some of the women wore décolleté dresses that wouldn't be appropriate anywhere for a modest person, and certainly not in a synagogue.

And this is the "cream" of what passes for Modern Orthodoxy!

We do so many things properly. We sacrifice so much to give our children good Jewish educations, to maintain Jewish homes, to support our community institutions. But we seem to be missing a key ingredient in religious life: the sense of holiness.

The external forces of secularization have taken a toll on our internal spiritual lives. We—wittingly or unwittingly—adopt a secular lifestyle that is dressed up in religious garb. As long as we generally keep kashruth and Shabbat and send our children to Day Schools, we think we're Orthodox enough. But the essence of holiness is missing. The awareness that we live our lives in the presence of God is lacking. Even in synagogue, even during prayers . . . we manage to block God from our consciousness. We seem to be secular people even as we sit in sacred space.

This week's Torah reading includes the priestly blessing that the Kohanim give to the children of Israel. Rabbi Ovadia Seforno, the great medieval Italian Jewish commentator, describes the tripartite blessing as follows: The first verse wishes us good material sustenance; the second verse wishes us good spiritual sustenance; the third verse wishes us eternal blessing in the World to Come.

Commenting on the second verse, he writes: "May [God] enlighten your eyes with the light of His countenance, so that you will see wonders in His Torah and His creations. . . . "

The blessing is for us to experience the divine light so that we can truly see and see truly; so that we can find enlightenment and excitement in our study and observance of Torah; so that we can look on God's creations with thoughtfulness and spiritual uplift.

Modern Orthodoxy is not a compromise position, but a principled approach to Judaism that demands religious observance and religious experience. It teaches us a way to live in the secular world without losing our souls in the process. It fosters intellectual and spiritual growth, the sense of wonder...the sense of holiness. When Torah and mitzvoth are lived on a superficial level without full awareness that we are in the presence of God, then they lack the key ingredient that endows them with meaning.

How can we regain and maintain a sense of holiness in a secular world? How can we inculcate ourselves and our children with an awareness of the presence of God in our lives?

The first step is to recognize our problem. The second step is to reorient our way of thinking, observing mitzvoth, and praying. The third step is to help our synagogues and Day Schools become bastions of religious life at its best.

If each of us would devote some time every day to thinking deeply about our spiritual lives, we could transform ourselves. If each of us would try to experience prayer as a genuine confrontation with God, we could enhance our sense of holiness. If each of us would insist that our homes, our schools and our synagogues be infused with lofty Torah values, we could re-generate a vibrant and thoughtful Modern Orthodox Judaism.

May God enlighten our eyes with the light of His countenance so that we will see wonders in His Torah and His creations.

Thoughts on בהעלתך

Demagogues and Pedagogues

🕊 This week's Torah portion includes a strange episode. A "mixed multitude" (*asafsuf*) riled up the Israelites so that they complained bitterly about their situation. They longed to eat meat. They reminisced about the diet they had in Egypt—fish, cucumbers, melons, leeks, onion, and garlic. The miraculous mannah from heaven, which was delivered to them daily in the wilderness, did not satisfy them.

Rabbinic commentators generally assume that the *asafsuf* was the non-Israelite group that attached itself to Israel at the time of the exodus from Egypt. However, this is a problematic assumption. Why would the Israelites have paid attention to complaints raised by the mixed multitude? They could have pointed out the obvious: We were slaves in Egypt! We would much rather eat mannah as free people, than whatever the Egyptians fed us when we were slaves.

The word *asafsuf* has the connotation of "adding on," or "gathering to." Instead of applying this term to the non-Israelites who attached themselves to Israel, I suggest that the term actually refers to charismatic Israelites who gathered people around them. These were demagogues who knew how to incite the public, to play on their fears and anxieties. Even though their message was easily refuted by facts, they were able to cause discontent among the masses by means of their fear-mongering and their complaining. Demagogues have that talent: They can talk nonsense and still arouse the public to panic.

When Moses was confronted by the angry masses of Israelites, he called to God in despair. He could not handle the situation. He needed help.

God replied: "Gather (*esfah*) unto Me 70 men of the elders of Israel whom you know to be the elders of the people and officers over them." God said He would give these men some of Moses' spirit, so that they would share in leadership with him. By using the word *esfah*—with the same root as *asafsuf*—the Torah is pointing out that demagogues can be quelled only by equally articulate and charismatic opponents who speak truth.

The Torah tells us that Moses "gathered 70 men of the elders of the people." These men "prophesied but they did so no more" (*va-yitnabe'u ve-lo yasa-*

153

fu). This verse is generally understood to mean that these men prophesied only this one time, but did not continue with this power subsequently. This would seem odd. Why would their prophecy be so short-lived?

I think *lo yasafu*—from the same root as *asafsuf* and *esfah*— should be understood to mean that they did not gather people around them; they were not successful against the demagogues. Why were they unsuccessful? Because Moses did not follow God's instructions correctly.

God had commanded Moses to choose 70 men who were elders and who were officers over the people. But when Moses chose these men, the Torah tells us that he chose elders—not that these elders were also officers. The occasion called not just for elders who were wise and reasonable—but for officers, who had the power and courage to act, to stand up against the crowd. To combat demagoguery, a correct message often is not enough. What is needed is strong, persuasive leadership who can rally people around them.

The *asafsuf* were charismatic Israelite trouble-makers and demagogues. Moses was told to gather—*esfah*—a team that could counterbalance the demagogues. But the team he chose did not have the requisite fortitude and eloquence to draw the public to them—*lo yasafu*.

The world always seems to have no shortage of demagogues who preach lies and vanities—and who nonetheless gather large crowds around themselves. To combat these demagogues, a true message does not necessarily persuade the masses. What is needed is not only a true message, but the courage and commitment to speak and lead clearly and passionately—to draw the masses to truth and away from demagoguery.

To fight the demagogues—we need real pedagogues, those who teach the truth in a powerful and convincing way.

Intellectual Humility

🖎 A seventh-grade student in a yeshiva Day School recently asked me a serious question. His rebbe was teaching the class about the sin of embarrassing another person. The rebbe stated that if A embarrasses B, then Hashem transfers all the mitzvoth of A to B, and all the sins of B to A. The student was puzzled by the severity of this punishment, and he asked me: "Is this really true?"

While not wanting to undermine the authority of the rebbe, I also did not want this student to think that the rebbe's words were literally true. Indeed, the rebbe's statement is problematic in various ways.

⟶ Does anyone (except for a prophet) have first-hand knowledge as to how God decides on rewards and punishments? Isn't it pretentious in the extreme to attribute policies to God, when in fact there is no way to verify such claims?

⟶ Is it proper religious education to present God in such a way as to make Him appear egregiously unjust? How is it fair to deprive a person of all his/her mitzvoth and to transfer them to one he/she has embarrassed? How is it fair for God to transfer all the sins of the victim to the one who embarrassed him/her?

⟶ Does the rebbe imagine that his simplistic lesson will be accepted blindly and unthinkingly by his students? Does he really think they will now be less likely to embarrass one another because they fear such dire consequences from God?

I told the seventh grader that the rebbe was drawing on a classic midrashic style of rhetoric. The lesson is not to be taken as literally true, but is a figurative way of saying that embarrassing another person is a very bad thing to do. Similarly, Hazal taught that embarrassing someone is akin to murder. They did not mean that one was literally guilty of murder and subject to a death penalty; they used hyperbole to express the seriousness of the transgression.

When teaching the words of our Sages, we need to have the literary tact to know how they used language. If we teach hyperbolic statements as being literally true, then we not only misconstrue the teachings of our Sages, but we unwittingly mislead our students into believing problematic things. As they grow older and wiser, they may say to themselves: If our rebbes were mistaken on this, perhaps they were mistaken on many other matters.

In this week's Torah portion, we read: "And the man Moses was very humble, more than any other person on the face of the earth" (*Bemidbar* 12:3).

When we read the accounts of Moses in the Torah, we do indeed see instances where he displayed humility. But we also see many examples of strong public action: He confronted Pharaoh fearlessly; he led the Israelites with fortitude. Although he described himself as having a "heavy tongue" and lacking eloquence, Moses spoke to the Israelites with strength and great oratorical skill. In what sense was Moses "very humble?"

We generally identify humility with meekness, shyness, quietude. Perhaps the Torah is indicating another perspective on true humility.

Moses was the most humble person specifically because he was the person who came closest to God, who spoke to God "face to face." Because he confronted God on such a high level, Moses was the human being who best understood the ultimate limitations of humanity. While others were living on the mundane level—filled with competitiveness and jealousy and interpersonal strife—Moses lived on an entirely different plane. He achieved exceeding humility by being as close as possible to the eternal and infinite God. His grand vision transcended petty human jealousies and strife.

The closer one is to God, the loftier one's religious vision becomes. The loftier one's religious vision, the more humble one becomes. This humility does not necessarily manifest itself in meekness and shyness. Rather, it manifests itself in a spiritual wisdom and serenity that rises above the human fray, and in an overwhelming desire to live life in context with eternal God. It necessarily leads to an honest evaluation of what we know, and what we do not know, and what we cannot know.

I believe that this lesson very much applies to the way we live and teach Torah. While none of us will reach the level of Moses, all of us can aspire to a true humility that entails intellectual honesty, compassion, and a genuine knowledge of our limitations. Since we are not prophets, we should not speak as though we are prophets; we should not speak with certainty of supernatural things beyond our ken; we should not make claims about how God does or doesn't mete out punishments. When we read rabbinic teachings that go beyond these basic guidelines, then we should understand them in their literary, rhetorical spirit.

I am very proud of the seventh-grade student who had the intellectual clarity to wonder about the veracity of his rebbe's statement, and who had the motivation to bring his question to me. He has given all of us the opportunity to think through this vital aspect of religious education and religious life.

שלח לך Thoughts on

Pessimism, Optimism, and Realism

An old joke has it that a pessimist says the glass is half empty; the optimist says the glass is half full; and the realist says—you're using the wrong size glass!

In this week's Torah portion, we read of the 12 spies who were sent to scout the land of Israel. Ten of them were pessimists. They told the Israelites that the land was inhabited by giants. "We are not able to go up against the people, for they are stronger than we."

Caleb and Joshua were optimists. They reported that the land was wonderful, and that the enemies would be easily defeated. "Do not fear the people of the land, for they are bread for us; their defense is removed from over them and the Lord is with us."

While the 10 spies were alarmists and defeatists, the two spies presented a rosy picture totally at odds with the report of their colleagues. The masses of people believed the pessimists; they slipped quickly into despair and mourning. As a result, the Israelites were condemned to wander 40 years in the wilderness before the next generation would be allowed to enter the Promised Land.

Where were the realists when they were so very much needed? In the Torah's narrative of this episode, we don't hear their voices.

How might this story have turned out happier? When the spies returned from their mission, they should have reported their findings to Moses in a closed meeting. The pessimists and the optimists could have made their cases. Moses could have been the realist who fashioned the report in such a way that it reflected the concerns of the pessimists while also expressing the confidence of the optimists. The entire group could have presented the people with a balanced report, honest about the dangers ahead but confident that God would bring them victory.

When people face a crisis, they need to be told the truth about the challenges ahead. But they also need to be given a realistic plan of action. It is

157

destructive to create alarm and panic; it is irresponsible to ignore genuine threats.

The story of the 12 spies demonstrates the serious flaws of going public without first having serious private consultations that are grounded in realism. This is true for government officials, for journalists, for opinion makers—for everyone. Responsible leadership entails careful analysis, concern for how one's words and deeds will affect the public, an honest and realistic plan of action that can gain public support and confidence.

In Israel's War of Independence in 1948, David Ben Gurion called a meeting of his military experts to address a serious crisis. Reinforcements were desperately needed in the north, but there seemed to be no way to get the troops there. The experts told Ben Gurion that it was impossible to move troops to the north, since the enemies' positions were too strong. Ben Gurion replied: "We do not need experts to tell us that something is impossible. Anyone can say this. We need experts who can tell us how to accomplish the impossible!" Upon further deliberation, the experts came up with a plan—and they succeeded in doing the "impossible." They found a way of getting the needed troops to the north, and ensuring a victory for Israel in the battles there.

In the many crises we face—individually as well as communally—it is tempting to give in to pessimism and judge things to be hopeless or impossible. It is also sometimes tempting to ignore the real dangers before us, and to be unrealistically optimistic about chances of success. It is vital, though, that we maintain clear-sighted realism—facing problems honestly, being neither fearful nor foolhardy. If we consider things from different perspectives, we often can gain clarity on how to move forward.

It is the realists who are best suited to achieve the "impossible."

Noise, Quiet, and Our Inner Music

✍ My wife and I recently went out with friends to a new kosher restaurant in New York City. Although the food we ate was not memorable, the noise level in the restaurant still has my ears ringing! Aside from the ongoing talking of the many customers, the restaurant featured loud music blasting in the background. It was difficult for us to carry on a conversation at our table, since we could hardly hear each other in the midst of the din.

When we looked around, though, it was evident that the other customers—mostly on the young side—were having a great time! The louder the background music played, the louder the people raised their voices. No problem. Noise is good, noise is fun. Right?

According to the Deafness Research Foundation, about one in three cases of hearing loss in the United States is not about aging—but purely about noise! And much of the noise is self-inflicted. We literally are making ourselves deaf! The noise levels in our society have increased dramatically in the areas of leisure and recreation: movies, discos, restaurants, wedding receptions, and so forth. Noise can cause permanent damage to our ears when it reaches about 85 decibels. A typical rock concert is around 120 decibels. With the ubiquitous use of iPods, often played at loud levels directly into peoples' ears, we can expect a growing number who will suffer serious loss of hearing.

If noise is so unhealthy, why do so many people enjoy environments where they are barraged by intense loud noise for protracted periods of time? Why are they oblivious to the permanent damage they cause to themselves?

Here is a possible answer.

Loud noise enables people to tune out from their own minds. It crowds out any thoughts or worries they may have. They become lost in the noise so that they literally can't think straight . . . or can't think at all. And for many people, that is fun...not to have to think, not to have to remember, not to have to worry. It is worth it to them to damage their eardrums in exchange for the satisfaction of escaping from their own selves.

The problem with loud noise, aside from its danger to our hearing, is that it does not provide a permanent framework for the serenity that people seek. It is a temporary escape into a pretend dream-world . . . but then we necessarily return to the thoughts, worries, and problems of the humdrum reality in which we live.

There is a healthier and wiser way to overcome our anxieties—not by escaping into a noisy situation that crushes our inner selves, but by contemplating a serene framework that gives us to ourselves and strengthens ourselves. We don't need to be afraid to think, we don't need to create artificial ways of temporarily hiding from our thoughts and our concerns. Noise isn't the answer; quiet is!

This week's Torah portion concludes with a description of the mitzvah of *tsitsith*. It states that when we look at the blue thread of the *tsitsith* (a mitzvah we can now observe again with the rediscovery of real "*tekhelet*") we will be reminded of all the commandments of the Lord. The talmudic sage, Rabbi Meir, commented that the blue thread reminds us of the sea, and the sea reminds us of the sky, and the sky reminds us of the Throne of Glory of the Almighty (Sifri on *Bemidbar* 15:39).

I think that Rabbi Meir is teaching that if we wish to gain a deeper, wiser approach to life, we need to engage in quiet contemplation. We gaze out at the ocean; we raise our eyes to the sky; we are lifted into a different zone of thinking. We view life more calmly, we put our lives in context with the Throne of Glory of the Almighty. We ponder the fleeting nature of our lives in comparison with the vastness of the sea and eternity of the sky. By "escaping" into quiet, we actually can find ourselves.

The great kabbalists emphasized the importance of periodic *hitbodedut*—seclusion, separating our minds from mundane realities. Rabbi Aryeh Kaplan understood *hitbodedut* to mean meditation. If we can devote even a few minutes a day to quiet contemplation, we will be doing ourselves far more good than if we were to spend hours at a noisy restaurant, movie, or party.

When we go out to a restaurant or social event, let us seek those environments that allow us to think and to converse without having to be overwhelmed by noise. Let's keep the iPods turned low so as to preserve our hearing as well as our inner peace.

When we phase out the external blaring music that damages our ears and our clarity of mind, we phase up the internal quiet music that satisfies our souls.

Thoughts on קרח

Healthy and Unhealthy Controversy

☙ The *Pirkei Aboth* describes the controversy of Korah and his cohorts to have been "not for the sake of Heaven." Their goal was to overthrow the leadership of Moses and Aaron, in the hope of seizing political power for themselves. They did not offer a positive agenda; rather, they preyed on the fears and frustrations of the public.

When controversies are "not for the sake of Heaven"—but rather for the sake of personal gain and egotistical gratification—they are resolved by a show of power. The side that is stronger defeats the opponent; the controversy is over; history continues. These controversies are a zero-sum game. One side wins, one side loses.

The *Pirkei Aboth* contrasts the Korah model of controversy with that of the debates between Hillel and Shammai. Those disputes were "for the sake of Heaven." Neither Hillel nor Shammai was seeking personal power or glory. Each was presenting his interpretation of the Torah and his application of halakha. Each had cogent arguments to support his view. Although they disagreed strongly on various issues, they were not opponents out to destroy each other but were colleagues in search of truth. The Talmud reflects this idea when it states that both of their views "were the words of the living God." In such debates, a ruling must be reached so that people will know what the law requires. Yet, the "losing" side has not really lost. His opinion is still quoted, still taken seriously. Although it did not prevail then, it might prevail at another time or in another context.

Hillel and Shammai ultimately were on the same side—on the side of truth, on the side of Heaven. Their controversies reflected honest and well-reasoned differences of opinion. What they shared in common far outweighed their relatively few differences of opinion.

Just as in antiquity, we have our share of controversies today. Some are clearly in the category of Korah controversies—not for the sake of Heaven.

People fight for power, seek to destroy their opponents, give vent to their ego-tistical ambitions in cruel and ruthless ways. These controversies are resolved through power struggle. The stronger side will win; the weaker side will be wiped out or forced to back down or surrender completely.

We also have controversies that are more akin to those of Hillel and Shammai. As long as the disputants realize they are ultimately on the same side, these controversies can be healthy aspects of our intellectual and cultur-al lives. We can weigh both sides calmly and reasonably. We can disagree on various points of theology or philosophy, and still remain respectful and friendly to each other.

A problem arises, though, when theological and philosophical debates transform themselves into battles for power that call for the total defeat of opponents. On the surface, these controversies may seem to be "for the sake of Heaven," yet, they are in fact fueled by egotism and the desire to crush opposition. Disputants in such controversies do not see the opinions of their opponents as being "words of the living God," but as blasphemies that cannot be tolerated in any way. When theological and philosophical disagreements slip into the category of Korah-controversies, this leads to violence and terror-ism. Instead of being reflections of a search for truth, they become vehicles for oppression, fueling the overwhelming urge to crush those who dissent.

In his essay, "The Pursuit of the Ideal," Sir Isaiah Berlin dealt with the question of how we deal with theological and philosophical disagreements. He rejected "relativism," which posits that all arguments have equal weight, that everything is a matter of personal choice and preference. No, the categories of truth and falsehood exist. Not every viewpoint has equal legitimacy. Berlin favored what he called "pluralism," an acceptance that different people might come to legitimate differences of opinion without seeing each other as mortal enemies or opponents. In his view, this pluralism is "the conception that there are many different ends that men may seek and still be fully rational, fully men, capable of understanding each other and sympathizing and deriving light from each other." In other words, I may be convinced that I have the real truth, but I may still see that others—who do not share my understanding of truth—are good, sincere, and thoughtful people trying to do their best. I can learn from them, respect them, and be friendly with them. We are dis-putants—not enemies.

In distinguishing between the Korah-type controversies and the Hillel-Shammai-type controversies, the *Pirkei Aboth* was providing insight on the nature of human conflict. By juxtaposing them, it may have been alluding to the thin line between these two types of controversies. Power struggles can dress themselves up as religious debates; theological and philosophical disputes can be mere camouflages for egotistical and unsavory oppression of opponents.

Perhaps if we can learn to see our conflicts with others in the Hillel-Shammai model, we can develop a more harmonious religious and social discourse. This does not call on us to surrender our notion of truth; but only to recognize that other good, honest and fine people have the right to see things differently than we do. And perhaps if the public at large would adopt the Hillel-Shammai model, this might impact on the politicians, warriors, terrorists, and oppressors who follow the Korah-model and who strew so much grief and bloodshed on our world.

Healthy controversy reflects an honest search for truth. Unhealthy controversy reflects the desire for power and ego gratification. Let us be sure that all of our own controversies are for the sake of Heaven.

Conversations, Not Diatribes

❧ Here are two views on fairness; with which one do you agree more?

A. It is only fair that those who are wealthier should share with those who have less. The essential health of a society is based on compassion and caring, a spirit of responsibility for all members of society.

B. It is only fair that people should be allowed to keep what they earn through their own hard work. The essential health of a society is based on respect for individual rights and individual choices.

Those who opt for A are most likely to be political liberals. Those who choose B are most likely to be conservatives.

Depending on one's view of fairness, one will favor particular policies relating to such things as welfare, benefits for illegal immigrants, role of government, taxation, and foreign aid. Some will view contemporary government as fostering neglect of basic social, educational, and healthcare needs of the weakest members of society; others will view it as fostering creeping socialism. Some will claim that the government doesn't intervene enough to help all members of society; others will argue that the government is too invasive and is infringing on our personal autonomy. Some will blame our society's ills on the "greed" of Wall Street; others will blame the "lazy anarchists" who don't work productively and who want to live off of the labor and enterprise of others.

Which view is correct?

Actually, there is truth in both positions. A problem arises, though, when demagogues and ideologues of either side assume that they are entirely wise and virtuous and that the others are entirely misguided and wicked. Radical liberals and radical conservatives are so convinced that Fairness and Truth are on their side, they do not really give heed to the opinions of the other side. As political views become more polarized, increasing numbers of people talk and listen only to those with whom they agree. Instead of reasoned public discourse, we often hear strident shouting matches where each side vilifies the other.

Dr. Jonathan Haidt, in his book *The Righteous Mind*, offers considerable insight into why good people are divided by politics and religion. He advises us to become aware of why we hold our moral views, and why others might hold views that differ from ours. He writes: "We are deeply intuitive creatures whose gut feelings drive our strategic reasoning. This makes it difficult—but not impossible—to connect with those who live in other matrices. . . . So the next time you find yourself seated beside someone from another matrix...don't just jump right in. Don't bring up morality until you've found a few points of commonality or in some other way established a bit of trust...We're all stuck here for a while, so let's try to work it out" (p. 318).

In this week's Torah portion, we read of a full blown rebellion among the ancient Israelites. Korah and his cohorts arose against the leadership of Moses. The rebels were masters of demagoguery. They protested to Moses: "All the congregation is holy and God is in their midst? Why do you lord over the congregation of God?" Factions arose among the Israelites. Tensions reached the breaking point.

Ultimately, Korah and his followers were miraculously swallowed up by the earth. But even after this divine vindication of Moses' leadership, the people murmured against him and Aaron: "You have killed God's people." Peoples' "gut feelings" were in control of their "strategic reasoning." Once they had been fired up by the oratory and demagoguery of Korah and company, they were not receptive to other points of view.

It is natural and normal for people to have different outlooks and to approach life from different moral matrices. However, when we assume that all truth and righteousness is on our side, and that there is no truth or righteousness on the other side—then we enter into hostile relationships that are destructive to the overall fabric of society.

It is healthy for society to have liberals and conservatives, and for both sides to air their views passionately and sincerely. At the same time, it is essential that both sides actually listen to each other, and see what they can learn from each other. Instead of shouting matches, we need to engage in calm conversation where we can build on those values we all share. And when we inevitably have unbridgeable differences of opinion, let us not allow these differences to undermine our basic civility and decency.

"We're all stuck here for a while, so let's try to work it out."

Thoughts on חקת

Maintaining Purity and Integrity

🐚 The laws of the Red Heifer are considered to be among the inscrutable commandments of the Torah. The elaborate ritual was ordained for the purpose of purifying those who had become ritually unclean through contact with a dead body.

One of the strange features of this procedure was that while it purified the impure, it simultaneously defiled all those who were connected with the preparation of the ashes and water of purification. How could the exact same ingredients lead to opposite results? I suggest a possible explanation.

Those engaged in purifying others might naturally come to think of themselves as being highly important individuals. The impure people must turn to them for help. Being in this position of spiritual power could easily lead the "purifiers" to aggrandize themselves, to subtly (or not so subtly) adopt feelings of superiority. To prevent this eventuality, the Torah declares that the purifiers must themselves be rendered impure. Thus, they will not develop an inflated sense of self-importance, because they will realize that they must become ritually defiled while they purify others. The process does not raise them above those they serve, but actually lowers their status of ritual purity.

The ancient Red Heifer ceremony relates to a deeply significant aspect of religious psychology. Its message continues to be relevant today.

Some years ago I attended a meeting of Orthodox rabbis to discuss policies relating to conversion to Judaism. One of the rabbis unabashedly proclaimed: "We have the power! We can demand prospective converts to do everything our way. We do not need to make any concessions because we have total control. They need us; we don't need them. We have the power!"

I responded: "Did we become rabbis so that we can gain and exert power? Isn't it our responsibility to help others and bring them closer to God and Torah, humbly and sincerely? Isn't it antithetical to our religious worldview to arrogate to ourselves "power" to make people squirm, and bend to our will, and meet our demands—even when these demands far exceed what the actual halakha requires?"

He responded: "We have the power; let's use it."

His attitude has largely prevailed in the Orthodox rabbinic establishment. I frequently receive emails and phone calls from prospective converts who have faced abuse and arrogance in their dealings with Orthodox rabbis and rabbinic courts. Among the criticisms I've recently heard: The would-be converts are treated like numbers, not like people; the rabbis don't return calls, don't keep scheduled meetings, keep delaying the actual conversion; the rabbis keep adding requirements, well beyond anything stated in Rambam and *Shulhan Arukh*; in some cases the rabbis have made rude comments, even questioning the morality or integrity of the would-be converts. "We have the power; let's use it!"

This is not "power" but arrogance and corruption. In halakhic terms, this is called "*inuy haDin*," a miscarriage of justice causing undue suffering. It is a mockery of the halakhic process, not a fulfillment of it.

It is not that the rabbis are bad people. Certainly, they consider themselves to be good people who seek to implement Jewish law and tradition in the best standards possible. The problem is that when people are in positions of "power," they are easily corrupted by this power. They come to see themselves as the ultimate arbiters of halakha and truth; they become part of a larger culture of power-grabbing and power-holding; they see themselves as representatives of real truth and they threaten or malign those who disagree with them.

The ritual of the Red Heifer provides a vital lesson for those in positions of religious leadership—whether rabbis or laypeople. It teaches us to see our roles with humility and sensitivity, not to inflate our self-importance, and certainly not to seek power over others. It reminds us to focus full attention on those who turn to us, to do our best to serve and to help.

It is not power that we seek, but compassion and justice. It is not lordship that we desire, but service to God and humanity.

The Ways of Pleasantness

🖎　The Talmud (*Taanit* 4a) cites the opinion of Rav Ashi that any rabbinic scholar who is not hard as iron is no rabbinic scholar! A *talmid hakham* must hold strong convictions and must not bend under pressure. Yet, a few lines later, the Talmud reports the opinion of Ravina: "Even so, a person must teach himself the quality of gentleness." Yes, commitment to principles is very important; but so is maintaining a compassionate and loving attitude.

The ideal religious personality strives to harmonize both of these qualities. One must be courageous in upholding Torah and mitzvoth, must be hard as iron to resist improper compromises. At the same time, one needs to maintain a gentle, non-confrontational attitude; one must not be overly rigid and inflexible.

In our tradition, Moses is often depicted as being hard as iron. He was unflinching in his commitments and strict in his judgments. By contrast, Aaron is described as being one who "loves peace and seeks peace"—a man of gentleness. There was a distance between Moses and the public; he was austere, not easily approachable; but people felt comfortable in the presence of Aaron. While they respected Moses, they loved Aaron.

This week's Torah portion reports the death of Aaron: "And when all the congregation saw that Aaron was dead, they wept for Aaron 30 days, even all the house of Israel (*Bemidbar* 20:29)." When the Torah recounts the death of Moses, it states: "And the children of Israel wept for Moses in the plains of Moab for 30 days (*Devarim* 34:8)." Rabbinic commentators have noted a significant difference between these two accounts. When Aaron died, "all the house of Israel" mourned. "All" the people—men, women, and children—suffered a loss; they all wept the passing of a friend, a gentle and kind leader. But when Moses died, the Torah does not say that "all" mourned for him; rather there is a general expression of grief among the children of Israel, but not everyone felt the loss with the same degree of intensity and sadness. The public mourned Moses out of respect; they mourned Aaron out of love.

In our times, it is vital that we be strongly dedicated to our principles and values. It is essential that we maintain the courage to stand up against those who would undermine Torah and mitzvoth. Yet, it is also vital—more than ever—that we teach ourselves to act with gentleness and kindness. Too often, religion is presented to the public with an angry, ugly and iron face; it is perceived as a mechanical, overly strict and authoritarian way of life. We need to be sure that religion is lived and presented to the public in a spirit of love, gentleness, and kindness. "Her ways are the ways of pleasantness, and all her paths are peace."

At a time when so many Jews are alienated from Torah, it is imperative that we put more emphasis on the view of Ravina—that we learn to conduct ourselves with pleasantness and gentleness. We need to draw more on the approach of Aaron who loved peace and pursued peace.

Insisting on unnecessary stringencies is not a sign of piety but of folly. It drives people away from Torah. It not only discourages people from adopting a Torah way of life; it also alienates people who grew up within the Orthodox fold.

An Orthodox rabbi recently issued an email to his community, in which he offered permissive views on several halakhic issues. He provided his reasoning, along with halakhic sources that supported his views. He was quickly and harshly condemned by "right-wing" rabbis who insisted on the more stringent views. One rabbi went so far as to declare that anyone who follows the opinions of the "lenient" rabbi will be condemned to severe punishments in the next world! Apparently, this rabbi believes he has the keys to the next world, and that he is empowered to speak on behalf of the Almighty!

Such arrogance in the name of Torah is reprehensible. "Lenient" views that are halakhically valid—are halakhically valid! It is appropriate for such views to be circulated. Being strict does not mean being more religious; it often means that a person has not studied the halakha well enough, or that he/she prefers stringencies even when lenience is justified and correct. If one has legitimate objections to a halakhic position, one should state them clearly and calmly, providing the relevant sources to support his/her position. Calling names, making threats, and condemning others is not the way of Torah, but authoritarianism gone amok.

The ways of the Torah are the ways of pleasantness. That is a fundamental principle no one should forget.

Thoughts on בְּרִיק

Spirituality Begins at Home

🕊 There is a feeling among many Jews, including many Orthodox Jews, that worship in the synagogue lacks adequate inspiration and spirituality. Among the complaints: the synagogue ritual is chanted by rote; the prayers are recited too quickly; the prayers are recited too slowly; the service is not understood by congregants; people talk too much in synagogue; the services do not involve everyone in a meaningful way.

Here are some of the "solutions" that have been suggested over the years, along with why they have not achieved full success:

1. Introduce Hassidic/Carlebach melodies. These may be more lively and inspirational than the usual synagogue music. Yes, for some people, singing such melodies is emotionally satisfying. But for many others, such music seems more like a hootenanny than a vehicle for addressing God.

2. Make the services more egalitarian. Yes, for some people this seems like a way of getting men and women more involved. Yet, the Reform and Conservative movements have been fully egalitarian for many years—without any perceptible improvement in the overall spiritual life of their communities. Indeed, these movements have been suffering from serious loss of membership, and from generally poor attendance at services. While newly established "partnership" services are popping up in the Orthodox world, it remains to be seen whether this represents a passing fad, or if these types of services will fall into the same patterns that have taken hold in the non-Orthodox egalitarian services.

3. Make services shorter; include more readings in the vernacular. Yes, for some people this makes the synagogue experience more palatable. But it is doubtful whether it brings people to a greater feeling of the presence of God, or whether it will inspire more people to actually attend services.

4. Introduce meditation practices. Yes, some people may find this helpful to their spiritual experience. But many others may find these prac-

170

tices an outside imposition on Jewish worship and may be repelled by this mode of spirituality.

Whatever suggestions are offered, one can come up with counter-arguments. Each individual and each community has different needs and expectations.

The "crisis of the synagogue" needs to be viewed, I suggest, in a much broader context. The synagogue is only one factor—and not the major factor—in the real problem we are facing. The real problem is: moderns are losing, or have already lost, their sense of intimacy with God. God is simply not a real presence in many of our lives. Even if we observe the commandments, study Torah, and say our prayers, we may still not feel the awesome, overwhelming experience of living in the light of the Eternal.

If we are losing, or have already lost, a sense of intimacy with God, making changes in the synagogue service will not restore that intimacy. Whatever gimmicks we introduce, while possibly helpful to some, will ultimately fail, because they are focusing on symptoms rather than on the malady itself.

To a religious Jew who feels God's presence in daily life, the synagogue service poses little or no problem. The synagogue is just one of many contexts in which one experiences the divine. It is not the center of religious life, and certainly not the only place to feel God's presence. One follows the synagogue ritual out of loyalty to tradition, out of solidarity with generations of Jews who have prayed in this manner, out of a spiritual quest to be part of the community's prayers to the Almighty. But one also says private prayers any time of the day, in almost any place.

If we have personal spirituality, we can bring this into our public spirituality. If we can maintain, or regain, a living relationship with God in our daily lives, then our synagogue experience becomes much higher and much deeper.

Surely, a synagogue needs to do its best to help congregants reestablish intimacy with God; and it needs to conduct its prayer services in a manner that is conducive to spiritual experience and development. But it also needs to realize that it is an enabler of spirituality, not a substitute for spirituality. God doesn't dwell only—or even primarily—in the synagogue. God dwells everywhere. Most of our lives are not spent in the synagogue, and most of our lives are deeply in need of relationship with the Almighty. If we can develop a full spiritual personality, we will find the synagogue experience to be a meaningful and vital aspect of our lives. We need to be working on how to become more sensitive to our souls, to our personal relationships with God. We need to imbue our daily lives with Torah and mitzvoth in such a way that these activities resonate within us, and raise our spirits.

When Bil'am blessed the people of Israel, he said: "How goodly are your tents, O Jacob; your dwellings O Israel." The "tents" refer to our homes, the centers of our everyday lives; the "dwellings" refer to our synagogues and study halls. When we first have our "tents" in order, it is a natural extension to have our "dwellings" in order.

It is far from a simple matter for moderns to maintain, or regain, a sense of intimacy with God. Much of the time, spirit militates against genuine religious experience. Religion is not an easy way to God, and is not a short cut to spirituality. Treating symptoms without going to the root of our problem only makes the problem worse.

If we want our synagogues to be more spiritual, we have to be more spiritual ourselves. If we want our "dwellings" to be spiritually alive, then we first have to be sure that our "tents" are spiritually alive.

A Generous or a Grudging Eye

🦋 The *Pirkei Aboth* (5:22) contrasts the virtues of Abraham with the vices of Bil'am: Whoever possesses these three qualities is a disciple of our father Abraham—a generous eye, a humble spirit, and a meek soul; but one who possesses the opposite qualities—a grudging eye, a proud spirit, and a haughty soul—is a disciple of the wicked Bil'am.

Why did the author of this passage specifically choose to contrast Abraham and Bil'am? The Torah is replete with examples of virtuous people, and also has no shortage of wicked characters. What is so unique about Abraham and Bil'am that makes them paradigms for good and evil?

Perhaps the answer is to be found in how each of them dealt with an external group of people with whom they had no particular connection.

The people of Sodom were wicked, and the Almighty planned to destroy the city. Abraham sought the Lord's mercy, pleading that the city should be spared if at least 10 righteous people could be found within it. Abraham might simply have prayed for the salvation of his nephew Lot and family. Why did he intercede on behalf of strangers—especially when God had informed him that the Sodomites were worthy of destruction due to their sinfulness? Abraham had "a generous eye," he was concerned for the wellbeing of others—even strangers, even sinners.

Bil'am was hired by the king Balak to curse the Israelites. It was believed that Bil'am had supernatural power, so that his curses would be effective in destroying the children of Israel. Bil'am had no reason to hate Israel or to curse Israel, but he was willing to use his powers against Israel; God intervened and made him utter blessings rather than curses. Bil'am had a "grudging eye." Unlike Abraham who prayed on behalf of Sodom, Bil'am was ready to curse a people who had done him no wrong and with whom he had no particular connection.

It is natural for people to be concerned about their own families, communities and in-groups. It is more of a challenge to be concerned about "outsiders," those of different backgrounds, nations, ethnicities. Disciples of Abraham demonstrate "a generous eye," an attitude that recognizes the essential humanity of all people and that feels responsibility for others, including "outsiders." Disciples of Bil'am demonstrate "a grudging eye," an attitude that feels no obligation to "outsiders," an attitude that is neutral or negative about the rights and feelings of others. Whereas Abraham prayed for a wicked people, Bil'am stood ready to curse an innocent people.

The paradigms of Abraham and Bil'am continue to be relevant to us in our own time. Many millions of people live in poverty, in war zones, in lands of oppression. Hundreds of thousands of them flee their homelands in search of a better environment for themselves and their families. Their favored destinations are lands of freedom and economic opportunity. However, even in these free and relatively wealthy countries, economic conditions are not ideal. The new immigrants—many of whom arrive illegally—create heavy burdens on the host countries, which are themselves struggling with economic downturns and high unemployment.

How do we view these "outsiders?" Do we have "a generous eye" like our father Abraham; or "a grudging eye" like the wicked Bil'am? Do we stop to remember that in recent generations, so many of our own parents and grandparents were refugees seeking safe havens—and who often confronted more Bil'ams than Abrahams during their times of danger and distress?

Surely, it can be argued that each country has limited resources and has the right to secure its borders from illegal immigrants. Surely, no country can allow itself to be inundated by waves of people who do not follow the proper legal channels for immigration.

But when policies are made and opinions are espoused, we need to step back and ask ourselves: Are we disciples of Abraham or disciples of Bil'am? Although even disciples of Abraham will have limits to how much they can do to help others, they will at least be approaching the issue with a humane and compassionate attitude. They will reach for their maximum, not settle for the bare minimum.

They will think and act with a generous eye, not with a grudging eye.

The Dangers of "Echo Reasoning"

🐚 The Book of Judges, chapter 11, tells the horrific story of Jephthah and his daughter. Jephthah was chosen to be the leader of the Israelites in their war against Amon. Before going to battle, he vowed that, if victorious, he would offer "whatsoever comes forth of the doors of my house to meet me" as a burnt offering to the Lord. When he returned triumphantly from the war, it was his daughter—his only child—who came out of the house to greet him with song and dance.

Though sorely grieved by the rash vow he had made, Jephthah said that he could not go back on his word. It appears from the biblical story that he did indeed sacrifice his daughter. Rabbinic tradition, though, includes the view that he did not murder his daughter, but had her life devoted to God. She was doomed to live the rest of her life in isolation from society.

The Midrash raises obvious questions: Why didn't Jephthah go to Pinehas, the high priest, and plead for his vow to be annulled? Or why didn't Pinehas take the initiative to go to Jephthah so as to annul the vow and thereby save the daughter's life?

Jephthah thought: I am the judge of Israel, and I will not humiliate myself by going to the high priest—a man of lower rank. Pinehas thought: I am the high priest, and I will not humiliate myself by showing deference to the judge—a man of lower spiritual rank. While each of them was jealous for his own dignity, the life of Jephthah's daughter was sacrificed. The Midrash points out that God punished both Jephthah and Pinehas for their callousness, willfulness, and egocentrism.

Why did these leaders allow their pride to prevent them from acting intelligently and morally? I think this Midrash is underscoring a problem endemic to powerful or charismatic leaders. These individuals are accustomed to being honored, to having a retinue of admirers who fawn over them and agree with their every word. They internalize a feeling of invincibility and infallibility; they think that they do not make mistakes, or that they are not allowed to admit that they make mistakes. Their personal honor becomes a "false god"— they worship themselves!

In her book, *The March of Folly*, Barbara Tuchman describes the immorality and corruption that characterized a group of Renaissance Popes. Rodrigo Borgia, known as Pope Alexander VI, was an egregious example of depraved and luxurious living. Late in life, he was stricken with a moment of remorse. He told a consistory of cardinals: "The most grievous danger for any Pope lies in the fact that encompassed as he is by flatterers, he never hears the truth about his own person and ends by not wishing to hear it."

I recently learned of a phenomenon called "echo reasoning." This refers not merely to leaders, but to everyone who speaks and listens only to those with similar views. These views are echoed from one to the other, and become louder and more entrenched. It becomes increasingly difficult to think beyond the "truths" of the group. Members of the closed circle become more extreme, less able to reason independently.

To be morally strong and intellectually sound, we need to be open to an array of views and to be open to criticism. We need to engage in honest self-evaluation—trying to avoid the egotism and pride that paralyzed Jephthah and Pinehas, Pope Alexander VI, and victims of "echo reasoning." We need to think; to challenge and be challenged; to express our views and listen to the views of others. Unless we have this intellectual and emotional flexibility, we run the risk of becoming our own "false gods." We surround ourselves with flatterers and sycophants—with the result that our own humanity becomes hollow and false.

When political or religious leaders succumb to the illusion of power and infallibility, they become dangerous to themselves and to others. A society or religious group that submits blindly to authoritarian leadership is dooming itself to perdition.

It is fashionable in some religious circles to idolize cult leaders and to refrain from (and even deeply resent) any criticism aimed at these great ones. It is fashionable in some circles to foster "echo reasoning," where it is only licit to speak with others who share the same views, where it is forbidden to hear opposing ideas and critiques. Such circles represent a genuine danger to healthy religious life. Such circles foster leaders who are likely to fall into the patterns of Jephthah and Pinehas.

When this happens, innocent people suffer. Religion grows rigid and intolerant. Voices are silenced.

We can fight "echo reasoning" by insisting on independent reasoning. We can fight autocracy by insisting on freedom of expression. We can combat religious rigidity and intolerance by raising our voices for intellectual vibrancy, compassion, and social responsibility.

Long Live the Happy!

❧ Researchers at the Albert Einstein College of Medicine and the Ferkauf Graduate School of Psychology of Yeshiva University conducted extensive studies on longevity. In one of these studies, they focused on 243 Ashkenazic Jews (average age 97.6 years, 75% women) to determine whether there is a genetic basis to living long lives. Their findings were reported in an article published online May 21, 2012, in the journal *Aging*.

Dr. Nir Barzilai, Director of Einstein's Institute for Aging Research, commented that when his team began their research, they had assumed that the very elderly would be mean and ornery individuals, whose stubbornness contributed to their longevity. Instead, they found qualities that reflected an optimistic, positive view of life. "Most were outgoing, optimistic and easygoing. They considered laughter an important part of life and had a large social network. They expressed emotions openly rather than bottling them up." Moreover, these very elderly people had lower scores for displaying neurotic personality, and higher scores for being conscientious, compared with a representative sample of the U.S. population.

While optimism and laughter don't guarantee longevity, they seem to be factors that enable people to live longer and to live happier.

In this week's Torah portion, we read of the festive days that mark the Jewish religious calendar. Maimonides, in his Guide for the Perplexed (III: 43), makes a significant comment about religion and happiness: "The festivals are all for rejoicings and pleasurable gatherings, which in most cases are indispensable for man; they are also useful in the establishment of friendship, which must exist among people living in political societies." Happy occasions are essential. Pleasurable gatherings enlarge our lives by linking us with family and friends, by enabling us to meet new people and interact with them in a positive environment.

Indeed, we not only have the festival days; we have the joy of Shabbat each week. We have the happiness of so many mitzvoth each day. Judaism promotes a positive, optimistic worldview and lifestyle. The hallmark of Jewish religious life is happiness!

The Talmud (*Taanit* 22b) relates a story that Elijah the Prophet pointed out two people who had a place in the World to Come. Who were these outstanding individuals? They were street comedians! They told jokes. When asked why they devoted their time to making people laugh, they answered: We try to relieve people's sufferings; we offer them a moment of laughter to free them from their woes; we use humor to bring peace among those who are arguing with each other.

The eighteenth-century sage, Rabbi Eliyahu ha-Cohen of Izmir, elaborated on the virtues of these street comedians. "Anyone who is happy all his days thereby indicates the greatness of his trust in God. This is why they [the street comedians] were always happy. . . . This quality [of accepting life with happiness] is enough to give a person merit to have a place in the World to Come; for great is trust [in the Lord], even if a person is not perfect in all other moral perfections" (*Midrash Talpiot*).

If longevity is a measure of the quantity of our lives, happiness is a measure of the quality of our lives.

Interestingly, research is demonstrating that quality has an impact on quantity.

As the Psalmist taught long ago: "Serve the Lord with gladness, come with exulting into His presence" (Psalms 100:2).

Thoughts on מצות

Linking the Generations

🐚 Rabbi Akiba believed that parents transmit to their children six character-istics: physical appearance, strength, wealth, wisdom, longevity, and "*mispar haDorot lefanav*"—the number of generations before (*Mishnah Eduyot* 2:9). What is meant by this last phrase?

Children are not born into a historical vacuum. They are heirs to the ear-lier generations of their families. In the case of Jewish children, they are not only heirs to their particular family traditions, but they "inherit" all the previ-ous generations of the Jewish people going back to the time of Abraham.

The challenge to parents, grandparents, and elders is to transmit to the new generations the secret of feeling united with the past generations, of feel-ing a kinship with historical personalities as though they are contemporary companions. We introduce our children and grandchildren to the number of generations before them, so that they come to realize that they are in a life-long dialogue among all the generations of their family and of their people. This is a wonderful gift: It provides historical memory, rootedness, an expan-sive vision of Jewish peoplehood, and strength to deal with life today and in the future.

The older generations communicate not merely with words, but by the living experience of Jewish observances and ideals. In sharing our deepest thoughts and emotions, in bringing our younger generations into lives of Torah and mitzvoth, we transmit the adventure of Jewish civilization and destiny.

Some time ago, a group of Jewish teenagers visited our synagogue for Friday night services. Obviously, they had not received a very intensive reli-gious education. They sat through the services with blank expressions on their faces; most of them did not even bother to open prayer books. They felt no connection—not even curiosity—about the religious traditions of our people. They were strangers to the generations who came before.

Too often, parents and grandparents see their responsibility as providing material wellbeing to the younger generations of their family. Indeed, this is a valid responsibility. But it is also vital to tend to the spiritual, moral, and emotional wellbeing of our children and grandchildren. If we don't give our children "the number of generations before," we have robbed them of their birthrights, and we have fostered their sense of spiritual deracination.

Some years ago, there was a well-publicized child custody battle, in which the mother sued the father for childcare in "a moderately luxurious mode." She asked for $4,400 a day! She explained that she needed this sum in order to provide her child with antique furniture, maids, horse-riding lessons, meals at restaurants, an apartment with a prestigious address, and a suitable summer home. The mother was indeed awarded a huge sum for child support, yet it is quite possible that the child is still deprived in the most important areas of life. Money cannot buy a feeling of belonging, a feeling of connectedness to deep and nourishing traditions. Money cannot buy a warm and loving relationship with "the number of generations before." Money cannot buy proper moral values or ethical proclivities. The mother worried about her child's horse-riding lessons and fancy living conditions, but she would have done a greater service to her child by worrying more about the child's soul.

In this week's Torah portion, we read that the tribes of Reuben and Gad asked Moses if they could remain on the other side of the Jordan River, and not enter the Promised Land along with the rest of the Israelites. They said: We have a great multitude of cattle. "We will build sheepfolds here for our cattle and cities for our children."

Moses was troubled by the fact that they first expressed concern for their cattle—their material wealth—and only then mentioned the needs of their children. Moses pointedly instructed them: "Build cities for your children and folds for your sheep." Your priority needs to be with your children's wellbeing, not with your sheep and cattle. You need to put your primary energies into raising proper children.

We can most effectively transmit "the number of generations before" not by sending our children to synagogue—but by taking them to synagogue with us. We can most successfully communicate the values of Torah not by sending our children to study Torah—but by studying Torah with them ourselves. If we want them to be connected to our people and our traditions, we ourselves need to be connected to our people and traditions.

"The number of generations before" does not only refer to those ancestors of the past. It also refers to us.

Thoughts on מסעי

The Past as Prelude

🕊 It is said that when Alexander the Great reached the peak of his career by conquering the entire known world—he broke down and cried.

One explanation for his crying is that he realized that there were no more battles for him to undertake. His best achievements were in the past. He had climbed to the top and had nowhere else to go. He cried in frustration.

Another explanation is that he realized that his tremendous accomplishment really amounted to very little. Earth is a speck in the universe; even if one were to rule the entire earth, there was a vast universe over which he did not rule. Moreover, humans are mortal; whatever we accomplish, however impressive, is short lived. In a thousand years or a million years— who will know or care what we've done? What difference will it have made? Thus, Alexander cried at the sheer vanity of life, the ultimate emptiness of his life's deeds.

How can we live happy and productive lives—and not break down crying like Alexander did? This week's Torah portion offers some guidance.

Parashat Masei records each of the stopping places of the Israelites during their 40-year trek in the wilderness. The Midrash explains that this detailed account reflects God's loving concern for the children of Israel. It is compared to a king who had taken his ailing child to a distant place in order to be cured. On the return journey, the king would stop at each resting place and remind his child: This is where we found shelter; this is where we cooled off at an oasis; this is where you had a headache. Each place evoked memories and created a deeper bond between the king and his child.

But the recounting of past stopping places was not a mere experience of nostalgia. Rather, it was coupled with the knowledge that we are now going home, that we are looking forward to a bright future with new challenges and opportunities.

The Israelites, in meticulously reviewing their past travels, were also anticipating their entry into the Promised Land.

Jewish tradition teaches us to review our past and to recount our historical achievements, but it teaches us to do so without breaking down and crying as did Alexander the Great. Judaism imbues us with a sense that every day has meaning, that we can grow and attain something new and better. Life is not a rut or a routine; we are not trapped or locked in one place. No matter how much we have accomplished, we have not reached the end of our possibilities. There is a Promised Land ahead.

We do not succumb to the frustration or despair that confronted Alexander the Great, because we have a different orientation to the meaning of life. We are not here to achieve egotistical goals such as fame and power, but to serve God and humanity. Greatness is not measured by the number of lines one receives in history books, but by the myriad small deeds of kindness and charity and goodness that we have performed, by our positive impact on family, friends, and society.

The detailed description of the Israelites' travels in the wilderness reminds us of the importance of the past stages of our lives. It also serves to call our attention to the future, to the Promised Land, to the goals not yet attained. Just as we are strengthened by our past, we are energized by the hopes for our future.

מטות-מסעי

"Shall Your Brethren Go to the War, and Shall You Sit Here?"

🐚 One of the burning issues in contemporary Israeli political/religious life relates to widespread exemptions from military service granted to Hareidim ("ultra" Orthodox Jews). The Hareidi leadership insists that all men who study Torah in their yeshivot are thereby serving the nation, and must not be asked to do anything more. Whereas other young Israeli men and women are required to serve in the military or national social services, Hareidi young men and women have generally been allowed to be exempted by dint of their religious commitments.

It must be pointed out that many religious Israelis serve conscientiously and valiantly in the Israel Defense Forces. Indeed, religious Zionists have proven to be among Israel's most dedicated and most effective soldiers, officers, and community workers.

The dilemma in Israel relates specifically to the Hareidi community. The increasing hostility toward the Hareidim is palpable among the wide spectrum of Israeli society, including many in the religious Zionist camp. Why, they ask, should their sons and daughters sacrifice so much for the nation while the Hareidi sons and daughters are asked to sacrifice nothing? Why should Israeli society/government provide so much financial support and welfare to a community that refuses to share in the responsibility of defending the nation? Echoing Moses' question to the tribes of Gad and Reuven, which we read in this week's Torah portion: "Shall your brethren go to the war, and shall you sit here?" (*Bemidbar* 32:6)

The Hareidim reply: We serve the nation by studying Torah! We are the spiritual soldiers of Israel without whom the nation of Israel cannot survive.

Surely, the study of Torah is meritorious. It can be legitimately argued that gifted young men who wish to devote themselves to high-level Torah study should be granted this opportunity, as long as they recognize their responsibility to the total Israeli society—not just to their Hareidi enclaves. The problem arises, though, in that the Hareidi leadership demands exemptions for all their many thousands of students, not just for the elite few very promising students.

The public stance of Hareidi leadership has been uncompromising and strident. One Hareidi rabbinic leader was quoted in the Israeli press as having stated that if the Israel Defense Forces were to draft 50,000 Hareidim, they will need to prepare 50,000 prison cells—since not one of the Hareidim will agree to serve!

How different is this approach from the normative religious view expressed by Moses himself. In this week's Torah portion, Moses made it clear to the tribes of Gad and Reuven—and to the Israelites in general—that all are obligated to fight for the nation. Any tribe that shirks responsibility is thereby undermining the strength and the morale of the entire people.

When Israel's War of Independence broke out in 1948, a group of yeshiva students came to the office of Rabbi Benzion Uziel, Sephardic Chief Rabbi of Israel. They asked Rabbi Uziel to write letters exempting them from military service. Rabbi Uziel expressed his unequivocal displeasure with these students. He told them that it was their religious duty to fight in defense of Israel. When the nation comes under attack, even brides and grooms must hasten from the wedding canopy in order to defend the people of Israel. Not only is there a religious obligation to fight in defense of the nation, but yeshiva students who claim exemptions inevitably bring disgrace to the religious community and to the Torah.

Rabbi Haim David Halevy, a devoted disciple of Rabbi Uziel, demonstrated by personal example that Torah students and scholars were an integral part of the nation's defense. During the War of Independence in 1948, he served in an army unit comprised of yeshiva students and graduates. This military experience did not detract from his Torah scholarship—he went on to become one of the greatest rabbinic scholars of his generation!

The State of Israel is seeking ways to include many more of the Hareidim in the Israel Defense Forces and in the related National Service programs. There is much political in-fighting and negotiating among the various parties. It is clear, though, that the overwhelming majority of Israelis are fed up with the status quo that offers sweeping exemptions and benefits to Hareidim.

Religious leadership should not be resisting the impending changes, but should be at the vanguard of suggesting ways in which all Israelis can share in the responsibilities and privileges of serving in defense of the nation. In the long run, this is not only better for the State of Israel; it is better for the Hareidi community itself—and is better for the status of religion and Torah in the Jewish State.

It is well past time to reclaim the religious vision of such sages as Rabbi Uziel and Rabbi Halevy.

Thoughts on תשעה באב

What Unifies the Jewish People?

א Elias Canetti, a Sephardic Jew who won the Nobel Prize for Literature in 1981, offers some interesting observations about Jews in his book *Crowds and Power*: "Fools may tell stories of their sameness everywhere, but anyone who knows them well will be inclined to think that there are more varied types among them than among any other people . . . Jews are different from other people, but, in reality, they are most different from each other" (p. 178).

Given the tremendous diversity among Jews, what is the unifying factor that makes us consider ourselves to be one people? Canetti writes: "One is driven to ask in what respect these people remain Jews; what makes them into Jews; what is the ultimate nature of the bond they feel when they say 'I am a Jew.' . . . This bond . . . is the Exodus from Egypt.' Canetti suggests that the Israelites' formative experience as a vast crowd leaving Egypt is the key to understanding the nature of Jewish peoplehood. As long as Jews—however different they are from each other—share historical memories of the Exodus from Egypt, they continue to identify as members of one people. We are bound together by the shared experience of redemption.

Although Canetti touches on a vital point in Jewish identity, his explanation is incomplete.

In his magnificent Haggadah, the artist David Moss has provided another vital ingredient in the mystery of Jewish peoplehood. The Passover Seder is, of course, the classic recounting of the Exodus experience. Early in his Haggadah, Moss incorporates a dirge chanted on *Tisha B'Av*, the quintessential day of Exile and tragedy for the Jewish people. The dirge contrasts the feelings of elation at the Exodus with the sense of despair at the Exile. (On a related note, the evening service of *Tisha B'Av* at Congregation Shearith Israel in New York features a poignant elegy—"*Mah Nishtanah*"—which highlights the contrasts between Passover and *Tisha B'Av*.)

Thus, the Jewish people are unified by two great national experiences: Redemption and Exile.

These experiences are not merely singular historical events, but are prototypes that imbue the entire span of Jewish history—past, present, and future. We are supposed to experience the Passover Seder as though we ourselves were redeemed from Egypt. We are supposed to experience *Tisha B'Av* as though we ourselves witnessed the razing of our Temples in Jerusalem and were forced into a long and distressing Exile. Our thousands of years of history are marked by periods of elation and mourning, redemptions and exiles. It is the personal connection with both of these themes that serves to unite us as one people. If one ceases to feel connected to the shared experiences and ramifications of Exodus and Exile, he/she ceases to identify as a Jew.

Just as we recall *Tisha B'Av* on Passover, so we remember Passover on *Tisha B'Av*. Even as we mourn the sufferings of Exile, we maintain perfect faith in our ultimate Redemption.

If Exodus and Exile are unifying factors in defining our Jewishness, the Torah itself is the ultimate source of our peoplehood.

In *Parashat Devarim*, read on the Shabbat before *Tisha B'Av*, we are told that Moses took it upon himself to expound the Torah to the Israelites (*Devarim* 1:5). A Midrash suggests that Moses explained the Torah to them in 70 languages. But why would Moses need to explain the Torah in 70 languages, since the Israelites could not possibly have known all these tongues?

The Midrash is obviously alluding to something of deeper significance. Perhaps it is suggesting that the Israelites would ultimately find themselves scattered throughout the world, and would learn many new languages. The scattered communities would become very different from each other, unable even to communicate clearly with each other. Moses explained the Torah in 70 languages so that the Israelites would know that they had a unifying foundation in the Torah. No matter what language they would speak, the Torah would be accessible to them in that language. No matter how separate they seemed to be from other communities of Jews, the Torah bound them together as one people.

As we prepare for the observance of *Tisha B'Av*, let us take time to ponder the mystery and the wonder of Jewish peoplehood. The Exodus was the formative experience that propelled our people into history, with the principles of freedom and human dignity. The Exile was the experience that underscored our national courage, resilience, compassion, and determination. The Torah was—and is—the foundation of our spiritual teachings, our ideas and our ideals.

Those who shed the mournful tears of Exile will ultimately shed the joyful tears of Redemption. And the Torah is, and will remain, our light.

Beyond Tears

❦ Our ancient Temples in Jerusalem were destroyed in 586 BCE and 70 CE...and we are still fasting and crying! If this made sense during our many centuries of exile, does it still make sense today? After all, we now have a vibrant and strong Jewish State of Israel. With all our problems, shouldn't we be enjoying our sovereignty and the first flowerings of redemption? Isn't it time to stop fasting and crying for an exile that has functionally come to an end?

Rabbi Haim David Halevy, late Sephardic Chief Rabbi of Tel Aviv, addressed this issue in his volume of Responsa, *Asei Lekha Rav*, 1:13, which was published in Tel Aviv in 1976. He wisely observed: "If a nation knows how to remember the days of its destructions and tragedies and fixes days for fasting and prayer, then it may be presumed that it will merit redemption. Fasting is a matter for the nation, not for God."

Tisha B'Av is commemorated to arouse our national memories and our national aspirations. Even with the establishment of the State of Israel, we have a long way to go before all is well with the Jewish people. Although our observance of *Tisha B'Av* is not as bleak and somber as that of our ancestors in pre-State days, we still derive value by devoting the day to fasting and prayer, to memory of tragedies past, to dreams of redemptions yet to come.

It is a day for spiritual and national reflection.

The Talmud (*Yoma* 9b) suggests that the Temple in Jerusalem was destroyed due to the sin of *sinat hinam*, baseless hatred. However, "baseless" hatred seems to be rare, if not impossible. Whenever people hate, they don't think their hatred is baseless. They hate others because of their race or religion, because they fear them or were hurt by them. The reasons for their hatred may be entirely false and unfounded—yet, in their minds it is not baseless. Indeed, it would be quite amazing to come across someone who states that he/she hates you for absolutely no reason...just for the sake of hatred!

I believe the phrase "*sinat hinam*" should be interpreted differently. It does not mean baseless hatred. Rather, the word *hinam* derives from the word *hen*—graciousness, loveable-ness. The Temple was destroyed because people hated to see the *hen* in others. They dehumanized their opponents, treating them as though they lacked human charm and worth.

At the time preceding the destruction of the Second Temple, Jews were divided into hostile factions. There were zealots and pacifists, war-mongers and peaceniks, religious extremists and moderates. The groups were so antagonistic to each other, that they could not see the *hen* in their opponents. They stereotyped and demonized each other. This led to the fragmentation of society and to the inability to work together in a unified fashion.

When we look into each other's eyes and see a fellow human being, it is quite difficult to hate. We realize that all of us—regardless of nationality and ideology—are human beings. We love; we fear; we care for our families; we can be kind and compassionate. When we see the *hen* in others, our emotions steer away from hatred and toward sympathy.

Too often, people do not seriously look for the *hen* in others who are not part of their own inner circle. They dehumanize, create stereotypes...and hate to see the *hen* in those who differ from them. They do not see the individual human being with a heart and soul and feelings; instead, they see Settlers and Peace Now; ultra-Orthodox and secular; Jews and Arabs; Sephardim and Ashkenazim. Instead of talking to each other as fellow human beings, we tend to shout at each other as enemies. It is easy to hate a stereotype; it is difficult to hate a fellow human being who has *hen*.

Don't we deeply lament the fact that our enemies constantly engage in dehumanizing us, in presenting us as hateful objects rather than as fellow human beings? Don't we profoundly wish that our enemies would take the time to look into our eyes and see our *hen*, realizing that we all are created by the same God and all are endowed with grace and lovingkindness? And if we are profoundly disappointed by the hatred aimed against us, shouldn't we strive our mightiest to avoid falling into that same vicious trap of hating others? Shouldn't we try to elevate our own humanity by seeing the *hen* in our fellow Jews and in all our fellow human beings?

Tisha B'Av certainly has meaning for us today. It is a day for fasting, prayer and introspection. It is a prod to national memory. It is a reminder of past failures. It is a clarion call for a wiser, more humane and happier future. It is a challenge to overcome the pernicious sin of *sinat hinam*, hating to see the *hen* in our fellow human beings.

It is a time for tears—and a time to move beyond tears.

Thoughts on דברים

A Balanced Approach to Religion

☙ *The New York Times* (July 15, 2012) included an important article by Ross Douthat entitled "Can Liberal Christianity Be Saved?" He points out that the liberal denominations of Christianity have increasingly identified themselves with "progressive" causes—and in the process have experienced a drastic drop in membership and church attendance! He writes that "...liberal Christianity has simply collapsed. Practically every denomination...that has tried to adapt itself to contemporary liberal values has seen an Episcopal-style plunge in church attendance."

One explanation for this precipitous decline is that the church's message has become so universal, that people do not see a sharp difference between "liberal Christianity" and secular humanism. One can simply be a good human being, without needing the trappings and expense of church membership.

A similar phenomenon has been noted within the Jewish community. The liberal denominations of Judaism have also experienced a dramatic decline in membership and synagogue/Temple attendance. They have increasingly focused on universal themes such as social justice and *tikkun olam*, while downplaying commitment to ritual observance of mitzvoth and engagement in Jewish theology and philosophy. People conclude that one can fulfill Jewishness by espousing universal ideals—without making a concomitant commitment to Torah and mitzvoth. While trying to be more "relevant," the liberal denominations are actually becoming more irrelevant.

On the other side of the spectrum, the more conservative religious denominations have been experiencing growth in membership and attendance. Indeed, the more extreme groups seem to be enjoying the most robust increases. Apparently, many people are looking for religious structure that is more demanding, more comprehensive, more "authentic."

Yet, many thinking people find the extreme conservative religious framework to be seriously deficient. It is too authoritarian, too conformist, too dogmatic, too coercive.

In the Jewish religious world, the position of Modern Orthodoxy is balanced between the universalism of the liberal denominations and the extreme

190

particularism of the right-wing groupings. Modern Orthodoxy stresses commitment to Jewish beliefs and ideas, and demands adherence to halakha. It provides a meaningful structure for life and a spiritually sensitive way for the individual to serve God and humanity. While unflinchingly devoted to the particularistic teachings of Torah and mitzvoth, Modern Orthodoxy encompasses the universal values of Judaism—values that flow from the ideas and ideals of Torah. It respects our autonomy, our intelligence, our ability to assume personal responsibility. It allows room for creative thought and action.

In this week's Torah portion, we read that "Moses took upon himself to expound the Torah" (*Devarim* 1:5). We might have expected the verses to continue with an explanation of the various laws of the Torah or interpretations of its key teachings. Instead, Moses continues by offering a review of the 40-year history of the Israelites since the Exodus from Egypt. Moses believed that this history lesson served in some way as a proper exposition of the Torah.

Apparently, Moses was teaching the Israelites an essential truth. In order to understand the ideas and mitzvoth of the Torah, they first had to understand their own history, their own experiences. The Torah is not an abstract set of rules designed for a utopian world. Rather the Torah is grounded in reality, in the practical concerns of human beings as they actually cope with the challenges of life. Moses taught that to understand the Torah, the Israelites first had to understand their own distinctive history and their own distinctive mission. Once they had a solid and clear sense of their specific context and their specific identity, they could go on to play their spiritual role in the unfolding of human civilization.

Only after Moses reviewed their history did he go on in future chapters to expound to them on the beliefs and mitzvoth as well as their future role among the nations of the world. He was teaching, in effect, the need to be grounded in particular history and observances, as a foundation for concern and work for the improvement of society in general.

In our contemporary efforts to transmit Judaism to our communities, we need to espouse a religious worldview that is clearly and authentically rooted in the history and experience of the Jewish people, that is unflinchingly committed to Torah and mitzvoth. At the same time, we need to balance our particularism with our concerns and actions on behalf of the universal betterment of humankind.

Short cuts often lead us to dead ends. Long cuts often lead us into labyrinths. Let us think carefully as we proceed in the unfolding of Judaism for our and future generations.

ואתחנן

Each Person Can Make a Difference

🐦 This week's Torah portion includes the instruction that we do that "which is right and good in the sight of the Lord" (*Devarim* 6:18). Rabbinic tradition has understood this phrase to mean that we are required not merely to follow the letter of the law (that which is right), but to be compassionate beyond what the exact law demands (that which is good). If we can conduct ourselves on this level of righteousness, we can live better lives for ourselves and can impact on the improvement of society.

People sometimes feel that the world is filled with cruelty and injustice but that they can do nothing to change things. The evils are simply too great, and we are too small and insignificant to make any real impact.

The Torah reminds us to do that which is right and good, to exert ourselves to the best of our ability. We should not be discouraged by the magnitude of the problems that face us, nor should we underestimate the role we can play if only we were to exert ourselves properly.

One of the inspiring personalities in the history of Congregation Shearith Israel in New York City is Maud Nathan (1862–1946). She was a Daughter of the American Revolution, with deep roots in American life. A founder and first President of Shearith Israel's Sisterhood (established in 1896), she was an indomitable activist on behalf of creating a just and harmonious society.

Maud Nathan was a leader in the women's suffrage movement, and became an international spokesperson for women's rights. Theodore Roosevelt appointed her as head of the women's suffrage movement of his National Progressive Party.

Among her singular achievements, she served as President of the Consumers' League of New York from 1897 to 1917. She and her colleagues strove to ameliorate the terrible working conditions of young women who worked in New York's department stores and shops. The basic insight of the Consumers' League was that social ills could be solved by positive action on the part of many. Instead of condemning the offending stores and shops, the Consumers' League created a "white list" of businesses that provided proper working conditions and pay. Consumers were urged to patronize stores on the "white list," thus creating pressure on all stores to upgrade working conditions so they could earn a place on this list. Through persistent hard work and ongoing negotiations with employers, the Consumers' League brought about a monumental change in the status quo. The success depended on the daily decisions of thousands of consumers. Individually, their decisions might have seemed unimportant. Cumulatively, though, the impact was enormous.

Just as Maud Nathan sought to enhance the civil rights of women and to improve the working conditions of store clerks, she strove to create greater harmony among the various segments of society. She was one of the few Jewish women of her era to work together with Christian women on joint social and philanthropic projects. She believed that anti-Semitism and racial prejudice could be diminished if people of all backgrounds had opportunities for positive interactions.

In her book, *Once Upon a Time and Today*, she reminded her readers: "Prejudice produces humiliation which is not easy to bear. And the sad part is that the nature becomes warped and the spirit of kindliness and friendliness is changed into bitterness and resentment. To live in peace, there must be mutual confidence, trust, cooperation, no antagonism. How often, instead of mutual respect for differing spiritual values, there is suspicion, intolerance."

Although she herself had felt the stings of anti-Semitism, she took pride in the fact that she had "been able to make her protest count." Through her persistence, hard work, and idealism, she did that which was right and good in the sight of the Lord—and in the sight of her fellow human beings.

Instead of feeling frustrated and powerless by the problems of our world, we need to remember the example set by Maud Nathan. If we energize ourselves and engage in joint action with others, we can achieve important progress. We should not become overwhelmed by the vastness of the problems that confront us, but should focus on the particular area/s where we can best succeed in fostering positive change. A lot of individual decisions can result in remarkable change for the good.

"And you shall do that which is right and good in the sight of the Lord."

Torah and Nature

❧ In the *Pirkei Aboth* (Ethics of the Fathers), the talmudic sage Rabbi Yaacov is quoted (3:9): "One who is walking along while studying [words of Torah] and interrupts his study and says 'how beautiful is this tree, how beautiful is this field'—the Torah considers him as though he is guilty of death." The source for this statement is usually given as a verse in this week's Torah portion that teaches that one is supposed to contemplate words of Torah when walking on one's way (*Devarim* 6:7). The assumption is that if one interrupts Torah study, even to admire the beauties of nature, one risks one's life.

Rabbi Yaacov's statement has often been understood to reflect a Torah-centered religious vision that denigrates the natural world. Presumably, one should be so engrossed in Torah so as not to be distracted by beautiful trees or fields!

I suggest that Rabbi Yaacov's statement actually may have something else in mind. It is not anti-nature or anti-aesthetics. It reflects an entirely different message.

There are two basic paths to the Almighty: Torah and Nature. These are not mutually exclusive paths, but are complementary. When we study Torah, we study the word of God. When we experience the beauties of nature, we confront the awesome creations of God. A proper religious worldview entails proper appreciation of both Torah and Nature, and sees the ultimate harmony and unity of both.

If one seeks God only through Torah, one's religious outlook lacks the sense of wonder and aesthetics that Nature provides. If one seeks God only through Nature, one's religious outlook lacks the direct contact with God's words.

Rabbi Yaacov was teaching that we need to maintain sensitivity to both pathways to God: to Torah and to Nature. If we are studying Torah while walking, and we see a beautiful tree, it is appropriate to praise the tree's beauty as a manifestation of God's wisdom. There is no problem with admiring the tree or field or any other feature of the natural world. A problem arises, though, if we see our admiration of nature as an "interruption" in our Torah study. If we do not view Torah and Nature as harmonious and complementary approaches to God, then we are "guilty of death." Rabbi Yaacov was reminding us to maintain a unified religious vision, not to view Torah and Nature as two separate and unrelated entities.

In his code of Jewish law, the *Mishneh Torah*, Maimonides highlighted the traditional emphasis on Torah study. "Among all the commandments, none is equal to the study of Torah. Study leads to proper action" (*Hilkhot Talmud Torah* 3:3). Through Torah study and mitzvah observance, a person can find a direct relationship with the Almighty.

Yet, Maimonides also highlighted the role of Nature in our religious development. "What is the way to love and fear Him? When a person contemplates His wondrous and great works and creations, and he sees in them His infinite wisdom, immediately he loves and praises and exalts and yearns with an overwhelming yearning to know His great Name....On meditating these very things, one immediately recoils, fears, and trembles, realizing that he is a tiny, low and obscure being of small intelligence standing before the One with perfect wisdom. . ." (*Hilkhot Yesodei haTorah* 2:2).

So we can read the message of Rabbi Yaacov as follows: Study Torah as a manifestation of God's words and will; admire Nature as a reflection of God's wisdom and creative powers. View Torah and Nature as complementary paths to God. Do not "interrupt" between them; do not see them as distinct and separate domains.

Righteousness Is Not Enough

🍃 In this week's Torah portion, we are reminded that God does justice on behalf of the orphan and the widow; He loves the stranger and provides food and clothing (*Devarim* 10:18). The implication is that we, too, should emulate these compassionate qualities of the Almighty, caring for those who need our assistance and protection.

The theme of God's mercy is echoed in Psalm 146. In listing His attributes, the Psalm states that God "provides justice for the oppressed; He gives food to the hungry; He frees those who are bound; He gives sight to the blind; He raises those who are bowed." But then, surprisingly, the Psalmist adds the phrase "God loves the righteous," and then goes on to state that "God watches over strangers and upholds the orphan and widow." The pattern of the above phrases is to describe a person who has a deficiency (e.g., is oppressed, hungry, bound, blind, bowed, in the weak social position of stranger, orphan or widow)—and then to indicate that God resolves the deficiency and restores the person to fullness.

The only exception to this pattern is the phrase that "God loves the righteous." What is that phrase doing in the midst of these descriptions? (Logically, it should be connected to a later phrase that God "thwarts the way of the wicked." Yet, it is not so placed in our Psalm.)

I would suggest that the phrase should be interpreted in the same pattern as the other phrases in which it is included. Just as in the other phrases, it refers to a human deficiency which the Almighty comes to heal. What is the deficiency of the righteous? The lack of love! Since the righteous lacks love, God fills this deficiency by showering love upon the righteous.

This can be understood in two ways. A righteous person—since she/he has high principles—is not always a beloved person. People don't necessarily like others who are righteous, seeing them rather as being self-righteous. Or they don't like righteous people who seem to stand in criticism of the lifestyles and opinions of others. Since a righteous person might feel lonely and unloved, he/she should take comfort in the fact that the Almighty will love him/her. That divine love makes up for the deficiency of human love that he/she experiences.

I would suggest a second interpretation—not that the righteous are deprived of the love of others, but that the righteous lack the ability to love others! A righteous person follows the rules carefully, and does that which is right. In being committed to these rules, he/she might become disdainful of others who aren't quite as meticulous. The righteous person becomes characterized by love of the rules, not by love of fellow human beings. Indeed, those people who do not conform to his/her standards of righteousness become objects of scorn or disgust.

The Talmud relates a strange passage about a father who prays on behalf of his ailing son. If the father says that he will give charity if God will heal the son, the father is considered to be totally righteous. Yet, this prayer seems to be less than ideal. Why should the father be considered to be righteous by making a bargain with God? Rabbi Hayyim Yosef David Azulai, one of the great sages of the eighteenth century, commented on this talmudic passage. He stated: The father is considered righteous—but not pious! He is righteous in that he strikes a bargain and meets its terms exactly. He has not deviated from the rules. Yet, he is not pious—his attitude reflects a low level of religiosity. It lacks true love of God.

A righteous person might not even realize that righteousness is insufficient to make one a good person, a religious person. A righteous person can be cold, calculating, unsympathetic to others—and still be following the rules meticulously. Such a person is lacking in piety—in love of God and love of fellow human beings. Such a person is devoted to the rules, but is not devoted to living by ideals that deepen and transcend the rules. The righteous person lacks love.

Thus, the Psalm lists the deficiency of the righteous as a deficiency of love—a deficiency in his/her ability to live with a loving attitude toward God and human beings. So God must intercede and teach the righteous person to love.

When the Bible describes God's love and compassion and His concern for the weak and downtrodden, it is presenting a model for emulation. Just as He is kind, so we are to be kind; just as He is merciful, so are we to be merciful. The essence of religion is not merely doing that which is right—but doing that which is imbued with compassion and love.

Our goal is not merely to be righteous—but to be pious. To be pious entails the qualities of empathy, compassion—and sincere love.

What Are Our Real Preferences?

❦ Economists speak of the "principle of revealed preferences." This principle teaches that we can better predict what people will do based on their current behavior patterns rather than on what they say they will do. People most accurately reveal their real selves by their deeds, not by what they espouse.

For example, a smoker may say that he/she places infinite value on his/her life. Yet, each time he/she lights up a cigarette, the action reveals that his/her words are not really true. The smoker demonstrates a willingness to endanger health and shorten life—and is likely to continue smoking. A person may claim to believe in this or that cause; and yet, his/her deeds point in a different direction. He/she does nothing to support that cause, exerts no effort or makes no contribution. A person may say he/she wants to keep at a healthy weight and stay fit. But these intentions are less indicative of the person's future behavior than whether he/she eats healthily and exercises regularly. If we want to predict how people will behave tomorrow, we are better off seeing how they behave today and ignoring what they claim to believe or what they say they will do.

Of course, people can and do change. Patterns of behavior are not fixed permanently. People can actually live up to the beliefs and ideals and goals they espouse—but it's a safer bet that people will not change. It is generally more accurate to judge people by their actions rather than by their words and their professed intentions. As a rule, we reveal our preferences by what we do, not by what we say.

In this week's Torah portion, we are enjoined to fear and love the Lord. How may we achieve these lofty goals? We are commanded "to walk in all His ways...to serve the Lord your God with all your heart and with all your soul; to keep for your benefit the commandments of the Lord and His statutes..." (*Devarim* 10:12–13).

The Torah understands that our highest spiritual goals are attained through and manifested in our actions. We serve God not by pious pronouncements of faith, but by "walking in all His ways," by the actual fulfillment of the Torah's commandments. We demonstrate piety not by artificial displays of "spirituality," but by solid and steady commitment to righteous living.

It should be emphasized that the Torah views the fulfillment of commandments as a means of coming into a relationship with the Almighty—to fear and to love God. If the commandments are performed in a mechanical and unthinking way, then this reveals one's preference for automatic ritualistic behavior rather than a dynamic living relationship with God.

People sometimes refer to themselves as being "religious" or being "not religious." We should not pay too much attention to these descriptions. Rather, we should see how people—and especially our own selves—actually conduct life. Over the years, I've known individuals who described themselves as being "religious"—but who were very far from leading upright and constructive lives. I've also known individuals who have described themselves as being "not religious"—but who have behaved with utmost righteousness and admirable devotion to the needs of the community.

When taking stock of our own lives, it is useful to ponder the "principle of revealed preferences." We most accurately reveal our beliefs, commitments, and ethical principles by how we act—not by what we say.

What are our real preferences? How can we bring our lives in line with our ideas and ideals?

We Are Caretakers, Not Owners

🖉 The sages of talmudic times often expressed profound ideas in terse, enigmatic statements. An example of this is found in the midrashic comment: "The world was created in the merit of three things: in the merit of [the mitzvoth of] Hallah, tithes, and first fruits" (*Yalkut Shimoni, Bereishith* 1:2). If we were to speculate as to which mitzvoth were absolutely vital to the creation, we might have chosen other—seemingly more important—commandments, such as the Sabbath, the laws of holiness, and the sanctification of One God.

What did the author of this Midrash have in mind? Why did he think that the laws of Hallah, tithes, and first fruits were so vital to the creation of the world? To answer these questions, we need to ponder the significance of these three mitzvoth.

All three of these commandments are reminders that we ultimately own nothing, that the universe belongs to God. God allows us to be guardians and caretakers of property, and we are expected to uphold our responsibilities faithfully. When we make a batch of dough, we take off a piece. In Temple days, this was given as a gift to the Kohanim, the priests in the Temple. Today, with the absence of the Temple in Jerusalem, we burn a bit of dough as a reminder that it is not ours. We may not use the rest of the dough until we've first taken out the Hallah.

A farmer works hard to bring in a crop. He might think: This all belongs to me; I've done the labor; I've invested time and money: the produce is all mine. The Torah reminds us: No, it is not yours, it is God's. One tenth must be given to the Levites, and a tenth of the remainder must be given to the poor, or must be brought to Jerusalem to be eaten there.

A farmer sees the first fruits budding on his trees; he has worked long and hard to earn the harvest. Yet, he must designate the very first fruits to be brought to the Temple as an offering to the Almighty.

These three mitzvoth underscore a vital fact of creation: The world was created by and belongs to God. We are transient guests here. The Almighty blesses us with property to sustain ourselves and our families—but we must always realize that what we have is not fully ours; it is ours only insofar as God enjoins us to be worthy caretakers.

These three mitzvoth point to the ultimate truth—well beyond the realm of agriculture—that all our property and assets are on temporary loan to us from the Almighty. This is not merely an abstract idea, but is a foundation for a wise philosophy of life. It keeps things in perspective. If we think that what we earn is all ours and only ours, we are sadly mistaken; it is ours only by virtue of the fact that God has allowed us to have it on loan. We literally cannot take it with us.

These three mitzvoth epitomize our sense of gratitude to the Almighty for what He gives us. They teach us humility and charity. They put life into a spiritual perspective.

In this week's *Parasha*, we read about the mitzvah of tithing. In commanding the bringing of tithes to the Temple, the Torah states that we are to bring the tithes of our grain, wine, oil, the firstlings of our herd and flock "that you may learn to fear the Lord your God always" (*Devarim* 14:23). It is precisely through bringing these offerings that we learn to fear the Lord, to recognize God's role as Creator and Master of the universe.

We all work hard to earn income, to invest wisely, to enjoy our worldly assets. When we understand on the profoundest level that all our material assets are simply temporary loans from God, we can live more responsibly and more wisely. By setting aside part of our material wealth to help the needy and to support charitable institutions, we thereby demonstrate our recognition of God as Master of the universe. Tithing and giving charity are not merely acts of kindness; they are fulfillments of practical obligations that God has placed on us.

This theme is highlighted by our making blessings before we eat or drink. Yes, we are allowed to enjoy our food and drink—but only after first giving recognition and gratitude that these are gifts from the Almighty. One who eats or drinks without first offering a blessing is considered by the Talmud to be a thief of sorts. He/she has "robbed" God of recognition as Creator. More importantly, he/she has robbed him/herself of an opportunity for putting material life into a spiritual context.

The midrashic sage taught that the world was created in the merit of the mitzvoth of Hallah, tithes, and first fruits. He was pointing to a deep truth that none of us should ever forget.

Religious Aspirations and the Entrepreneurial Spirit

❦ I recently met with a friend who is a very successful entrepreneur who deals with top people at leading high-tech companies such as Microsoft, Google, and Amazon. He told me that when these companies look to hire new employees, they especially value applicants with entrepreneurial experience—even if these applicants had run their own businesses and failed!

Why would they want to hire "failed" entrepreneurs?

My friend explained: A high percentage of start-up companies fail. To start such businesses requires imagination, risk-taking ability, creativity, and hard work. These are exactly the qualities the big high-tech companies are looking for. Even if the entrepreneurs failed in their own businesses, they have demonstrated unique courage and willingness to think "out of the box." They showed that they were willing to try something new and to invest their lives in it.

If people are willing to think imaginatively and to work hard at developing their plans, they increase their odds of success. Even if their original businesses did not turn out well, they eventually can find the right framework for their talents and energies.

It is not "failure" to have high aspirations that one has not fulfilled. It is failure for one not to have had high aspirations in the first place.

This week's Torah portion begins with the words, "Behold I set before you this day. . .". Rabbi Hayyim Benattar, in his Torah commentary *Ohr haHayyim*, offers an interesting interpretation based on the words *re'eh anokhi*. He suggests that these words might be understood in the sense of Moses telling the people of Israel: "Behold me," that is, see how high I've been able to rise, to have related to God "face to face." In setting himself as a model, Moses was reminding the Israelites that each of them could rise to great spiritual heights. If they would each strive to the best of their abilities, they could achieve great things.

Moses was calling on the Israelites to have high religious aspirations. Even if they experienced many failures along the way, they ultimately would maximize their opportunities for spiritual growth if they kept striving to attain their ideals. It is not "failure" to have been unable to fulfill all one's aspirations; rather, it is failure not to have aspired in the first place.

Religious life is not static. Indeed, the hallmark of religion at its best is an ongoing sense of striving, failing, growing, falling back, moving forward.

Religion at its best is dynamic and life-transforming. Those who are masters of religious life are precisely those who demonstrate "entrepreneurial" spirit: the willingness to try, to take risks, to invest oneself totally in a set of grand ideas and ideals, to fail, but then to pick oneself up and try again.

Religious life is deficient when it lacks enthusiasm and energy. Unless we are growing and developing, we are stagnating or regressing. Religion isn't about maintaining a dull status quo; it is about dynamic self-transformation and spiritual growth. It is looking to the example of Moses and other great men and women—and aspiring to raise ourselves to their models.

Rabbi Abraham Isaac Kook, who was the Ashkenazic Chief Rabbi of Israel in the early twentieth century, once compared religious life to being on a ladder. Was someone on a higher rung more "religious" than one on a lower rung? Rabbi Kook answered: It depends on which direction the people were going. A person might be on a higher rung—with more knowledge and greater level of mitzvah observance—and yet be stagnant or actually on the way down the ladder. Another person might be on a lower rung of religious knowledge and observance, yet be ascending, moving up with each passing day. So the one who is ascending is experiencing a dynamic and growing religious life, whereas the one on the higher rung is experiencing a dry and diminishing religious life. The one on the lower rung is aspiring to grow, while the one on the higher rung has surrendered to rote and dullness.

Religion is not a part-time sideline, or something to do in our spare time. It isn't a collection of laws and customs for us to perform in a mechanical way. It is, at root, a framework for striving toward a dynamic relationship with the Almighty. It is not so much a pattern of life as an attitude toward living, of reaching beyond ourselves, of aspiring to raise ourselves above the mundane, of climbing one more rung in our quest for self-understanding and confrontation with the divine.

Yes, we will surely experience failures along the way. But it is not these failures that define who we are. What defines us is our aspirations—and our willingness to strive to attain them.

שפטים

"Groupthink" or Independent Thinking

🐚 Professor Eliezer Schnall of Yeshiva University and his student Michael Greenberg presented a paper at the annual convention of the American Psychological Association on August 7, 2011. They discussed an influential theory developed by the psychologist Irving Janis, known as "groupthink." Janis posited that tight-knit, smart, and well-informed cliques can suppress dissent and create a "groupthink" phenomenon—where the general public goes along with the ideas of the inner-power group. People either come to accept the dictates of the power group, or they are de-legitimized or ostracized. Dissent is crushed. Open and free discussion is not tolerated.

Dr. Schnall demonstrated how the deleterious effects of groupthink were consciously counteracted by the methods of operation of the Sanhedrin, the classic judicial system of ancient Israel. For example, when discussing cases in the Sanhedrin, the judges of lesser authority spoke first. The more senior judges offered their own opinions later. This system was adopted in order to ensure free and open discussion. If the veteran "expert" judges spoke first, the other judges might be reluctant to express disagreement with them. The result would be groupthink—control of discussion by a small, powerful clique.

The Sanhedrin sought to avoid becoming insular. Outside experts were consulted. Disciples who watched the proceedings were allowed to offer their opinions. If the Sanhedrin reached a unanimous guilty verdict in capital cases, the defendant was acquitted! It was assumed that absence of dissension meant that group conformity was operating and that the defendant did not have a fair trial.

Groupthink is a highly dangerous phenomenon. It arrogates considerable authority into the hands of a small inner circle, and essentially causes the public to conform to the views of this power clique. This is the method employed by tyrannies. This is the method that enables small elite groups to impose their views on a passive or frightened public. Groupthink is quite evident in anti-Jewish and anti-Israel propaganda and in the "politically correct" move-

204

ment. Individuals stop thinking for themselves, stop demanding facts, stop evaluating the "truths" that are imposed on them. If they resist the pressures of groupthink, they risk being branded as social and intellectual outcasts. They risk being isolated and ostracized.

In this week's Torah portion, we read that the courts are to pursue justice: *tsedek tsedek tirdof.* Many commentators have understood this phrase to mean: You must pursue justice in a just way. The search for truth must be conducted in an open and free environment, without coercion or intimidation. People must feel free to offer their insights and opinions, and must not succumb to groupthink. Discussion and dissension are to be encouraged, not stifled.

Manifestations of groupthink are ubiquitous in our society, and it requires considerable astuteness and courage to resist its pressures. Groupthink is increasingly evident in religious life, where small groups of clerics/intellectuals seek to impose their narrow views on the public. They state what is "true" and expect the public to go along with their pronouncements. Those who don't follow the dictates of the power group are branded as heretics. The tyranny of groupthink is rampant in religious fundamentalist circles of whatever religion. Small cliques of "authorities" are granted incredible status, bordering on or including infallibility, and they proclaim what is "true" and what is "heresy." Discussion, debate, and dissent are ruled out. Woe unto the person who does not conform in thought or behavior to the dictates of the "authorities."

If groupthink is highly dangerous for society at large, it is perhaps even more pernicious for religious life. It injects a spiritual poison into religion, gradually sapping religious life of vitality, creativity, and dynamism. Instead of fostering a spirit of discussion and free inquiry, it demands a ruthless conformity. Instead of empowering religious people to think and analyze and debate, it forces religious people to stop thinking independently, to refrain from analysis and debate, and to suppress any ideas that do not conform to the framework of groupthink. It insists on abject obedience to "authorities"—even when we don't agree with them, even when we don't acknowledge them as our "authorities," even when we are convinced that these "authorities" are leading the public in an entirely incorrect direction.

If we are to be responsible individuals, we must resist the tyranny of groupthink. We must insist on the freedom to think for ourselves, to evaluate ideas independently, to stand up against coercion and intimidation. We must strive for a religious life that is alive and dynamic.

We must pursue truth and justice in a true and just way.

Truth and Consequences

Rabbi Akabia ben Mahalel lived in the generation before the destruction of the Temple by the Romans in 70 CE. He was known for his piety and profound erudition. The Talmud reports (*Mishnah Eduyot* 5:6) that he disputed with the other rabbis on various issues of Jewish law.

Akabia's colleagues wanted him to back down from his views and to accept the majority opinions. He refused. They offered to appoint him as the Av Bet Din, head of the authoritative rabbinic court—if only he would withdraw his opinions and accept theirs. Akabia replied: "It would be better for me to be called a fool all my life rather than to be wicked in the eyes of God for even one moment." He would prefer to be disdained by his colleagues rather than betray his integrity, rather than appear false in the eyes of God.

Akabia is a model of intellectual courage and moral strength. Truth is not for sale, not to be traded in exchange for power or honor. We are answerable, after all, to Almighty God.

Akabia's attitude is reflected in the words of this week's Torah portion: "*Tsedek tsedek tirdof*," you shall surely pursue justice. Our commentators have understood this phrase to mean: You shall pursue justice in a just way, using just means. We are commanded to be scrupulously just, through and through.

Akabia's commitment to truth was uncompromising. He would not succumb to the blandishments and flattery of his colleagues. He would not issue a ruling that he considered wrong, even as a means of keeping peace among his colleagues.

Yet, before Akabia died, he instructed his son to accept the rulings of the rabbis, who were the majority! Although he himself could not accede to the majority views since these views contradicted the teachings Akabia had received from his teachers—the son was obligated to follow the views of the majority—the leaders and teachers of the son's generation.

Akabia was willing to withstand a lifetime of suffering as a lonely "minority of one" due to his commitment to truth. At the same time, he fully understood that his colleagues had other views as to what the truth was; normative Jewish law was determined by majority opinion. While Akabia was a "martyr" to his view of truth, he wanted this martyrdom to be limited only to himself, not to future generations.

Akabia is a classic example of principled commitment to one's traditions and truths, even at high personal cost. But he is also a classic example of broad-visioned wisdom. He understood that minority opinions, however valid they may seem, ultimately must give way to the views of the majority of sages. The sages, after all, are also seekers of truth and perfect justice; they are also learned and thoughtful people who seek to be faithful to God's word.

When mediating between our personal opinions and the differing views of the majority of our colleagues, we need to keep Akabia's example in mind. It is right and proper to stand up for the truth as we see it. But it is also right and proper that our disputes not be passed down through the generations.

Thoughts on כִּי תֵצֵא

Electronic Lashon HaRa

☙ At a recent lunch meeting with friends, we were discussing the ugliness and lack of civility that too frequently characterize blog sites and online comments. Modern technology makes it quite easy for people to post hostile remarks against those with whom they disagree. These ad hominem attacks gain lives of their own, being forwarded to readers who then forward them to others. In a matter of a few seconds, people can spread *lashon haRa* to a wide audience.

My friend told me of a woman who had been viciously attacked by online critics for statements she had made. She patiently searched for the telephone numbers of as many of the critics as she could identify. And then she called each of them.

They were startled to actually be speaking with the person they had so harshly maligned online. When they realized that the person they had attacked was a real human being with real feelings, they became somewhat apologetic for the rashness of their remarks. It is one thing to write an anonymous comment against an anonymous person; it is another thing to confront the person directly, as a fellow human being.

Modern technology makes it easy to dehumanize others. People can lodge the cruelest and most outlandish charges—without ever having to face the victims of their venom, without ever having to consider the ultimate impact of their *lashon haRa*. They feel that it's perfectly fine for them to vent, to call names, to discredit others—because they don't see these "others" as fellow human beings. The victims are merely targets on a computer screen, to be shot down just as one shoots down enemies in other computer games.

Rabbi Eliezer Papo, one of the great sages of the nineteenth century, offered an important insight to authors. He suggested that if author A wished to write a critique of a work by author B—even if author B had died long ago—author A should imagine that author B was in the same room with him. He should not write down even one word that he wouldn't say to author B face to face. This advice inculcates respectfulness to fellow human beings. If we wish to critique ideas or opinions, we should not use ad hominem attacks. Rather, we should focus on the issues themselves, and offer calm and cogent arguments. Name-calling never establishes truth; only careful and thoughtful reasoning can lead us to truth.

In this week's Torah reading, we are commanded to "remember what the Lord your God did unto Miriam by the way as you came forth from Egypt" (*Devarim* 24:9). According to rabbinic tradition, Miriam was struck with leprosy due to her sin of speaking *lashon haRa*, evil-spirited gossip against Moses. The Torah insists that we remember the consequences of *lashon haRa*, that we recognize that it plagues the speaker as well as the victim.

Lashon haRa has always been considered by Jewish tradition to be among the most heinous sins. It is a sin that causes affliction to the speaker, to the listener, and to the victim. In the modern era, *lashon haRa* has reached new magnitudes of danger and harmfulness, due to the instant communications made possible by new technologies. If Miriam was punished for spreading a little gossip among a relatively few people, imagine the culpability of one who electronically spreads slander and disparagement to many thousands of people.

Here is some advice for coping with electronic *lashon haRa*:

1. Don't post any comment or critique that you would not say to the victim in person.

2. Don't write ad hominem attacks or engage in character assassination. If you object to someone's opinions, then focus on the opinions. Show why they are wrong. Offer cogent arguments. Be respectful. If you receive a comment/blog/email that contains *lashon haRa*, delete it immediately. Do not forward it to anyone else. If possible, communicate with the sender and register your disapproval of his/her spreading of *lashon haRa*. Do not trust the reliability of anyone who sends around ad hominem attacks.

3. Remember what the Lord your God did unto Miriam by the way as you came forth from Egypt.

Me First!

❧ Americans spend about 37 billion hours a year waiting in lines—and few of us enjoy the experience. What really irks us, though, is when we experience someone trying to cut into line. These "cutters" offend us with their bad manners, their lack of fairness, and their apparent feeling that their time is more valuable than ours.

Cutters are despicable to us because they show disdain for us and everyone else on line. They think only of themselves, without casting a thought as to how the rest of us feel. We are not irritated with them only because they cost us a few more seconds in line; we are agitated because they depreciate and insult us by their arrogant selfishness in thinking themselves more important than the rest of us who are patiently waiting our turn.

This week's Torah portion includes various commandments that aim at increasing our sensitivity to the feelings of others. We need to think not only about what is best for ourselves, but also about how our actions impact on others. If we find a lost object, we are supposed to try to return it to its owner even if this takes time and energy on our part. We need to think about the feelings of the person who has lost this possession. Workers in vineyards are allowed to eat grapes as they work, so that their feelings are respected and their natural hunger is satisfied. When coming to collect a loan, one must wait outside the home of the borrower and wait courteously for him/her to make payment.

The Torah insists that workers be paid on time. To delay payment is considered "oppression" of the worker. "In the same day you shall pay the wages, neither shall the sun go down upon it; for he is poor, and sets his heart upon it: lest he cry against you unto the Lord and it be counted a sin against you" (*Devarim* 24:15). Delay in paying one's worker is not simply an act of financial negligence, but a bitter affront to the laborer who depends on his daily income. Delaying payment is a sin against the worker's dignity and self-respect.

Postponing payment reflects an attitude of disregard and disdain toward the one who has provided service and who is entitled to receive pay. It was said of Rabbi Yitzhak Luria, the great kabbalist of sixteenth-century Safed, that he would not allow himself to pray Minhah (the afternoon prayer) until he first paid his debts to his workers. He reasoned: How can I stand in prayer before God when I have not fulfilled my basic obligation to my workers?

We might extend Rabbi Luria's reasoning to those who cut in line, who take shortcuts at the expense of others, who think themselves more important and more entitled than the rest of us. How can these self-centered and disrespectful people come before God in prayer, when they have shown callousness to their fellow human beings?

The Talmud (*Berakhot* 6b) states that if one does not respond to the greeting of another, it is considered as though he/she were a thief! By ignoring the greeting of another person, it is as though one is indicating: You are not important enough to merit a simple word of response from me; you simply do not matter to me! The non-responder is considered a "thief" because he/she has robbed another person's dignity and feeling of self-worth.

The greatest people are precisely those who are most generous and sensitive to the feelings of others. They conduct themselves with good manners and thoughtfulness. They are humble, natural, and kind. They do not cut in lines; they pay their debts on time; they demand no extra honors or privileges.

Rabbi Bahya Ibn Pekuda, in his classic *Hovot haLevavot*, teaches: "No moral quality can possibly exist in anyone whose heart is devoid of humility before God or has in it anything of pride, haughtiness or conceit."

כי תבוא

"The Paper Towel Syndrome"

🦌 How many times has this happened to you? You've gone out of your way to help someone. You've spent time and energy, and possibly even incurred financial expense. Yet, once the person has benefitted from your kindness, he/she doesn't bother to show appreciation, not even to say a sincere thank you.

I call this the "paper towel syndrome." People use you like a paper towel, and then toss you out without a second thought. They've gotten what they needed out of you, and then they move right along with their lives as though they had always been entitled to your acts of kindness.

This week's Torah portion includes the text that a farmer is supposed to recite when bringing the first fruits to the priest. In thanking God for His beneficence, the farmer first recounts the experience of the Israelites in Egypt and states: "The Egyptians dealt ill with us, and afflicted us, and laid upon us hard bondage" (*Devarim* 26:6).

Rabbi Yitzhak Shemuel Reggio, a nineteenth-century Italian Jewish commentator, notes that this passage indicates that the Egyptians were *kefuyei tovah*—ingrates. With all the benefits they had derived from Joseph, they nevertheless returned his kindness with acts of cruelty against his people. Joseph was essentially a "paper towel"—to be used and unceremoniously discarded. The Israelites were enslaved—to be exploited as "paper towels" without any thought as to their human rights and dignity. No need to say thank you, no need to show appreciation, no need to demonstrate gratitude.

While we may remember instances when we were treated like paper towels, we might be less likely to keep in mind cases when we ourselves treated others with the paper towel syndrome. We have benefitted from the time, trouble, and expense which others have devoted to help us—and yet we may not have always shown appreciation. We may have taken this kindness for granted, as though we were entitled to it.

The Torah's description of the first fruits and tithe offerings underscores how important it is for us to be grateful—and to express gratitude. The hallmark of a religiously sensitive person is to thank all those who have benefitted him/her, and not to take kindness for granted.

Treating others as paper towels is obviously to dehumanize them. It is to reduce them to utilitarian objects whose purpose is merely to fulfill our needs.

In his essay, "The Community," Rabbi Joseph B. Soloveitchik underscored that halakha demands high respect for the dignity of others. "To recognize a person is not just to identify him physically. It is more than that: it is an act of identifying him existentially. . . . To recognize a person means to affirm that he is irreplaceable. To hurt a person means to tell him that he is expendable, that there is no need for him." In other words, to recognize a person means to affirm that he/she has human value, that he/she is appreciated, that he/she matters to us. To hurt a person means to treat him/her as a paper towel, expendable, to be used and discarded.

Certainly, we do not act kindly because we want or expect a show of gratitude. We do what is good and what is right because it is good and because it is right. Yet, how much nicer our world would be if we and others avoided the paper towel syndrome, if we all could develop that sensitivity and graciousness to recognize the human dignity of others. Just as others should not treat us as paper towels, so we need to be very careful not to treat others as such.

Physical and Spiritual Survival

❧ In his essay "Fate and Destiny," Rabbi Joseph B. Soloveitchik delineates two aspects of Jewish peoplehood: the camp and the congregation. "The camp is created as a result of the desire for self-defense and is nurtured by a sense of fear; the congregation is created as a result of the longing for the realization of an exalted ethical idea and is nurtured by the sentiment of love. Fate reigns in unbounded fashion in the camp; destiny reigns in the congregation...."

The camp is concerned with our physical survival. We join together to fight against our enemies. We mobilize our resources to defend ourselves from attack. The camp is our means of maintaining our existence in a hostile world.

The congregation is concerned with our spiritual survival. Yes, we need the camp to protect us from danger; but we also need to know the purpose and meaning of our community. Why are we fighting? What are our goals? Survival in and of itself is not enough; we need to survive in order to fulfill our role as a congregation. Rabbi Soloveitchik notes: "The congregation is a group of individuals possessing a common past, a common future, common goals and desires, a common aspiration for a world which is wholly good and beautiful and a common unique and unified destiny."

This week's Torah portion includes the passages to be recited by farmers when they brought their first fruits to the Temple. This recitation reviews Israelite history: Our ancestor was a wandering Aramean; we were slaves in Egypt; we overcame many obstacles and much suffering. The text reminds us of our history as a camp. We were endangered; we were afraid; we were victims of a negative fate.

But then the recitation continues by expressing gratitude to the Almighty for bringing us to the land of milk and honey. It puts life in context of the divine promises to Israel, and the many blessings enjoyed by the people of Israel. The Torah then makes it clear that we are a congregation with a destiny, not merely a camp forced to defend itself. "This day the Lord your God commands you to do these statutes and ordinances; you shall therefore observe and do them with all your heart and with all your soul. You have avouched the Lord this day to be your God and that you would walk in His ways, and keep His statutes, and His commandments, and His ordinances, and hearken unto His voice" (*Devarim* 26: 17–18).

Throughout our history, the people of Israel has had to view itself and act as a camp. This continues in our own time. The State of Israel and the Jewish People are constantly under physical and political attack. Our survival is threatened by tyrants and pundits, by extremists and bigots, by missiles and potential nuclear attack.

First and foremost, we need to strengthen ourselves as a camp, as a strong and determined people dedicated to defending ourselves from vicious enemies. Not one of us is safe unless we ensure the safety and security of all our camp.

Yet, throughout our history, the people of Israel has understood its nature as a holy congregation. We have stood tall and strong in promoting the great vision of the Torah; the messianic idea that teaches peace for all people; the dedication to God and kindness to our fellow human beings. We have known *why* we survive; we have been a people with a revolutionary and powerful devotion to righteousness, compassion, respect for all human beings.

Just as we need to devote tremendous energy and strength to maintaining our camp, so we need to devote tremendous energy and strength to maintaining ourselves as a congregation. Our physical survival is a primary responsibility; our spiritual flowering is equally vital.

Some Jews are "Jewish" only (or mainly) in response to anti-Semitism or anti-Israel attacks. They are "camp" Jews. Some Jews are "Jewish" only (or mainly) in their fulfillment of the rituals of our religious tradition. They are "congregation" Jews. In fact, though, we each need to play our role in both domains. We need to fortify our camp and activate our congregation.

Some years ago, Israeli families were forcibly evacuated from Gush Katif as a peace gesture on the part of the Sharon government. One of the families, whose son was murdered by Palestinian terrorists, was reluctant to leave their home. The Israeli military insisted that the evacuation had to take place by orders of the Israeli government. The family left its home, but the father asked to return to his house to retrieve two items. The army officer gave him permission to do so.

The man returned with two items: an Israeli flag from above the front door; and the mezuzah that had been on the doorpost of the front door.

The Israeli flag: a reminder of our need to be a camp, a powerful State that can defend itself from its enemies. The mezuzah: a reminder of our need to be a congregation, a spiritually vibrant, compassionate and idealistic Torah community.

May the camp of Israel forever be strong in defending our nation. May the congregation of Israel forever be a beacon of light, illuminating ourselves and others with the ideas and ideals of a compassionate, righteous, and meaningful Torah.

Thoughts on נצבים

Renewing the Covenant between God and Israel

🔊 "You are standing this day all of you before the Lord your God; your heads, your tribes, your elders, your officers, all the people of Israel; your little ones, your wives, and the stranger/convert that is in the midst of your camp, from the hewer of your wood unto the drawer of your water" (*Devarim* 29:9–10).

Over the years, I have received many hundreds of inquiries from people interested in converting to Judaism. Some have been spiritual seekers who have found meaning in the great teachings of Torah. Some have discovered Jewish ancestry and now want to reconnect with their Jewish roots. Some have fallen in love with a Jew, and have wanted to become part of the Jewish people and raise a Jewish family. Whatever the motivation for their contacting me, I have derived much satisfaction and joy in dealing with this large and diverse group of people.

Recently, though, I received an email inquiry that was entirely new to my previous experience. The note came from a person who had converted to Judaism with an Orthodox Bet Din—and now wanted to know if it would be possible to annul his conversion!

I informed him that once a person becomes halakhically Jewish, there are no annulments. But then I asked him why he wanted to annul his conversion? I wondered if he had lost faith in God and Torah, or if he had experienced anti-Semitism, or if there were other factors which motivated this unusual request.

His answer relieved me...and pained me deeply.

It relieved me because he assured me that he loved God and Torah, that he studied Torah regularly, and that he found great satisfaction in observing mitzvoth. His problem wasn't with Judaism and the Jewish way of life.

It pained me deeply because he informed me that the problem was the Jewish community in which he lived! He felt that members of the community treated him like an outsider. Being a single man, he was having great difficulty establishing a positive social life. Whether this was his own impression or whether it was objectively true, he felt that he was discriminated against

216

because he was a convert, because he was of a different background from the mainstream of the community. So he decided he wanted to annul his conversion because Jews had rejected him.

I told him that he should stay true to God, Torah, and mitzvoth—but that he might be happier moving to another community! He seemed reassured by this answer, and wrote to me that he indeed would continue to study and observe Torah...but that he would try to find a more congenial Jewish community in which to live.

In describing the covenant between God and the people of Israel, the Torah informs us that *all* Israelites were to stand before God—from the elite leaders, to the humble masses, men and women, old and young, born Israelites and converts. The essential quality of the covenant is that it included every Israelite—all as equals before God. If Israelites did not recognize the ultimate equality of each member of the group, this would constitute a breach in the covenant itself.

Maimonides (*Hilkhot De'ot* 6:3) provides the parameters for what it means to "love one's neighbor as oneself." His words are of profound importance: "A person must speak in praise of his neighbor and be careful of his neighbor's property as he is careful with his own property and solicitous about his own honor. Whoever glorifies himself by humiliating another person will have no portion in the world to come." In the very next law, Maimonides notes that it is incumbent to love the proselyte, first because he/she is a fellow Jew, and second because there is a special Torah obligation to love the proselyte. All Jews are equal before God; all are equal partners in the covenant with God; all must be treated with the same respect and consideration that we want others to show to ourselves.

As we prepare to observe *Rosh Hashana*, it is important that we refocus on the framework of the covenant between God and Israel, that we recognize how important it is for each Jew to be treated as a fellow partner in our adventure with the Almighty. Our communities need to reflect a sincere inclusiveness, a feeling of mutual respect among ourselves. One of the great strengths of the Jewish people is our diversity, our richness of traditions and backgrounds; we stand as one people before God, each of us equal in the eyes of God.

If even one Jew feels rejected or alienated because he/she is of a "different" background, race, or ethnic group—then the structure of the Jewish covenant with God is shaken. If even one Jew wants to annul his/her Jewishness because of feelings of rejection by other Jews, then the Jewish religious enterprise is challenged. Self-righteousness and smugness are antithetical to the ideals of Jewish peoplehood.

"You are standing this day all of you before the Lord your God. . . ."

Let us each stand before the Lord imbued with love of God, love of our fellow Jews, love of our fellow human beings. Let our communities reflect love, compassion, spiritual vitality. Let us renew the covenant between God and Israel.

Thoughts about Thinking

🕊 The Torah calls on us to think, to evaluate, and to act righteously. It challenges us to serve the Almighty with our intelligence and personal responsibility; not from blind obedience.

In this week's Torah portion, we read: "For this command that I command you today is not a wonder to you, and it is not distant....For the thing is very near to you, in your mouth, and in your heart, to do it." The Torah is not an esoteric document that can be deciphered only by an elite group of prophets or sages; rather, it is the heritage of the entire people. Each of us has access to the truths of the Torah by means of our own intellectual and emotional efforts.

In his book, *The Philosophy of Hebrew Scripture* (Cambridge University Press, 2012), Dr. Yoram Hazony makes an impassioned case that the Bible is essentially a reasonable and philosophically sound literary corpus. While so many have mistakenly characterized the Hebrew Bible as a simplistic work that demands nothing but blind obedience to the word of God, Dr. Hazony demonstrates that the Bible is actually a very sophisticated intellectual enterprise. If one is able to study the Bible on its own terms, understanding its own literary and philosophical methods, then one will find it to be not only a magnificent collection of literature and laws, but also a profound exploration of ideas and ethics.

The Hebrew Bible includes a wide range of texts, with varying—and sometimes contradictory—viewpoints. Rather than presenting us with dogmatic "truths" in the form of a catechism, it offers historical narratives, laws, prophetic orations, wisdom literature. Dr. Hazony notes that

> the purpose of the biblical editors, in gathering together such diverse and often sharply conflicting texts, was not to construct a unitary work with an unequivocal message. It was rather to assemble a work capable of capturing and reflecting a given tradition of inquiry so readers could strive to understand the various perspectives embraced by this tradition, and in so doing build up an understanding of their own.. . . . The reader who takes up the Hebrew Bible is thus invited and challenged to take up a place within this tradition of inquiry, and to continue its elaboration out of his or her own resources. (p. 65)

Judaism calls on us to engage in this "tradition of inquiry," to be seekers of truth. Certainly, the Torah offers laws that we are commanded to obey. But it offers vastly more than this; it offers a spiritual context for life, a respect for our personal religious and philosophic strivings, a realistic and humble awareness of our strengths and limitations as human beings.

Judaism is at its best when its adherents are intellectually and emotionally engaged with its teachings. It is far below its best when its adherents sink into the abyss of blind obedience.

Some months ago, *Forbes Magazine* published a list of the 10 richest rabbis in Israel. The rabbis' net worths ranged from 9 million dollars to 335 million dollars! It appears that all (or nearly all) of these rabbis have reputations as wonder workers, Sephardic kabbalists, or Hasidic rebbes of huge dynasties. These rabbis have amassed huge fortunes because the public is willing to pay them for their blessings, amulets, holy water, and so forth. It seems that a considerable segment of the public does not believe in its own ability to pray to God, but wants the intercession of holy men who supposedly have an inside track with God. Many people aren't interested in a "spirit of inquiry"—they want "truth" as promised to them by wonder working rabbis.

If these wonder working rabbis indeed have such magical powers and can control God, then why don't they use these powers to disarm Israel's enemies; to uproot anti-Semitism; to punish the wicked; to provide for all the sick, poor, and hungry of the world?

A tendency has arisen in segments of the Jewish world that grants magical, even infallible, powers to certain "sages." This tendency leads to a vast perversion of Judaism, and veers in the direction of superstition and cultic behavior. It fosters authoritarianism, obscurantism, and dogmatism. It undermines freedom of thought, religious inquiry, independence of spirit. The fact that cultic rabbinic figures can amass so many millions of dollars is an indication of how deeply this negative tendency has taken root.

It is essential that we reclaim Judaism as an intellectually vibrant, creative, and dynamic religious way of life. This entails personal commitment, a sense of responsibility, and a commitment to the "spirit of inquiry" that characterizes a healthy Judaism. We need to have the self-respect and religious dignity to think . . . and to keep thinking.

Thoughts on האזינו

Three Tendencies

In his essay, "The Messianic Idea in Judaism," Professor Gershom Scholem points to three tendencies within the spiritual life of the Jewish people: conservative, restorative, and utopian.

The conservative element stresses the need to maintain things as they've always been. It is manifested in a deep commitment to Jewish law and custom; it focuses on detail and ritual. This tendency wants to ensure stability and continuity. It worries that any change in the system can lead to the unraveling of the entire structure.

The restorative element longs for the "good old days." It wants to renew our days as of old, to reestablish the kingdom of King David, to rebuild the Temple in Jerusalem. Its underlying thought is that the greatest eras and personalities are in the past, and that our wish is to return to a past "Golden Age."

The utopian element longs for a messianic era. It is characterized by spiritual restlessness and idealistic fervor. It contains within it bubbling emotions, and can be creative, nerve-wracking, even painful. It calls on us to change our focus from the safety of the past to the uncertainty of the future.

Throughout Jewish history, these three elements have reflected themselves in our religious lives. In some eras, one element has predominated; in other eras, another element has predominated. But all three have always been with us to some degree.

The challenge is to balance the claims of all three tendencies, and to develop a Jewish life that draws on the strengths of each. The conservative element maintains the religious structure of our daily lives. Without adherence to halakha on a regular basis, Judaism is sapped of its influence on our lives. It becomes a nostalgic pastime to be experienced on special occasions. It becomes a matter of personal preference rather than a commitment to a divinely ordained way of life. Without the conservative element, Judaism becomes watered down to such a degree as to lose its real spiritual power.

The restorative element reminds us that we indeed did enjoy "golden ages" and we did indeed produce great personalities. Although we in fact do not want to return to the past, we can derive tremendous inspiration from the great events and personalities of Jewish history. If we can restore the best elements of our past, this can be a boon to us and to the future of our people.

The utopian element reminds us to focus on the future. Without the idealism and hopefulness of utopianism, we risk becoming mired in the past. This tendency keeps us focused on developing new ideas, new ways of approaching an imperfect world, new aspirations for improving society.

In this week's Torah portion, we read: "Remember the days of old; think about the years of the past generations. Ask your father and he will tell you, your elders and they will explain to you" (*Devarim* 32:7). I believe this verse can be understood as providing us insight on maintaining a vibrant Judaism that maintains a keen balance among the conservative, restorative, and utopian tendencies.

"Remember the days of old . . . ". Tradition is vital to our wellbeing. By rooting ourselves in our traditions and teachings, we retain continuity with our past and we deepen our sense of rootedness and structure. This is the conservative tendency.

"Ask your father . . .". Rashi comments that "father" refers to our prophets. This is a nod to the restorative element. We lack prophecy today; yet we long for the "good old days" when we had divinely inspired prophets who could lead us, who could deliver direct messages from God. Lacking the presence of living prophets, we must depend on the words of the prophets as recorded in the Bible.

"Your elders . . .". Rashi comments that "elders" refers to our sages. The hallmark of a genuine sage is wisdom to apply ancient teachings to the needs of the current generation. Historically, our greatest sages have also been the most utopian, the most tuned in to the coming generations of the Jewish people, the most concerned about a messianic future.

Judaism that is based primarily on the conservative tendency becomes dry and over-ritualized. Judaism that is based primarily on the restorative element becomes quixotic and irrelevant. Judaism that is based primarily on the utopian element becomes deracinated, flailing out in various directions while disconnecting itself from the wellsprings of Jewish tradition.

In truth, we need all three elements and we need to balance them wisely. This was true of the Jewish past. It is true for the Jewish present. It is the foundation of the Jewish future.

Thoughts on ראש השנה

Eyes Open and Eyes Shut

☙ Paul Gaugin, the famous nineteenth-century French artist, once commented: "When I want to see clearly, I shut my eyes." He was referring to two different ways of perceiving reality. With our eyes open, we see surface reality—size, shape, color, and so forth. But with our eyes shut, we contemplate the context of things, our relationship to them, the hidden meanings.

Take, for example, a dozen roses. With our eyes open they are 12 beautiful flowers. With our eyes shut, they may be full of memories and associations—roses given or received on our first date; roses at our wedding; roses growing in our childhood home's backyard; roses on our grandmother's Shabbat table.

The way we see fellow human beings is also very different with open or closed eyes. With our eyes open, we see their physical features. With our eyes shut, we remember shared experiences, friendships, happy and sad moments. When we want to see clearly—comprehensively—we shut our eyes.

Mircea Eliade, a specialist in world religions, has written in his book, *The Sacred and the Profane*, about the pagan view of New Year. For pagans, human life is a series of recurring cycles, always on the verge of chaos. On New Year, people descend into this primordial chaos: drunkenness, debauchery, chaotic noise. Elements of this view continue to pervade modern society in the observance of the beginning of a new year.

The Jewish view is radically different from the pagan view. For Jews, reality isn't a hopeless cycle of returns to chaos, but a progression, however slow, of humanity. We aim for a messianic day. *Rosh Hashana* is not a return to primeval chaos, but a return to God, a return to our basic selves. Our New Year is observed with prayer, repentance, solemnity, and a faith that we can—and the world can—be better. We are not trapped in a vicious and hopeless series of cycles, but are moving toward a better time.

The pagan New Year is an example of seeing reality with open eyes. Things really do seem to be chaotic when viewed on the surface. Humanity does not seem to improve over the generations. We always do seem to be on the verge or self-destruction.

The Jewish New Year is an example of viewing reality with our eyes shut, of seeing things more deeply, more carefully. While being fully aware of the surface failings of humanity, we look for the hidden signs of progress and redemption. We attempt to maintain a grand, long-range vision. This is the key to the secret of Jewish optimism. While not denying the negatives around us, we stay faithful to a vision of a world that is not governed by chaos, but by a deeper, hidden, mysterious unity.

The Talmud reports (*Baba Batra* 60b) that when the Second Temple in Jerusalem was destroyed by the Romans in 70 CE, everything seemed lost for the Jews. A group of pious Jews were so distraught that they stopped eating meat or drinking wine as a sign of mourning. Rabbi Yehoshua spoke with them: Why are you not eating meat and not drinking wine? They replied: How can we eat meat or drink wine when we remember the destroyed Temple, where offerings of meat and wine were brought on the altar? Rabbi Yehoshua replied: Then you shouldn't eat bread, because meal offerings were brought in the Temple. You shouldn't eat fruit, because first fruits were brought as offerings. You shouldn't drink water, because there were water libations.

Rabbi Yehoshua continued: Not to mourn at all is impossible, since we have undergone a terrible tragedy. But to mourn excessively is impossible, because the public cannot go on mourning forever.

The sages taught that we should leave part of our homes unpainted, or leave out a bit of food from our meals, or wear a bit less jewelry—all as a sign of mourning, *zekher leHurban*, recalling the destruction of the Temple. But other than these few signs of mourning, we need to live as happily and vibrantly as possible. We need to get beyond the tragedy.

With our eyes open, we see destruction and chaos. We descend into endless mourning. With eyes shut, we remain aware of the tragedy—but we see more deeply. We think beyond the immediate sadness. We consider the needs of the community at large, we plan for future generations. Tragedy hurts, but we cannot allow it to debilitate us.

The problem of faith today is not how to have faith in God. We can come to terms with God if we are philosophers or mystics. The problem is how can we have faith in humanity? How can we believe in the goodness and truthfulness of human beings?

With our eyes open, we must view current events with profound despair and trepidation. We see the threats and challenges that face the United States, Israel, and all humanity. We see leaders who are liars and hypocrites. We see wars and hatred and violence and vicious anti-Semitism. We are tempted to think that chaos reigns.

But with our eyes shut, we know that redemption will come. We know that there are good, heroic people struggling for change. We know that just as we have overcome sorrows in the past, we will overcome oppressions and oppressors of today.

Rosh Hashana reminds us to learn to view our lives and our world with our eyes open—but also with our eyes shut. We are challenged to dream great dreams, to seek that which is hidden, to thank God for our blessings, to see beyond the moment, to let our minds encompass the past and strive for the future.

Rosh Hashana is a call to each individual to move to a higher level of understanding, behavior, and activism. *Teshuva*—repentance—means that we can improve ourselves, and that others can improve, and that the world can improve.

This is the key to Jewish optimism, the key to the Jewish revolutionary vision for humanity, the key to personal happiness.

ראש השנה
ושבת
תשובה

Separation and Reunion

🦋 The root of deepest human sadness is embodied in the word "separation." We feel this sadness especially at moments of transition: when we say goodbye to a child who is leaving for college or moving out of town; when we say goodbye to a loved one whom we won't be seeing for a long time. Parents cry at the weddings of their children. Their tears, to be sure, are tears of happiness; yet, they are also tears of pathos, of separation.

There is the poignant separation of divorce, of breaking off close relationships; and the ultimate separation of death. Saying goodbye to a dying parent, spouse, relative, or friend must be counted among the saddest of human experiences.

It is at moments of separation that we feel our emotions surging in uncontrollable waves. We are at our best and at our worst. We come to recognize that we are not in control of everything, that we cannot hold things still, freeze time, freeze relationships. We cannot prevent death.

Reunion and reconciliation are at the root of the deepest human joy and satisfaction. Seeing a loved one after years of separation, reuniting with family and friends—these experiences bring tears of happiness. We feel the completeness of our lives. Things are now right. The joys of reunion are implied by our belief in an afterlife where we will ultimately be reunited with loved ones who have passed on. Death, in other words, is not a final separation. It, too, will be followed eventually by reunion.

Separation and reunion seem like opposites. They are not. They are two sides of one coin, two harmonious notes in the rhythm of life. One without the other is impossible, just as it is impossible for there always to be light and no darkness, always sunshine and no rain.

The three themes in the *Musaf* service of *Rosh Hashana* may be considered in light of the themes of separation and reunion. The first section describes God as King, the Being that has control over life and death. When we contemplate this image of God, we react with fear, with a sense of separation. We realize that we are not ultimately in control of our lives—God is. We feel awed by God's power, we feel separated, even alienated.

The next theme, though, is *zikhronot*—God remembers. He acts with kindness. God is a compassionate Parent who is concerned with our lives. We are not forgotten or forsaken. Our lives are not random or anonymous. We are remembered, we are brought closer to God and to each other.

The third theme, *shofarot*, serves as a bridge between the poles of separation and reunion. The shofar reminds us of the *Akedah* story, a symbol of separation, where a father was to sacrifice his beloved son. Abraham, alone with Isaac on a forsaken mountain, realizes that God is the ultimate king with control over life and death.

But the shofar is also reminiscent of the revelation at Mt. Sinai. At that time, the Israelites were crowded together, united, touching shoulders. There was reconciliation between the people and God.

Rosh Hashana reminds us of the root of our greatest sadness and our greatest happiness. Memories of past separations come to mind, memories that will never leave us and that we experience intensely. But we also experience reunion. We are together in the synagogue. Members of our family have returned; friends and neighbors have come together. We are glad.

Separation is an inevitable part of life. The family and the community help us deal with these separations as best we can. A synagogue provides us the opportunity to pray and to study together, to increase our happiness, to enable us to participate in acts of kindness, caring and sharing.

We seldom have the power to prevent separation and the anguish that goes with it. But we do have the possibility of increasing our sense of completeness by uniting with our family, loved ones, friends; by sharing, encouraging, by being part of the life of our community. Separation and sadness often come of themselves. Reunion and reconciliation require us to take the initiative.

It is the beginning of a New Year. The rhythm of life and death continues, the rhythm of separation and reunion. Let us be strong in facing the challenges and losses that confront us. Let us gain strength from reuniting with family and friends—and with God.

שבת
תשובה
ויום כפור

Roads to Atonement

ꙮ Although we popularly refer to the upcoming fast day as *Yom Kippur*, the Torah calls it *Yom haKippurim*—the day of atonements (in the plural). The plural form reminds us that there are many roads to atonement. Each person is different and is on a unique spiritual level; each comes with different insights, experiences, memories. The roads to atonement are plural, because no two of us have identical needs.

This season of *teshuva* and *kappara*—repentance and atonement—provides us with a special challenge and opportunity. We are granted a yearly period of time for intense evaluation of our lives. This period should serve as a springboard to deeper understanding and personal growth.

The first step in the process of spiritual renewal is to become humbly aware of our frailties. No matter how successful we think we are, we are mortal! We have limited physical capacities and a limited time of life on this earth. Aside from our physical limitations, we have moral and religious shortcomings that must be confronted. The Spanish thinker, Ortega y Gasset, suggested that a person grows only after confronting deep existential crisis. "These are the only genuine ideas; the ideas of the shipwrecked. All the rest is rhetoric, posturing, farce. He who does not really feel himself lost, is without remission; that is to say, he never finds himself, never comes up against his own reality." The first goal of this season is to feel "shipwrecked."

But when we do "come up against our own reality" we often reach a point of perplexity. How are we to make ultimate sense of our lives? How are we to understand the vagaries of human existence—disease, wars, injustice? How are we to deal with all the social and professional pressures? How can we cope with problems in our families and communities? How can we advance beyond the quagmire of fear and self-doubt?

The famous Hasidic Rabbi Menachem Mendel of Kotzk once asked: Where is God? And he answered: Whereever a human being lets Him in! If we want to feel the presence of God, we need to open ourselves to that experience. The season of *teshuva* and Yom *haKippurim* is a time to restore our relationship with the Almighty, to express our perplexities. This genuine experience of relationship with God gives us the inner strength to cope with our problems and perplexities.

A further step in the process of *teshuva* and *kappara* is balancing the feelings of alienation and belonging. We say to the Almighty: *"ki ger anokhi imakh; toshav kekhol avotai,"* I am a stranger with You, a sojourner as were all of my ancestors. What does this mean? I feel as though I am a stranger, alienated from God; there are barriers between me and You. But I want to be a sojourner, a permanent resident in Your presence, not a stranger or a passing visitor. I want to come home to the teachings and traditions of my ancestors who have maintained faith and courage for the past 3,500 years.

A parable: A person tries to cut down a tree with a dull-edged saw. He works very hard but achieves little progress. A passerby sees this and asks: Why don't you sharpen the saw? The person responds: I don't have time, I can't stop working, I need to cut down this tree. The passerby says: But if you would stop working for a few minutes to sharpen the saw, you would actually save time and effort, and you would better be able to accomplish your goal! The person replies: No, I don't have time to stop working, I must keep sawing. Without the proper tools, we exert great energy but achieve inadequate results.

In spiritual life, too, we need proper tools. If we work with old habits, with stubborn attachment to stale and futile patterns, we will not grow. We need to think more clearly about our goals and how we can best attain them. *Yom haKippurim* provides a day when we take off from our usual routine. It is an entirely different kind of day from any other day of the year. It is a time to sharpen ourselves spiritually; to humbly face our limitations; to cope with our perplexities; to seek atonement and purification, to return to our spiritual core.

The season of *teshuva* and *kappara* provides us with a unique spiritual opportunity. Happy are they who can experience this season with an acute mind and alert spirit.

Searching for Ultimate Clarity

❦ The Talmud (*Pesahim* 50a) tells a remarkable story. The great sage, Rabbi Yehoshua ben Levi, had a promising and learned son who took ill—and died. The grief at the loss of this young man was immeasurable. But then, amazingly, the son somehow revived. And the joy at his coming back to life was no doubt even greater than the grief at his supposed death.

Rabbi Yehoshua realized that his son had undergone a unique experience, having tasted death but then having been returned to life. So the father asked the son: What did you see on the other side? What is the nature of the world after death? The son responded: *"olam hafukh ra'iti,"* I saw a topsy-turvy world. Those who are great here are small there; and those who are small here are great there. Rabbi Yehoshua told his son: *"olam barur ra'ita,"* you saw a clear world; you saw things the way they really are.

In this world, we cannot easily judge who is actually great or insignificant. We live in a world of illusions and shadows, and we are easily deceived. How can we know the real essence of anyone, if they are truly great or not, if they are truly good or not? How can we see things here as they ultimately are in the eyes of God? Only in the next world, the world of spirit and truth, does clarity prevail. In this world, not only are we not able to clearly understand others, but we often have difficulty even evaluating our own true selves.

But how can we attain clarity of insight? How can we see things with the lucidity of genuine truth? Dr. Elisabeth Kubler-Ross has found that when people reach the last stage of life, when they have accepted their impending death, they often become infused with remarkable clarity. There is no more reason for deception; one has nothing to lose by being totally honest. At this last stage of life, a person can give a clear evaluation of his or her life.

In his studies of individuals who underwent near-death experiences, Professor Raymond Moody has found common elements in the experiences of all his subjects, regardless of their gender, race, or religion. Having "gone to the other side" and returned, they all tended to reach two conclusions: One must love others; one must learn as much as possible. This extreme experience jarred them into a world of spiritual clarity; they somehow learned to focus on what is truly important in life, on what has ultimate value for our souls.

But all of us want to gain clarity of insight without having to wait until the very end of our lives! Very few of us will undergo a near-death experience. So how are we to gain this insight here and now?

It seems to me that *Yom Kippur* plays a special role in this regard. It attempts to place us, albeit symbolically, into a crisis mode. The imagery of the day is that we are, in fact, on trial for our lives. We come before God and plead with Him to inscribe us in the Book of Life. Yet, we know fully that He may decide otherwise. On *Yom Kippur*, we are supposed to feel as though we are dangling between life and death. We fast, we deprive ourselves of physical needs and pleasures. These are symbolic gestures expressing how seriously we take this day of judgment. It is as though we are saying that we are so concerned about our life and death, that we simply have lost interest in eating and drinking. We are too agitated to be concerned with our physical wants.

Each of us experiences *Yom Kippur* differently, because each of us is a different person. We respond to the prayers and the ritual to the degree that we bring our knowledge, feelings, and sensitivity to them. If we spend *Yom Kippur* in serious contemplation and prayer, we can gain much. *Yom Kippur* is a gift that God has given to the Jewish people. It is one day a year when we can devote ourselves to serious meditation, to search for genuine clarity in our lives. Whether we understand Hebrew more or less, whether we can follow the prayers fluently or imperfectly—each of us has the opportunity to enter the mood and spirit of the day, to ponder the theme of this occasion.

Rabbinic tradition speaks of *"teshuva sheleima,"* a complete repentance. This entails not merely repenting for this sin or that sin, or asking forgiveness for this transgression or that error. Complete repentance means transforming our personalities, transforming the way we lead our lives, seeing our lives organically, comprehensively, clearly.

This is the challenge of *Yom Kippur*—to judge ourselves truly. Through this exercise of prayer and meditation, we may gain the spiritual insight which leads us to a dynamic self-transformation.

We should not be the same person the day after *Yom Kippur* that we were the day before *Yom Kippur*. We should be moving ahead, raising our lives to a higher level. May we merit to see *"olam barur"*—a clear world, a true world. May we merit the insight to understand the ultimate reality of our lives and the lives of others.

And with this clarity, may we have the merit to make our lives and our world a better, more spiritual, wiser place for all of us.

סוכות

The Business of Life

❧ Healthy societies and communities depend on their members' loyalty and sense of responsibility. They thrive when people work for the general good and not just for their own self-interest. People realize that if they are to enjoy the benefits of a society/community, they should rightfully share in the responsibilities of its maintenance.

Happily, many people understand this and govern their lives accordingly. They are good citizens, good community members. They pay their way and do their share.

Unhappily, there is a growing trend in our society that undermines these values. Professor Barry Schwartz of Swarthmore College has written extensively and cogently on how the market economy—where people look out primarily for themselves rather than the public good—is eroding the quality of our lives. In almost every profession and every business, there is a "free agent" attitude that says: Let me take as much as I can for myself; I'm not going to worry about how this affects others. Business is business. My first concern is for the bottom line; let others fend for themselves.

We read in our newspapers how major corporations, with billions of dollars of annual profits, pay little or no taxes. They hire lawyers to find loopholes, and they pay lobbyists to make the tax loopholes in the first place. Their explanation is: Business is business. We need to maximize profits. We owe this to our stockholders.

But what about responsibility for the country, the society that enables them to do business and make profits? What about a sense of loyalty for the rest of the citizenry, who must pay all the taxes that these corporations avoid? The answer: Business is business. We take what we can; if the burden falls on others, that's their problem, not ours.

While this philosophy of the market economy increases, the quality of our lives decreases. Some few get very rich, and the masses are left to pay the bills. This causes a breakdown in trust, a festering of social antagonisms and resentments. As the level of public responsibility decreases, personal relationships suffer as well. The conclusion is that people are disposable. Loyalty to others is not the top concern; money is.

Judaism is a powerful voice that stands for social responsibility. The Torah reminds us that we were slaves in Egypt. We are to have mercy on the stranger, for we were strangers in the land of Egypt. The Torah and rabbinic tradition insist that we see the humanity in others, that we put the concerns of human beings first. We are instructed to be constructive, caring, responsible people.

Each of us is an ambassador of this great idea, this great vision. The hallmark of who we are as a Jewish people is our commitment to humanity—our own humanity and the humanity of others. We rebel against oppression; we reject the philosophy of business is business, that profits come first; we embrace social responsibility and mutual trust. Each of us who strives to live by these Jewish ideals is a moral hero who defies the dehumanizing tendencies evident in our society.

In describing *Sukkoth* as the time of our rejoicing, our tradition reminds us that we are to rejoice by sharing our blessings with others. It is not a time to hoard our harvest for our own benefit, but a time to remember the poor and the stranger—to share and reach out to others.

The *sukkah* is a temporary dwelling reminding us that our own lives are temporary—we are transient visitors in this world. Our personal fulfillment comes through sharing with others, through playing our part for the betterment of all.

Professor Gershon Galil of the Department of Biblical Studies at the University of Haifa recently deciphered an inscription dating from the tenth century BCE—the earliest known fragment of Hebrew writing. How wonderful that this oldest Hebrew inscription captures the spirit of the Jewish people:

> You shall not do it, but worship the Lord. Judge the slave and the widow, judge the orphan and the stranger. Plead for the infant, plead for the poor and the widow. Rehabilitate the poor at the hands of the king. Protect the poor and the slave, support the stranger.

Some people think it's fine to say that business is business, that people are disposable, that people don't matter as much as profits. Look out for yourself, and let others look out for themselves.

We say with full voice: This is not the way. *Hessed* is the way. Social responsibility is the way. Building a righteous society is the way.

Disraeli's Thoughts on Sukkoth

❧ Interesting insights about *Sukkoth* have come from the pen of Benjamin Disraeli (1804–1881), the First Earl of Beaconsfield. Disraeli was of Jewish birth, and his family had been associated with the Spanish and Portuguese Congregation in London. Although his father had Benjamin baptized to Anglicanism at age 12, Disraeli never denied his Jewish roots. He rose to become the first—and thus far only—British Prime Minister of Jewish ancestry.

Anti-Semites never forgave Disraeli's Jewishness and constantly identified him as a Jew in spite of his conversion to Anglicanism. In response to a vicious anti-Semitic comment made in the British parliament, Disraeli famously retorted: "Yes, I am a Jew, and when the ancestors of the Right Honourable Gentleman were brutal savages in an unknown island, mine were priests in the Temple of Solomon."

Disraeli writes about *Sukkoth* in his novel, *Tancred*, originally published in 1847. Tancred was a young British nobleman who had a spiritual longing to visit the Holy Land. When he arrived, he spent time with a Jewish family and became acquainted with Jewish religious life. His visit coincided with *Sukkoth*, and he was told that this is a great national festival celebrating the harvest. He was shown the *lulav* and *etrog*, symbols of the autumn harvest. Tancred was deeply impressed.

Disraeli writes: "The vineyards of Israel have ceased to exist, but the eternal law enjoins the children of Israel still to celebrate the vintage. A race that persist in celebrating their vintage, although they have no fruits to gather, will regain their vineyards. What sublime inexorability in the law! But what indomitable spirit in the people!"

Disraeli notes that it is easier for "the happier Sephardim, the Hebrews who have never quitted the sunny regions that are laved by the Midland Ocean," to observe the festival, since they can identify with the climate and setting of the early generations of Israelites who celebrated *Sukkoth*. "But picture to yourself the child of Israel in the dingy suburb or the squalid quarter of some bleak northern town, where there is never a sun that can at any rate ripen grapes. Yet he must celebrate the vintage of purple Palestine! The law has told him, though a denizen in an icy clime, that he must dwell for seven days in a bower. . . ."

He continues with a description of the ignominies that Jews suffer in their ghettos in Europe "living amid fogs and filth, never treated with kindness, seldom with justice. . . . Conceive such a being, an object to you of prejudice, dislike, disgust, perhaps hatred. The season arrives, and the mind and heart of that being are filled with images and passions that have been ranked in all ages among the most beautiful and the most genial of human experience; filled with a subject the most vivid, the most graceful, the most joyous, and the most exuberant . . . the harvest of the grape in the native regions of the vine."

The downtrodden Jews, in observance of *Sukkoth*, find real joy in life. They decorate their *sukkahs* as beautifully as they can; their families gather together to eat festive meals in the *sukkah*. The outside world may be cruel and ugly; but their inner life is joyous and noble. Their external conditions may not seem too happy, but their internal happiness is real.

The Jews, while remembering the glories of the Israelite past, also dream of the future glories of the Israelites when their people will be restored to their ancient greatness. Disraeli points to an important truth: Happiness is essentially an internal phenomenon, a matter of one's attitude and interpretation of reality. External conditions are less vital to genuine happiness than one's internal state of mind.

By celebrating *Sukkoth* over the many centuries of exile, the Jewish people was able to maintain an inner strength and happiness, a vivid sense of the past and a powerful vision for the future. We are fortunate today to be living at a time when the sovereign State of Israel has been re-established. We may celebrate *Sukkoth* with the added joy of knowing that our historic dreams have begun to be realized.

We have regained our vineyards. We must aspire to the day when we may enjoy our vineyards in peace and security, free from the threats and hatred that continue to be aimed against our people. "A race that persist in celebrating their vintage . . . will regain their vineyards." A people who persist in dreaming of a messianic era will ultimately see that dream fulfilled.

Thoughts on

שוכות ושמיני חג עצרת

Israel and the Nations

🌿 This has been a very difficult time for us as Americans and as Jews. Anti-American and anti-Israel attitudes are sources of great distress and sadness. How frustrating it is that these two nations, representatives of the highest humanitarian ideals, should be the victims of such deep, irrational hatred.

As Jews, we are particularly sensitive and troubled by anti-Jewish and anti-Israel propaganda and violence. We are pained that new generations of children are bred on vicious anti-Semitic stereotypes, and that they are taught that it is virtuous to be suicide bombers if in the process they murder Jews. We are troubled by anti-Jewish and anti-Israel bias in the media. It is ever so difficult to maintain equanimity when reading one-sided articles or seeing one-sided news reports that insidiously vilify the people of Israel.

When we take our current frustrations and add to them all of our people's frustrations throughout history, we have good reason to be bitter about the nations of the world. The Jewish people have suffered discrimination, persecution, violence, and the ultimate Nazi atrocities. The Arab world has inflicted untold suffering on the people of Israel, and it is due to the mercy of God and the heroism of the Israelis that the State of Israel continues to exist and to flourish.

So, if we want to vent our anger at the nations of the world, we certainly have had more than enough provocation.

But the festivals of *Sukkoth* and *Shemini Hag Atsereth* remind us that the Jewish people have a different approach. We do not wish evil on our enemies; we only wish them to repent, to see the light of reason and justice. We do not

236

pray for their destruction; we pray for their wellbeing!

An ancient rabbinic teaching notes that on the festival of *Sukkoth*, the ancient Israelites brought 70 offerings to the Temple in Jerusalem. In antiquity, it was believed that the world consisted of 70 nations. Thus, the Jews offered sacrifices on behalf of all the nations of the world. In the words of the *Midrash Shir ha-Shirim*: "Israel atones for all peoples, for the 70 calves that were burned on the altar at the feast of *Sukkoth* were offered on behalf of the nations, in order that their existence might be maintained in this world." Many of those nations were not kind to Israel, and many were actually hostile. Nevertheless, the Jews prayed for all the nations of the world.

The offerings were a way of demonstrating moral responsibility for the world and a positive relationship with all people. For those who were bad, we prayed that they would become better. For those who were good, we prayed that their goodness would be rewarded. For those who were neutral, we prayed that they might become enlightened with truth, and learn to act in righteousness. These offerings helped us keep things in proper perspective. They prevented us from becoming angry and bitter. They helped fire our sense of optimism and humanitarianism.

Whereas *Sukkoth* offerings in the Temple reflected concern for the nations of the world, the Temple service on *Shemini Hag Atsereth* focused on Israel alone. We had one day for a "private" dialogue between ourselves and God. It was a day to look inward, to strengthen ourselves spiritually. Yes, we need to keep in mind the wellbeing of all people: but we also need to have time to tend to our own specific needs and concerns.

During this festival season, we offer a prayer in the spirit of our ancestors:

"Almighty God, we the people of Israel pray for the wellbeing of all the nations of the world. Please grant your blessings to all those nations and individuals who have acted with kindness and understanding toward us, who have had the moral courage to stand with the Jewish people in good times and bad.

Please grant inspiration and courage to all those nations and individuals who turn the other way when we are in trouble, who offer us no help, who abstain when we are being maligned. May they grow braver. May they soon join us in our battle for universal righteousness and human dignity.

Please grant loving hearts to those nations and individuals who are filled with hatred. Inspire them with true love of God and humanity. May their evil thoughts and intentions be nullified, and may they repent their ways speedily and in our days.

Help us, the Jewish people, to maintain our inner strength, our courage and faith, our idealism and commitment to a better future for ourselves and all humankind."

The Challenge of the "Blank Wall"

🕊 On August 21, 1911, Leonardo da Vinci's *Mona Lisa*, one of the world's most famous paintings, was stolen right off the wall of the Louvre museum in Paris. The crime wasn't discovered until the next day. The Louvre was closed for a week due to the police investigation.

When the Louvre was re-opened, a line of people visited the museum to stare solemnly at the empty space on the wall where the *Mona Lisa* had once hung. One visitor left a bouquet of flowers. Indeed, until the painting was ultimately returned to the Louvre on December 30, 1913, throngs of visitors came to the museum to gaze at the blank wall! More people seem to have come to see the blank wall than had come in the previous two years to see the actual painting.

What motivated so many visitors to come to see the blank wall?

Perhaps it was sadness at the loss of a great art treasure.

Perhaps it was due to regret. Why hadn't we come to see it more often while it was hanging? Why was security at the museum so lax?

Perhaps it was concern for the future. Will the *Mona Lisa* ever be found and returned?

Whatever the motivation, thousands of people came to the Louvre to stare at an empty space.

I think this episode can be understood as a parable of life. Our lives are a collection of pieces of art—our family, friends, experiences, careers,successes.

We come to a blank wall: failures, losses.

We are struck with sadness. We have lost possibilities, opportunities, relationships.

We are struck with regret. We could have and should have done better with our lives.

We are concerned for the future. Can we restore our losses, or can we at least learn to live with our losses and failures?

We have come to the closing days of our holy day period. *Rosh Hashana* is a time to tour events of our past year and to re-examine the artwork of our lives. *Yom Kippur* is a time to recount sins and errors and to think about what we could have done better. *Sukkoth* is a time to celebrate our accomplishments in a spirit of happiness.

Then we come to *Shemini Hag Atsereth*—a blank wall. This is a holiday with no frills, no shofar, no fasting, no *lulav*, no *sukkah*. The blank wall symbolizes our sadness, regrets, possibilities, hopes, and aspirations.

After what we have experienced during the holiday season, we now reach a blank wall; we are called upon to start working on our new masterpiece—the life still ahead of us. It is time to rally our strength, our wisdom, our sensitivities to the needs of others.

The "blank wall" attracts us because it is latent with opportunities; it opens new challenges; it calls on us to imagine what we can be and what we can create in the year and years ahead.

It is fitting that *Simhat Torah* is associated with *Shemini Hag Atsereth*. This is a reminder that the art of the blank wall can be meaningfully restored if we ourselves rejoice in our Torah heritage. The spiritual power of Torah has infused the Jewish people for thousands of years—and it has the power to help each of us develop our lives into a new, beautiful masterpiece.